Adoption in Old Babylonian Nippur and the Archive of Mannum-mešu-liṣṣur

MESOPOTAMIAN CIVILIZATIONS

1. *The Lamentation over the Destruction of Sumer and Ur*
   Piotr Michalowski

2. *Schlaf, Kindchen, schlaf! Mesopotamische Baby-Beschwörungen und -Rituale*
   Walter Farber

3. *Adoption in Old Babylonian Nippur and the Archive of Mannum-mešu-liṣṣur*
   Elizabeth C. Stone and David I. Owen

4. *Third-Millennium Legal and Administrative Texts in the Iraq Museum, Baghdad*
   Piotr Steinkeller and J. N. Postgate

Adoption in Old Babylonian Nippur and the Archive of Mannum-mešu-liṣṣur

Elizabeth C. Stone
and
David I. Owen

with a contribution by
John R. Mitchell

Eisenbrauns
Winona Lake, Indiana
1991

Library of Congress Cataloging-in-Publication Data

Stone, Elizabeth Caecilia, 1949–
Adoption in Old Babylonian Nippur and the Archive of Mannum-mešu-liṣṣur / Elizabeth C. Stone and David I. Owen with a contribution by John R. Mitchell.
p. cm. — (Mesopotamian civilizations ; 3)
Includes bibliographical references and index.
ISBN 0-931464-53-6
1. Akkadian language—Texts. 2. Adoption—Iraq—Babylonia—History. 3. Contracts—Iraq—Babylonia—History. 4. Nippur (Ancient city)—History. 5. Mannum-mešu-liṣṣur—Archives. I. Owen, David I. II. Mitchell, John R. (John Robert), 1949–. III. Title. IV. Series.
PJ3870.S76 1991
492′.1—dc20 91-346

Contents

Acknowledgments

Work on the two major parts of this volume was begun independently by both authors over ten years ago. The actual collaboration on this volume started in 1980, and the final product edited together into a single volume by Stone in 1988. In retrospect, the frequent, unanticipated delays we each encountered probably resulted in a more accurate final product. During this time numerous individuals and institutions provided help and support. Access to the texts at the Ashmolean Museum, Oxford, and permission to publish the OECT photographs were graciously provided by the Visitors of the Ashmolean Museum and Roger Moorey, who also provided the photographs of OECT 8 1 [no. 42] and OECT 8 2 [no. 38]; to those at the Iraq Museum, Baghdad, by Fawzi Rashid; to those at the University Museum, Philadelphia, by Åke Sjöberg; to those at the Oriental Institute, Chicago, by John A. Brinkman, Miguel Civil, and McGuire Gibson, who also kindly granted permission to work on unpublished Nippur tablets; and to those in the Rare Book Collection, Olin Library, Cornell University by Herb Finch. The departments of Anthropology at the State University of New York at Stony Brook and Near Eastern Studies at Cornell University provided secretarial help and logistical support. Paul Zimansky undertook the laborious task of making photos of many of the tablets in Cornell and Miguel Civil offered help with philological problems encountered with the Chicago Nippur tablets. Margaret Green and Piotr Steinkeller provided invaluable advice on the proper translation of the texts in question, and Norman Yoffee and Marten Stol read through the manuscript and provided us with invaluable advice. Jerrold Cooper invited the authors to submit this volume for publication in this series and we are grateful to him for his interest and help. Eisenbrauns, and particularly David P. Aiken, is responsible for the handsome layout of this book and for the meticulous attention to detail which characterize the work of this press and its staff. To all these individuals and institutions we offer our sincerest thanks, while at the same time taking full responsibility for any errors of fact or interpretation which may be contained in this work, for the latter we have only ourselves to blame.

° ° °

I would like to take this opportunity to express a debt of gratitude to a number of people who helped me in preparation of this work. David I. Owen drew my attention to the existence of the Cornell texts and was most generous in allowing me advanced access to those materials, and he has given me many helpful suggestions. Joachim Oelsner not only checked the two unpublished texts in Jena with which I was concerned and provided me with a precis of their contents, but also read and commented on an earlier draft of this paper, as did McGuire Gibson. Last, but not least, Margaret Green helped me in the preparation of the translations of the text. I have benefited greatly from their help, but all errors of fact or interpretation are entirely my own.

Elizabeth C. Stone
SUNY, Stony Brook

* * *

I would like to thank the staff of the Rare Book Room in the Olin Library for their interest and cordial cooperation during my frequent visits to the collection. Herbert Finch was particularly helpful in securing funding for the baking of the tablets and Donald D. Eddy allowed occasional loans of the texts for extended study. Norman Yoffee and Marten Stol have read this manuscript and provided their typically astute observations and corrections. I am particularly grateful for their help but they are in no way responsible for any errors of commission or omission on my part.

David I. Owen
Cornell University

Abbreviations

ARN — M. Çığ, H. Kızılyay, and F. R. Kraus, *Altbabylonische Rechtsurkunden aus Nippur* (Istanbul: Millî Eğitim Basımevi/Istanbul Arkeoloji Müzeleri, 1952)

BE — Babylonian Expedition of the University of Pennsylvania, Series A: Cuneiform Texts (Philadelphia: Department of Archaeology, University of Pennsylvania)
- 6/2 Arno Poebel, *Babylonian Legal and Business Documents from the Time of the First Dynasty of Babylon, Chiefly from Nippur* (1909)

CBS — siglum for tablets in the collections of the University Museum, University of Pennsylvania

Cornell — siglum for tablets in the Olin Library, Cornell University

HS — siglum for tablets in the Hilprecht collection, Friedrich-Schiller-Universität, Jena

Ni — siglum for Nippur tablets in the collections of the Archaeological Museum of Istanbul

OECT — Oxford Editions of Cuneiform Texts (London: Oxford University Press)
- 8 Guy G. R. Hunter, *Sumerian Contracts from Nippur: The Sayce and H. Weld Collection in the Ashmolean Museum* (1930)

OIMA — Oriental Institute Microfiche Archives (Chicago: Oriental Institute, University of Chicago)
- 1 Elizabeth C. Stone and Paul E. Zimansky, *Old Babylonian Contracts from Nippur*, vol. 1 (1976)

PBS — Publications of the Babylonian Section (Philadelphia: University Museum, University of Pennsylvania)
- 5 Arno Poebel, *Historical and Grammatical Texts* (1914)
- 8/1 Edward Chiera, *Legal and Administrative Documents from Nippur, Chiefly from the Dynasties of Isin and Larsa* (1914)
- 8/2 Edward Chiera, *Old Babylonian Contracts* (1922)
- 13 Leon Legrain, *Historical Fragments* (1922)

SAOC — Studies in Ancient Oriental Civilization (Chicago: Oriental Institute, University of Chicago)
- 44 Elizabeth C. Stone, *Nippur Neighborhoods* (1987)

TIM — Texts in the Iraq Museum (Wiesbaden: Harrassowitz)
- 4 Johannes J. A. van Dijk, *Cuneiform Texts: Old Babylonian Contracts and Juridical Texts* (1967)

Tables

Figures

Symbols

( )	addition made to translation for clarity
[ ]	broken text
⌜ ⌝	partially broken text
⟨ ⟩	accidental omission by scribe
⟪ ⟫	accidental addition by scribe

Plates

Adoption in Old Babylonian Nippur

Elizabeth C. Stone

> Without . . . the Fiction of Adoption which permits the family tie to be artificially created, it is difficult to understand how society would ever have escaped from its swaddling-clothes, and taken its first steps towards civilization."
>
> Sir Henry Maine, *Ancient Law*

Sir Henry Maine's stress on the importance of adoption in social change has enjoyed little favor in recent times. Indeed, both ancient historians and anthropologists have concentrated on synchronic rather than diachronic analyses, particularistic rather than generalizing approaches. While ancient historians have tended simply to describe adoptive behavior,[1] social anthropologists—with their bias toward simple rather than complex societies, toward structural rather than processual analyses—tend to view adoptions as "transactions in parenthood as a form of property."[2] In neither instance are adoption practices viewed within the context of changes in socioeconomic behavior.

A rare generalizing approach is that used by Jack Goody in his article, "Adoption in Cross-Cultural Perspective."[3] As a preliminary to his comparison of adoption as practiced by ancient civilizations and by modern simple societies, he outlines the functions of adoption as follows:

1. to provide homes for orphans, bastards, foundlings, and the children of impaired families

[1] See, for example, M. David, *Die Adoption im altbabylonischen Recht* (Leipziger Rechtswissenschaftlische Studien 23; Leipzig: T. Weicher, 1927); J. A. Cook, *Law and Life of Rome* (Ithaca: Cornell University Press, 1967); Hui-Chen W. Liu, *The Traditional Chinese Clan Rules* (Monographs of the Association for Asian Studies 7; Locust Valley, NY: J. J. Augustin, 1959), and W. K. Lacey, *The Family in Classical Greece* (Ithaca: Cornell University Press, 1968).

[2] Ward H. Goodenough, "Epilogue: Transactions in Parenthood," in *Adoption in Eastern Oceania* (ed. Vern Carroll; Association for Social Anthropology in Oceania Monograph 1; Honolulu: University of Hawaii Press, 1970) 399. See also the other articles in the same volume, and Ivan Brady (ed.), *Transactions in Kinship* (Association for Social Anthropology in Oceania Monograph 4; Honolulu: University Press of Hawaii, 1976).

[3] Jack Goody, "Adoption in Cross-Cultural Perspective," *Comparative Studies in Society and History* 2 (1969) 55–78.

2. to provide childless couples with social progeny
3. to provide an individual or couple with an heir to their property[4]

For Goody these three categories are exhaustive, yet any student of ancient Mesopotamian society knows that this is not so; "fictive adoption" at Nuzi clearly served as a means of property transfer and implied no parent-child relationship between the two transactors.[5]

No society is static, and the seeds of change are to be found where fictive relationships mask the inadequacies of the status quo. Since adoption automatically implies a fictive relationship between adopter and adoptee, adoption practices should prove a sensitive indicator of the conflicts within a society. The "fictive adoption" texts from Nuzi, written in the mid-second millennium B.C., which serve to transfer real estate, thus represent the transformation of traditional adoption practices to serve new functions, to fulfill new societal needs. The types of adoptions described by Goody are designed to redress deficits in family makeup, and may be termed familial adoptions; those documented from Nuzi, on the other hand, are motivated primarily by economic concerns, and will therefore be called economic adoptions. In this paper, adoptions in Old Babylonian Nippur (ca. 1920–1720 B.C.)[6] will be examined with these two types of adoption in mind.

Types of Adoptions at Nippur

To attain a full understanding of the roles played by adoption in Old Babylonian Nippur, it is first necessary to describe briefly the socioeconomic system. An examination of all available contracts from Nippur suggests that the basic units in society were shallow patrilineal lineages. This social system placed certain constraints on economic activities. The alienation of real estate, especially field property, was restricted. Fields and orchards could only be sold within a very narrow range of close agnatic kin, while the group of potential house purchasers was somewhat larger. Temple offices, on the other hand, were heritable, but not alienable before around 1800 B.C.; once they became alienable they were apparently governed by few restrictions. Nevertheless, these data indicate that even such unrestricted property as temple offices could be purchased only by one whose inheritance had already made him a property owner.[7] It may be argued that the alienation restrictions described above stem from traditional patterns of land use, patterns which were based on the principle of communal land ownership by kinship groups.

[4] Ibid., 57.

[5] E. M. Cassin, *L'Adoption à Nuzi* (Paris: Adrien-Maissoneuve, 1938).

[6] For simplicity, all dates have been converted into years B.C. following the system outlined by J. A. Brinkman in A. Leo Oppenheim, *Ancient Mesopotamia: Portrait of a Dead Civilization* (Chicago: University of Chicago Press, 1977) 336–37.

[7] Elizabeth C. Stone, *Nippur Neighborhoods* (Studies in Ancient Oriental Civilization 44; Chicago: Oriental Institute, 1987) 13–28.

At the time with which we are concerned, this ideology had to coexist with a system of individual land registration.[8]

It is within the context of this conflict between traditional and state ideologies that the impetus for social change can be found. The most useful way to approach the study of the Nippur adoption texts is to attempt to isolate the social and the economic components of the transaction. Clearly, all adoptions have elements of both components; the adoptee takes on the social role of the son or daughter, while accepting its economic benefits. At Nippur, although it is clear that the transactions were only recorded to ensure the protection of economic rights, the terms of the transaction should reveal the nature of the relationship between adopter and adoptee.

The adoption contracts at Nippur are far from uniform, although all are witnessed, dated, and sealed. Generally, they begin with a statement of adoption which is followed by a discussion of the settlements in cash or property that result from the adoption. Usually the adoptee stands to receive property through inheritance, while the adopter may receive an adoption payment. This is often followed by a section in which the penalties for breaking the contract are spelled out. Finally—either before or after the oath, before or after the witness list—the text may describe the monthly and annual rations which are to be delivered by the adoptee to support his new father until his death.

The twenty-five surviving Old Babylonian Nippur adoption contracts[9] can be classified into four broad categories, which apparently differ in both form and function. This chapter will begin with a discussion of these four categories, and will follow with an examination of those instances where additional texts concerning the adopting parties allow us to place this relationship in a broader context.

The four classes of adoption can be distinguished by classifying the participants in the transaction and the circumstances surrounding that adoption. As seen in criteria 2 to 4 in table 1, these classes are (1) a man alone adopts one or more sons,[10] (2) a man and his wife adopt one or more sons,[11]

[8] See Elizabeth C. Stone, "Economic Crisis and Social Upheaval in Old Babylonian Nippur," in *Mountains and Lowlands* (ed. Louis D. Levine and T. Cuyler Young Jr.; Bibliotheca Mesopotamica 7; Malibu, CA: Undena, 1977) 267–89.

[9] Approximately five hundred Nippur contracts are currently available for study, while an additional one hundred and fifty such contracts remain unpublished in the Hilprecht Sammlung, Freidrich Schiller-Universität, Jena (DDR); see J. Oelsner, "Neue Daten zur sozialen und wirtschaftlichen Situation Nippurs in altbabylonischer Zeit," *Acta Antiqua* 1974: 259–65.

[10] The texts that fall into this category are PBS 8/1 16 [no. 2], PBS 8/2 153 [no. 5], *ARN* 45 [no. 7], *ARN* 65 [no. 8], OECT 8 20 [no. 23], BE 6/2 28 [no. 4], TIM 4 13 [no. 1], TIM 4 14 [no. 3], and SAOC 44 10 [no. 6].

[11] The texts that fall into this category are OECT 8 21 [no. 32], BE 6/2 24 [no. 9], BE 6/2 57 [no. 11], SAOC 44 15 [no. 10], and SAOC 44 30 [no. 12]. PBS 8/2 107 [no. 13] is included in this group, although it should really be placed in a category of its own since it concerns the adoption of a newborn from its parents.

TABLE 1. *Adoptions in Old Babylonian Nippur*

			Criteria					
Text No.	*Publication*	*Date*	1 *Name first*	2 *Heirs*	3 *Property*	4 *Support*	5 *Slavery*	6 *Payment*
Type 1: Adoption by a man								
23	OECT 8 20	1873–1869	yes	yes	yes	yes	...	no
1	TIM 4 13[a]	1860–1837	yes	yes	yes	yes	no	no
2	PBS 8/1 16	1816–1794	...	yes	yes	yes	...	...
3	TIM 4 14	1791	yes	yes	no	yes[b]	no	no
4	BE 6/2 28	1742	no	yes	yes	yes	...	yes
5	PBS 8/2 153	1737	no	yes	no	yes	no	yes
6	SAOC 44 10	n.d.	...	yes	yes	...	...	no
7	*ARN* 45	1764	yes	yes	no	no	no	no
8	*ARN* 65[c]	1763	yes	yes	yes	no	yes	no
Type 2: Adoption by a man and wife								
9	BE 6/2 24	1746	yes	yes	no	no	no	no
32	OECT 8 21	1739	no	yes	no	no	no	yes
10	SAOC 44 15	1734	no	yes	no	no	no	no
11	BE 6/2 57	1728	no	yes	no	no	yes	no
12	SAOC 44 30	1749–1721	...	...	...	no	yes	...
13	PBS 8/2 107[d]	1749–1721	yes	no	...	no	...	yes
Type 3: Adoptions with marriages								
14	SAOC 44 1	1792	...	no	...	no	yes	no
15	*ARN* 37	1781	...	yes	no	no	no	no
27	Cornell 4	1744	...	yes	no	no	no	...
16	BE 6/2 48	1732	...	yes	no	yes	no	no
17	PBS 8/2 155	1749–1721	...	yes	yes	no	no	no
Type 4: Adoption by a woman alone								
18	*ARN* 9	1860–1837	...	...	...	...	...	...
19	SAOC 44 62	1860–1837	...	...	...	...	...	...
20	BE 6/2 4	1816	yes	no	...	yes	...	yes
21	BE 6/2 46	1735	...	...	...	...	...	...
22	*ARN* 100	1734	...	...	...	...	...	...

... Signifies the unavailability of this information, either due to a break in the text, or to its absence.

Criteria:
1. The name(s) of the adoptee(s) precede those of the adopter(s).
2. The adoptee(s) are named as heir(s) of the adopter(s).
3. The property to be inherited by the adoptee(s) is described in detail.
4. The adoptee(s) swear to contribute to the support of the adopter(s).
5. The adoptee(s) may be sold into slavery if they break the contract.
6. The adoption includes an adoption payment.

Notes:
a. This text is a restatement of an earlier adoption.
b. The support was given to a third person.
c. This text is a restatement of the *ARN* 45 [no. 7] adoption.
d. This text concerns the adoption of a suckling baby; the payment was made by the adoptive parents to the natural parents.

(3) the sons from a previous marriage are adopted by the new spouse,[12] and (4) a woman alone is the adopter (probable) or the adoptee.[13] The validity of these distinctions is confirmed both by the terms of the transactions (see table 1, criteria 2 to 6) and by the social and economic functions of the adoptions; these show distinct patterns that vary from class to class.

The most common type of adoption is type 1, where a man adopts one or more sons. This type of text has a temporal distribution that spans the entire two centuries covered by the texts. With the exception of *ARN* 45 [no. 7] and *ARN* 65 [no. 8], which will be discussed in more detail below, all texts in this category have the adopted son or sons receiving an inheritance of property (criterion 2) from the father in exchange for a contribution toward the future support of that adoptive father (criterion 4). None of the texts with these provisions threatens the adoptive son with slavery if he does not comply; indeed, many of them have no disinheritance clause at all (criterion 5). Thus the salient features of this type of adoption are that the adopter received security in his old age, while the adoptee received an inheritance of real property.

The second type of adoption is one in which the wife joins her husband as the adopter. In this case, there is never any clause in which the adopted son promises to support his adoptive parents in their old age (criterion 4), in spite of the fact that property inheritance (criterion 2) always accompanies such adoptions. The inclusion of the wife in type 2 adoptions suggests that in this instance the parenting aspects of adoption dominated.

The third group of adoptions consists of those which are associated with a second marriage. In these texts, sons by a previous marriage are adopted by the new spouse. Indeed, since marriage texts without adoptions are rare, adoption was apparently the reason for the tablet recording the marriage being written in the first place. In the one instance, BE 6/2 48 [no. 16], where the father was the surviving parent of the adoptive sons, they had to promise to contribute to the support of their stepmother in her old age, presumably thus accepting obligations which would have been automatic in the case of their natural mother. Where the mother contracts a second marriage, the treatment of her sons was apparently dependent upon her status. If she were to be sold into slavery in the case of a divorce, then, similarly, her sons would be sold if they denied their adoptive father. This type of adoption shows more variability than any other (see tables 1 and 2), apparently due to differences in the relative social positions of the new spouses. In general, however, it is clear that the motivations behind these adoptions were a restructuring of the families to be consistent with the social realities of a second marriage.

[12] The texts which fall into this category are PBS 8/2 155 [no. 17], *ARN* 37 [no. 15], BE 6/2 48 [no. 16], SAOC 44 1 [no. 14], and Cornell 4 [no. 27].

[13] The texts which fall into this category are *ARN* 100 [no. 22], BE 6/2 4 [no. 20], BE 6/2 46 [no. 21], SAOC 44 62 [no. 19], and possibly *ARN* 9 [no. 18] and SAOC 44 58.

Unfortunately, it is almost impossible to come to any understanding of the fourth type of adoption, which concerns women. Four of the five tablets are so badly damaged that even the determination of who was the adopter and who the adoptee is largely impeded, while the one complete text concerns unique circumstances. In most instances, one of the participants was a *nadītu*, or unmarried votary, and by analogy with the situation at Sippar where *nadītu* texts are more common, one would expect the *nadītu* to have been the adopter.[14] If this were the case, then the texts should refer to the designation by a *nadītu* of a girl who could follow her calling and inherit her property. However, unlike Sippar, in the Nippur texts the other participants in the transactions are all either men or married women, none of whom could become *nadītus*. In HS 2213 the adopter is clearly a *nadītu* and the adoptee a man. Indeed, other information (see pp. 15–16 below) makes it clear that this particular *nadītu* participated in more than one such adoption. Thus *nadītus* at Nippur used adoption differently from those at Sippar.[15] Unfortunately, the extremely fragmentary condition of these texts precludes penetration into the range of these practices.

With the completion of the description of the four basic types of adoption at Nippur, it is possible to begin a closer examination of the first two types of adoption, omitting for the moment types 3 and 4, which occur only under special circumstances. The evidence indicates that types 1 and 2 reflect contrasting socioeconomic relations between the adopter and the adoptee. In type 1 the support promised by the adoptive sons stresses the economic gain afforded to the adopter; while in type 2 the inclusion of the wife as adopter places more emphasis on the nurturing aspect of parent-child relations. An examination of the penalty clauses in the texts (table 2) may help to clarify this distinction. In type 1 texts (again with the exception of *ARN* 45 [no. 7] and *ARN* 65 [no. 8]), the penalty clauses are either identical for adopter and adoptee, or property inheritance is held hostage for support, or, in PBS 8/2 153 [no. 5], the adopter has more to lose if he breaks the contract than the adoptee. In type 2 texts, on the other hand, the penalty clauses are either equal or the adoptees are threatened with slavery if they break the contract. Thus very different relationships can pertain between the adopter and adoptee in the two types of adoption. In some type 1 texts the adoptee appears to

[14] However, in all cases, the name of the *nadītu* precedes the name of the other individuals; yet table 1 shows that in two cases out of three, the first name on the texts was that of the adoptee. It could be argued that the *nadītus* were of such importance that their names were places first; but it should be noted that in marriage documents the name of the wife, the passive role in the texts, is always mentioned first. On *nadītu* texts at Sippar, see Rivkah Harris, *Ancient Sippar* (Uitgaven van het Nederlands Historisch-Archaeologisch Instituut te Istanbul 36; Leiden: Nederlands Historisch-Archaeologisch Instituut te Istanbul, 1975).

[15] See also Elizabeth C. Stone, "The Social Role of the *nadītu* Women of Nippur," *Journal of the Economic and Social History of the Orient* 25 (1982) 50–70.

TABLE 2. *Penalty Clauses in the Adoption Texts*

		Penalty							
Text No.	*Publication*	1	2	3	4	5	6	7	8
23	OECT 8 20					x			
1	TIM 4 13				x				
2	PBS 8/1 16			x					
3	TIM 4 14				x				
4	BE 6/2 28			x					
5	PBS 8/2 153						x		
6	SAOC 44 10								x
7	*ARN* 45						x		
8	*ARN* 65	x							
9	BE 6/2 24				x				
32	OECT 8 21				x				
10	SAOC 44 15				x				
11	BE 6/2 57	x							
12	SAOC 44 30	x							
13	PBS 8/2 107					x			
14	SAOC 44 1	x							
15	*ARN* 37		x						
27	Cornell 4					x			
16	BE 6/2 48							x	
17	PBS 8/2 155				x				
18	*ARN* 9								x
19	SAOC 44 62								x
20	BE 6/2 4				x				
21	BE 6/2 46								x
22	*ARN* 100								x

Penalties

1. Adoptee may be sold into slavery if he breaks the contract.
2. Penalty clauses are more severe for adoptee than for adopter, but exclude slavery.
3. Adoptee loses inheritance if he withdraws support.
4. Penalty clauses are equal.
5. Penalty clauses are absent.
6. Penalty clauses are more severe for adopter than for adoptee, but exclude slavery.
7. Adopter may be sold into slavery if he breaks the contract.
8. This section not preserved in the text.

Table 3. *Annual Rations*

		Grain		*Oil*		*Wool*	*Total*
Text No.	*Publication*	*sila*	*KWE*	*sila*	*KWE*	*mana*	*KWE*
Adoptions							
23	OECT 8 20	600	450	48[a]	121/10	4	571/460
1	TIM 4 13	600	450	5	13	4	463
2	PBS 8/1 16	720	540	4	10	3	550
3	TIM 4 14	240	180	3	8	0.25[b]	188
4	BE 6/2 28	720	540	3	8	3	548
5	PBS 8/2 153	360	270	6	15	x	285
16	BE 6/2 48	864	648	x	x	6	648+
Other Nippur contracts							
—	*ARN* 29	3,600	2,700	12	30	10	2,730
—	TIM 4 27	740	555	4	10	5	565[c]
—	PBS 8/2 116	720	540	8	20	8	560[d]

KWE = kilograms wheat equivalent, calculated according to the system of Colin Clark and Margaret Haswell, *The Economics of Subsistence Agriculture* (London: Macmillan, 1970).

Notes

a. The scribe probably intended to write 4 *sila* per year, instead of 4 *sila* per month; therefore wheat equivalent has been calculated using both figures.
b. This figure is ¼ *gín* silver.
c. This is the amount which three brothers give to their mother.
d. PBS 8/2 116 is a restatement of the support given by brothers to their *nadītu* sister in *ARN* 29.

have the upper hand, whereas in type 2 texts it is the adopters who have the advantage.

Confirmation that the penalty clauses are in fact indicators of different relationships between adopter and adoptee comes from an examination of the levels of support stipulated by the adoption contracts (table 3).[16] Both the highest (BE 6/2 48 [no. 16]) and the lowest (TIM 4 14 [no. 3]) figures concern atypical circumstances; in the former the support is to be provided to a

[16] I have converted the grain and oil into "wheat equivalent" using the system devised by Colin Clark and Margaret Haswell, *The Economics of Subsistence Agriculture* (London: Macmillan, 1970). My figures are based on measurements taken from whole grain barley and sesame oil obtained commercially in Chicago. A sila was taken to be equivalent to a quart. Since, however, the size of the sila is not well defined, and since we do not know how modern barley and oil might differ from their ancient counterparts, these figures must be taken as only rough estimates.

stepmother, while in the latter it is to be provided to an otherwise unidentified third person.[17] Of the other adoption texts, the highest levels of support are recorded in those texts (PBS 8/1 16 [no. 2] and BE 6/2 28 [no. 4]) in which the penalty for the withdrawal of support was the loss of inheritance rights; the middle levels of support are associated with texts with equal or absent penalty clauses (TIM 4 13 [no. 1] and OECT 8 20 [no. 23]); while the lowest level of support is found in the text in which the penalty for the adopter breaking the contract is more severe than that for the adoptee (PBS 8/2 153 [no. 5]). The relationship between the penalty clauses and the levels of support is thus confirmed.

These levels of support may be compared both with support levels found in other Nippur texts (see table 3), and with modern subsistence figures from Iraq. It is significant that the higher levels of support in the adoption texts, and two of the three support clauses found in non-adoption texts, are all around 550 kg wheat equivalent per year—close to the figure of 536 kg wheat equivalent that Clark and Haswell calculated as the average subsistence level in Iraq during the 1950s.[18]

Further evidence on the nature of the relationships between all parties in type 1 adoptions may be found through an examination of OECT 8 20 [no. 23] and OECT 8 17/18 [nos. 24 and 53], written over thirty years apart. In the earlier text, Ur-Lumma adopts Lu-Bau as his heir in exchange for support. The text includes an oath in which Ur-Lumma and his heirs forswear all claims to Lu-Bau's new inheritance. In OECT 8 17/18 [no. 24 and 53], it appears that Lu-Bau has died, apparently without issue, and that the natural sons of his adoptive father, Ur-Lumma, therefore inherit his property, which includes much of that originally owned by Ur-Lumma, their father. Although Ur-Lumma's inheritance document has not been preserved, it seems safe to assume that his two natural sons lost their inheritance rights at the time of the adoption of Lu-Bau.[19] If the natural and adoptive sons had all been co-heirs, one would expect the two natural sons to have owned real estate contiguous to that of their adoptive brother since Nippur inheritances typically divided each plot between all heirs. That was not the case. Thus, if my interpretation of these two texts is correct, it becomes clear that Ur-Lumma's family expected to lose all future rights to their property as a result of this adoption; and it was only through the accident of Lu-Bau's childlessness that they were able to regain control. These data suggest that the adopter in this case must somehow have been forced into this transaction, since on the surface he had little to gain. It seems likely that Ur-Lumma was a debt-ridden

[17] BE 6/2 48 [no. 16] and TIM 4 27 suggest that sons were expected to provide support for their mothers after their father's death. The wording of TIM 4 14 [no. 3] suggests that it may be a restatement of an earlier adoption, rather than the original text.

[18] Clark and Haswell, *Economics of Subsistence Agriculture*, 81.

[19] In the intervening thirty or forty years, Lu-Bau presumably made other transactions whose texts have not been preserved, explaining why not all the property that he had received from Ur-Lumma is to be found in his later inheritance document.

property owner who was prevented by contemporary alienation restrictions from converting his property into cash through sale. Lu-Bau, on the other hand, the son of an *agrig*, a temple official, was probably a wealthy, but perhaps property-less or property-poor individual[20] who, while relieving Ur-Lumma from the burden of debt and want in his old age, also relieved him of his property. Even if he already owned some real property, since this text predates the time when temple offices become alienable and since the bulk of his adoptive inheritance was made up of these offices, adoption would still have been the only way for Lu-Bau to have gained control over such prestigious property.[21] In this example, the familial motives for adoption as outlined by Goody are absent. It is my contention that, similarly, largely economic motives dominated in other type 1 adoptions; the impoverished father received cash and security in his old age in exchange for the real property desired by his new son.[22]

The texts *ARN* 45 [no. 7] and *ARN* 65 [no. 8] do not fit comfortably into our four types. In the earlier text, *ARN* 45 [no. 7], a type 1 adoption was written, but without the usual support clause. In this text the penalty clause for the adopter was considerably harsher than for the adoptees. In *ARN* 65 [no. 8], written one year later, the terms of the adoption were changed. In this case, the property to be received by the adoptees was spelled out, and turns out to be quite meager, omitting the house property promised in the earlier text. In addition, the penalty clauses are altered so that the adoptees now face slavery if they break the contract. On the other hand, the support clause is still missing from the text. It is extremely difficult to understand how such a radical change in the relationship between the adopting parties could have taken place in only ten months. The second text could have been the result of litigation, perhaps due to the failure of the adoptive sons to live up to the unwritten part of their agreement. Unfortunately, since, as always, no clues as to the exact circumstances surrounding the writing to these contracts are given, one must simply accept them as anomalous.

[20] Although the *agrig*, or temple administrator, occurs not infrequently in the Nippur contracts, there is no conclusive evidence to suggest that *agrig*s were property owners. In all cases but one, the *agrig* is listed as a neighbor. Although such an occurrence suggests property ownership, residence may have been all that was implied. My general understanding of the title is that it referred to a position in the bureaucracy.

[21] It is not entirely clear what, other than prestige, was implied by temple-office ownership. In rare cases, the texts indicate that a prebend field was attached. Otherwise, it seems probable that ownership of such an office entitled the holder to a share in temple revenues. It seems clear, though, that the duties of such office holders were largely nonexistent.

[22] Such a relationship between adopter and adoptee was not unique to Old Babylonian Nippur, as Claus Wilcke has kindly brought to my attention. Both an Old Babylonian text from Sippar (C. Wilcke, "Notes Breves," *Revue d'Assyriologie* 73 [1979] 93 n. 11) and an Ur III text from Nippur (David I. Owen, *Neo-Sumerian Archival Texts Primarily from Nippur, in the University Museum, the Oriental Institute and the Iraq Museum* [Winona Lake, IN: Eisenbrauns, 1982], text 131 [CBS 8372]) record adoptees paying the debts of their adoptive fathers.

Although type 1 adoptions seem to have served primarily as means of property transfer, it must not be assumed that no Old Babylonian adoptions served the social functions outlined by Goody. Certainly in the case of PBS 8/2 107 [no. 13], in which a married couple adopted an infant from its natural parents, parallels can be drawn with the actions of childless couples everywhere. In other adoptions, the social implications are more complicated, but the evidence suggests that type 2 and 3 adoptions served to redress familial deficits. The terms of type 2 adoptions suggest that they were usually written when childless couples (hence the inclusion of the wife) adopted disadvantaged children (hence the somewhat stiff penalty clauses), in order to provide themselves with heirs (hence the clear statement of the inheritance rights of the adoptees). In type 3 adoptions the situation is clearer. The texts serve to turn two broken families into one whole one. These type 2 and 3 texts suggest that under these circumstances adopters and adoptees were expected to live together as families; for this reason the obligations owed to parents by their children did not have to be spelled out.

In the previous pages, adoption texts have been analyzed in isolation, but to understand how they functioned as one part of the socioeconomic system, the act of adoption must be examined within the context of an individual's total transactional activities. I will therefore continue with two case studies which illustrate how adoption, combined with marriage, property sale, and litigation, was used to achieve desired social or economic goals.

Case Study 1: Ur-Pabilsag Archive

The archive which concerns the activities of Ur-Pabilsag, previously discussed by Kraus, illustrates the interweaving of the social and economic aspects of adoption.[23] Although only one adoption text has been preserved, at least three adoptions took place, creating a web of social relations that was extremely complicated. The texts from this archive (see table 4 and fig. 1) show four distinct periods of transactional activity. The earliest texts (*ARN* 118, *ARN* 113) describe the inheritance of Ur-Pabilsag and his siblings, and the rearrangements of property which immediately followed the death of their father. In the second period (*ARN* 35, Ni 9232, *ARN* 112) Ur-Pabilsag and his brother are active as property owners involved in the transfer of property. It is the third phase of activity that concerns us the most (the texts in question are HS 2362a + HS 2395 + Ni 9220, HS 2213, *ARN* 41, and BE 6/2 23 + *ARN* 76). Ur-Pabilsag married, and along with Migir-Enlil, was

[23] F. R. Kraus, "Nippur und Isin nach altbabylonischen Rechtsurkunden," *Journal of Cuneiform Studies* 3 (1949). Half of the texts of this archive are in Jena (DDR) (Oelsner, "Neue Daten"). Dr. J. Oelsner has most kindly provided me with a brief description of the contents of the two most significant of the fourteen Jena texts, so that when the other texts from Jena are published they should not radically alter the conclusions drawn here. The published texts are *ARN* 35, *ARN* 41, *ARN* 112, *ARN* 113, *ARN* 118, Ni 9220, Ni 9232, Ni 9309 (these last three are published in *ARN*); PBS 8/1 81, PBS 8/1 82, BE 6/2 11, BE 6/2 23 + *ARN* 76, OIMA 1 18, OIMA 1 20 + *ARN* 136.

TABLE 4. *The Ur-Pabilsag Archive*

Publication	*Date*	*Transaction*
ARN 118	n.d.	Lugal-zimu, Lugal-ḫegal, Ur-Pabilsag, and perhaps Ninlil-meša inherit from Ubarum.
ARN 113	n.d.	Lugal-zimu, Lugal-ḫegal, and Ur-Pabilsag buy orchard and rations from Ninlil-meša.
ARN 112	n.d.	Lugal-zimu sells a field to Lugal-ḫegal.
ARN 35	1784/10	Girni-iša sells a temple office to Ur-Pabilsag.
Ni 9232	n.d.	Ur-Pabilsag sells property.
HS 2362a + HS 2395 + Ni 9220	1779	Ur-Pabilsag marries Ali-aḫati.
HS 2213	1778	Naramtum adopts Ur-Pabilsag.
Ni 9309	n.d.	Naramtum sells property.
ARN 41	1768/8	Ur-Pabilsag and Narubtum exchange a slave for some fields.
PBS 8/1 81	1762/6	Lugal-zimu and Ur-Pabilsag go to court to balance the account of some fields.
PBS 8/1 82	1762/7	Lugal-zimu goes to court to protect his sister's interest in a house.
BE 6/2 11	1758/9	Damiq-ilišu and Narubtum exchange houses with Nabi-Šamaš.
BE 6/2 23 + *ARN* 76	1746/10	Narubtum and Ur-Pabilsag inherit from Migir-Enlil.
OIMA 1 20 + *ARN* 136	1739/-	Damu-eribam, Nuska-nišu, and Rabut-Sin inherit from Damiq-ilišu.
OIMA 1 18	1739/10	Damu-eribam and Nuska-nišu sell a field to Ur-dukuga.

adopted by Naramtum, a *nadītu*. This provided him with close ties with the families of both his wife and his adoptive brother. When his adoptive brother Migir-Enlil later made Ur-Pabilsag his heir, this latter tie was made doubly strong. In the last period of activity, the texts (*OIMA* 1 20 + *ARN* 136, and *OIMA* 1 18) describe transactions of the next generation of Ur-Pabilsag's family and show how ties which were originally established through marriage[24] and adoption continued to be important in later generations. Since the concern of this chapter is adoption, our discussion will concentrate on the last two periods of activity, using the first two merely to set the scene.

[24] It has not been definitively established whether agnatic endogamy such as is practiced in the area today was also practiced in the past. If it were, as some of the evidence from this and other archives suggest (see p. 18 below), then Ur-Pabilsag's marriage could represent no more than the cementing of already established kinship ties and not the creation of new ones. However, if this were the case, then one would expect this marriage, like most marriages, to have remained unrecorded.

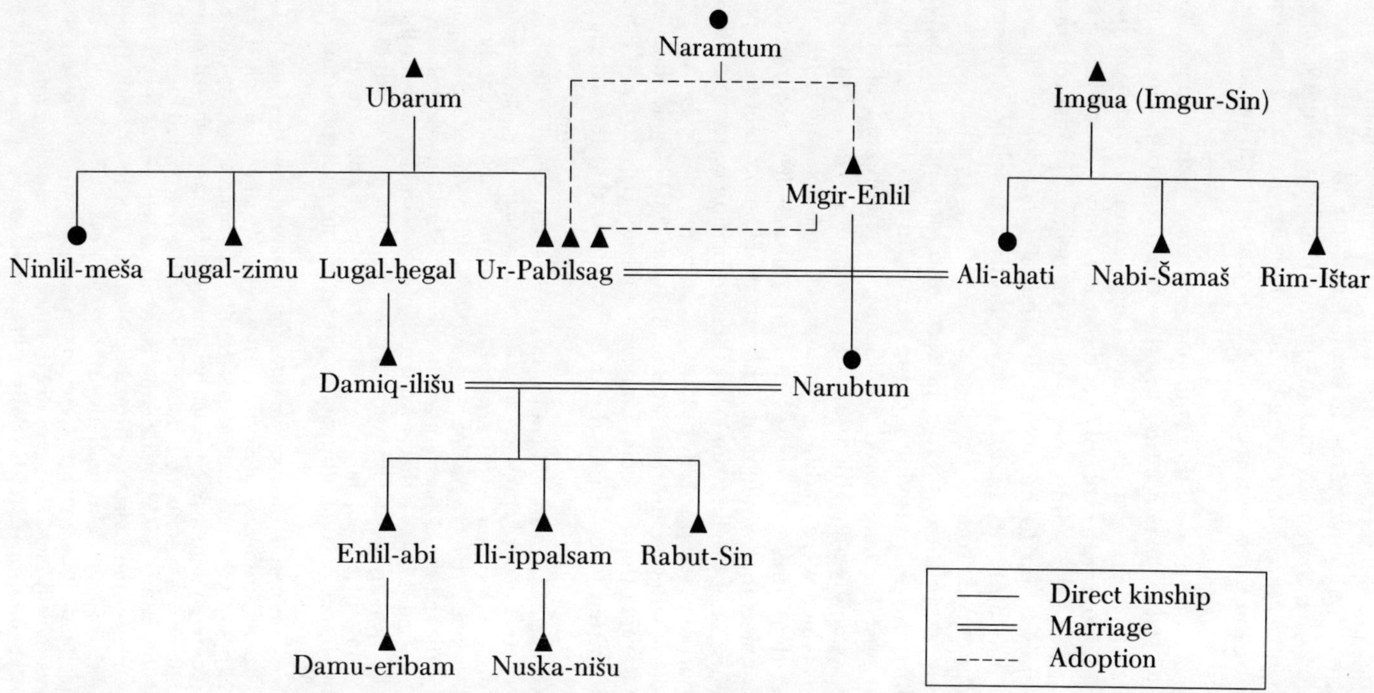

Fig. 1. Genealogy of Ur-Pabilsag

The text *ARN* 118 shows that Ur-Pabilsag, his brothers Lugal-zimu and Lugal-ḫegal, and probably their *nadītu* sister Ninlil-meša inherited property from their father.[25] Although only a small fragment of this text has been preserved, it may be concluded that the original tablet was quite large, but still written in a single column, suggesting a fair-sized estate, and that the order of birth of the three brothers was Lugal-zimu, Lugal-ḫegal, and lastly Ur-Pabilsag.

Ur-Pabilsag's position as the youngest son may help explain his subsequent actions. If the texts relating to other families from Nippur may be used as models, the eldest son, in this case Lugal-zimu, would have been the most likely candidate for the role of "head of the family." Indeed, PBS 8/1 82, a later text in which Lugal-zimu goes to court on behalf of his sister (probably Ninlil-meša), shows him to be acting in precisely that role.[26] Under these circumstances, any authority that a younger brother may have attained must have come from outside sources.[27]

Ur-Pabilsag established such a pattern of independent activity quite early. In 1784 B.C. he purchased a *nar*-ship from Girni-iša. This purchase of a temple office must be considered significant; as mentioned above (p. 2), temple offices, as newly alienable property, were not governed by the alienation restrictions which were traditionally imposed on house and field property. This purchase, therefore, may represent Ur-Pabilsag's first attempt to make extra-family contacts that would enable him to attain some degree of authority for himself. This is not the first time that the acquisition of temple offices was used for this purpose (see pp. 19ff. below).

It is not clear whether his marriage to Ali-aḫati in 1779 B.C. falls into this category, but the fact that a special marriage contract (HS 2362a + HS 2395 + Ni 9220) was written to celebrate the event suggests that the marriage itself

[25] In *ARN* the authors read and copied the fragmentary name of the heir as ^{d}en-líl-[ ]. However, (1) since "nin" and "en" are not dissimilar signs, (2) since in almost all cases the "dingir" and "en" signs are written together, not separately as in this instance, and (3) since *ARN* 113 records the *nadītu* Ninlil-meša selling her patrimony of orchard property and the rights to rations to her three brothers Ur-Pabilsag, Lugal-zimu, and Lugal-ḫegal, I believe that it is most likely that Ninlil-meša was the co-heir with her three brothers, rather than postulating an otherwise unattested third brother Enlil-[ ]. It must be noted, however, that if this were the case, it is the only attestation from Nippur of a *nadītu* receiving property through inheritance (see also Stone, "*Nadītu* Women").

[26] In this text, not only is the sister in question unnamed, but the Lugal-zimu who brings the suit has no further identification. However, (1) since the only Lugal-zimu attested from Nippur is the member of this family, (2) since this text, PBS 8/1 82 is published consecutively and has consecutive museum numbers, shared one witness with, and took place one month later than PBS 8/1 81, a text which clearly describes the activities of this family, and (3) since the sister about whom this text is concerned was a property owner, and therefore probably a *nadītu*, it is most likely that this text describes the affairs of Lugal-zimu and his sister Ninlil-meša.

[27] Such independent behavior patterns on the part of younger brothers have been attested ethnographically; see, for example, Barbara C. Aswad, *Property Control and Social Strategies: Settlers on a Middle Eastern Plain* (University of Michigan, Museum of Anthropology, Anthropological Papers 44; Ann Arbor: University of Michigan, 1971).

TABLE 5. *Participants in the Ur-Pabilsag Archive*

Name	*ARN* 118	*ARN* 113	*ARN* 112	*ARN* 35	Ni 9232	HS 2362a + HS 2395 + Ni 9220	HS 2213	Ni 9309	*ARN* 41	PBS 8/1 81	PBS 8/1 82	BE 6/2 11	BE 6/2 23 + *ARN* 76	OIMA 1 20 + *ARN* 136	OIMA 1 18
Ninlil-meša daughter of Ubarum	A?	A									A?				
Lugal-zimu son of Ubarum	A	A	A							A	A				
Lugal-ḫegal son of Ubarum	A	A							W	W?					
Ur-Pabilsag son of Ubarum	A	A		A	A	A	A	W?	A	A					
Naramtum, *nadītu*, daughter of Bau-a . . .						A		A					A		
Narubtum daughter of Migir-Enlil									A			A	A		
Damiq-ilišu son of Lugal-ḫegal			W									A			
Damu-eribam son of Enlil-abi														A	A
Nuska-nišu son of Ili-ippalsa														A	A
Rabut-Sin son of Damiq-ilišu														A	W
Imgua												N			
Ali-aḫati daughter of Imgua					A										
Nabi-Šamaš son of Imgua												A			
Rim-Ištar son of Imgua															N

A = actor N = neighbor W = witness

was unusual. Ties between the members of Ali-aḫati's and Ur-Pabilsag's families can be documented subsequent to their marriage (see table 5), but whether these were cause or consequence cannot be ascertained. Be that as it may, there is no question that when Ur-Pabilsag was adopted by the *nadītu* Naramtum in the following year, he was establishing firm extra-familial ties. The importance of these outside ties was confirmed when Ur-Pabilsag received a number of fields in exchange for a slave girl from Narubtum the daughter of Migir-Enlil, the other man adopted by Naramtum, Narubtum being his adoptive niece.[28] This avuncular relationship is supported by the terminology used in text, *ARN* 41. While in the text, Ur-Pabilsag refers to Narubtum as his daughter, and she refers to him as her father, the seal impressions record their true biological affiliations.[29]

It seems that, although Naramtum's actions had made Ur-Pabilsag and Migir-Enlil adoptive brothers, this tie did not necessarily imply full fraternal relations between the two men. Thus the repeated use of father-daughter kinship terms in *ARN* 41 may have been used to signify that Ur-Pabilsag was accepting the full role of father's brother to Narubtum.[30]

[28] Migir-Enlil's adoption document has not been preserved, but in BE 6/2 23 + *ARN* 136 he refers to Naramtum as his mother, and since she was a *nadītu* and therefore forbidden to bear children, she must have been his adoptive rather than his natural mother.

[29] The transliteration and translation of the text are as follows:

1. ^{I}*a-li-a-ḫu-ša*
2. geme$_2$ ur-^{d}pa-bil-sag
3. kù-bi ⅓ ma-na
4. ^{I}*na-ru-ub-tum* dumu-ni-ra
6. in-na-an-sum
7. ^{I}*na-ru-ub-tum* dumu-munus-a-ni
8. ^{I}ur-^{d}pa-bil-sag ad-da-ni-ra
9. 3 gán a-šà sur-^{d}gilgameš
10. ús-a-du ^{d}en-zu-*be-el-ap-li*
11. 2 gín 20 sar a-šà egir-sum-lá
12. ús-a-du ^{d}en-zu-*ri-me-ni*
13. 2 gín a-šà ka-ús-sa-^{d}nin-imma
14. ús-a-du kú-^{d}nin-imma
15. in-na-an-sum
16. u$_4$-kúr-sé lú-lú-ù
17. nu-un-gi$_4$-gi$_4$-da
18. mu lugal-bi in-pá-dé-eš

SEAL: ur-^{d}pa-bil-sag
dumu *u-bar-ru-um*

SEAL: *na-ru-ub-tum*
dumu-munus *mi-gir*-^{d}en-líl

Ali-aḫuša, the female slave of Ur-Pabilsag, valued at ⅓ mina of silver, has been given by Ur-Pabilsag her owner to his daughter Narubtum. Narubtum his daughter has in turn given to her father Ur-Pabilsag, 3 *iku*s of land in the Sur-Gilgameš field next to the plot of Sin-bel-apli, 2 *iku*s 20 sar of land in the Egir-sumla field next to the plot of Sin-rimeni, and 2 *iku*s of land in the Kaussa-Ninurta field next to the plot of Ku-Ninimma. In future neither will make a claim against the other. In the name of the king they have sworn. Sealed by Ur-Pabilsag son of Ubarum, and Narubtum daughter of Migir-Enlil.

[30] In other Nippur texts there is evidence of close kinship terms being extended to more distant relatives. One example will suffice. In BE 6/2 30 Mutum-ilu and Mar-erṣetim are described as sons of Dama-gugu, who was in fact their father's father. Similarly, in BE 6/2 10 these same individuals (this time identified with their true patronymic) refer to Ududu as their father's brother. In fact, genealogical reconstruction shows that he cannot be closer than their father's father's brother's son. As in the present instance, these closer kinship terms were used to emphasize the obligations of kinship.

The full implications of these new relationships is not clear without an examination of the much later text BE 6/2 23 + *ARN* 76. Here Migir-Enlil's property is inherited by his daughter Narubtum and by his adoptive brother Ur-Pabilsag. A brief, not altogether clear, phrase at the end may shed some light on the situation. I prefer to translate this colophon to the effect that when Migir-Enlil's wife died (and left him without male issue), he adopted Ur-Pabilsag (already his adoptive brother) as his heir.[31]

The implication of such an interpretation is that while adoption implied a restructuring of relationships between those directly involved in the transaction, these new relationships did not necessarily extend throughout the kinship system. Thus although Ur-Pabilsag and Migir-Enlil were both the adopted sons of Naramtum, without an additional statement Ur-Pabilsag could not have inheritance expectations as Migir-Enlil's residual heir, nor could Migir-Enlil's daughter Narubtum, when orphaned, expect Ur-Pabilsag to accept the protective role normally expected of the father's brother. Thus, by designating Ur-Pabilsag as his heir, Migir-Enlil consolidated relationships which were already implied by Naramtum's adoptions and provided his daughter with a protector. Ur-Pabilsag, on the other hand, not only received an inheritance, but with it control over the heiress Narubtum. He apparently exercised this control by arranging for the marriage of Narubtum with his nephew Damiq-ilišu, the son of his older brother Lugal-ḫegal.[32]

It is at about this time that the very real hostility that existed between Lugal-zimu, the head of the family, and his youngest brother Ur-Pabilsag becomes apparent. In PBS 8/1 81 the two brothers had to go to court before they were able to settle their accounts over shared residential property. This

[31] Kraus, "Nippur und Isin," 144, takes the kinship-term evidence in *ARN* 41 literally and presents an alternative translation to BE 6/2 23, suggesting that it was Ur-Pabilsag's wife who had died and that he had adopted Narubtum. The transliteration of the relevant passage reads as follows:

> ⅓ nam *na-ra-am-tum* ama *mi-gir-*ᵈen-líl
> *na-ru-ub-tum* dumu-munus *mi-gir-*ᵈen-líl
> ú ur-ᵈpa-bil-sag-ga egir dam-a-na-ka
> nam-ibila-ni-šè ba-da-an-ri-a
> téš-a-sì-ga-bi in-ba-eš

Both translations are grammatically possible, but Kraus's interpretation of the passage seems implausible. It fails to explain why Ur-Pabilsag received an inheritance from Migir-Enlil: while an adoptive brother could be declared an heir and thus be expected to inherit, surely a man adopting a daughter had no claim to her father's estate.

[32] Text BE 6/2 11, in which Damiq-ilišu and Narubtum are described as husband and wife, unfortunately lacks all patronymics. Several features suggest that this text refers to members of the Ur-Pabilsag family: the witness list of *ARN* 112 indicates that Lugal-ḫegal had a son named Damiq-ilišu; it is unusual for a wife to participate with her husband in a property transaction unless she were an heiress; and, finally, the purchaser, neighbor, and witnesses to this text are all drawn from families which had established ties both with Ur-Pabilsag's family and with that of his wife. Thus the circumstantial evidence that the text concerns the activities of members of this family is compelling.

court case implies that Ur-Pabilsag had successfully used marriage and adoption to build up sufficient authority to challenge his eldest brother. When he achieved the marriage between his second brother's son Damiq-ilišu and the niece that he had acquired through adoption, this marriage may have represented a takeover of his eldest brother's role, since through his relationship with Lugal-ḫegal's daughter-in-law he would have been in a position of dominance over both his and Lugal-ḫegal's branches of the family. Such a scenario has strong parallels with the activities of younger sons in modern Syria described by Aswad.[33]

The remaining texts relating to this family concern the activities of the heirs of Damiq-ilišu and Narubtum. Little needs to be said here, save that they indicate a continuation of the relationship that had existed with the family of Ur-Pabilsag's wife Ali-aḫati.

To summarize the significance of this archive, an examination of the implications of the adoptions both from the point of view of the adoptee, Ur-Pabilsag, and from that of the adopters may be profitable. Ur-Pabilsag appears to have been an ambitious youngest son who used marriage and adoption to amass both wealth and prestige to challenge the dominance of his eldest brother. His motivation for involvement in the adoption (and probably also in his marriage) was apparently to achieve sufficient wealth and power to successfully challenge his eldest brother's dominance over the family. His adopters, on the other hand, were rich in wealth and property, but poor in kinsmen. The key to understanding Naramtum's and Migir-Enlil's desire to form bonds with Ur-Pabilsag was the extremely dependent position of women in Old Babylonian Nippur.[34] Narubtum's exchange of field property for a slave girl in *ARN* 41 reflects this position; if unmarried women were secluded, slave girls were needed for them to make contacts with the outside world. Furthermore, both *nadītus* and married women were dependent on their brothers and sons for protection, as illustrated by PBS 8/1 82, where Lugalzimu goes to court on behalf of his sister. The adoptions of Ur-Pabilsag and Migir-Enlil by Naramtum may therefore be understood as acts which provided her with the security of a family in her old age, a role normally filled by the sons her calling denied her. Similarly, when Migir-Enlil made his adoptive brother co-heir with his daughter, he was ensuring that Narubtum would have a protector after his death.

All three adoptions documented in this archive fall within Goody's definition of adoption. Two of these adoptions are of the type 4 category, adoptions by *nadītus*, while the adoption of Ur-Pabilsag by Migir-Enlil is probably best placed in the type 2 category. In all three instances the functions of the adoption fall in Goody's category 3—"to provide an individual or couple with an heir to their property."[35]

[33] Aswad, *Property Control and Social Strategies.*
[34] Stone, "*Nadītu* Women."
[35] Goody, "Adoption in Cross-Cultural Perspective," 5.

For an understanding of the familial functions of adoption, it is irrelevant that Ur-Pabilsag's ambition led to his adoption by the heir-seekers Naramtum and Migir-Enlil. Nevertheless, not only does this archive shed light on the role of alliance in ancient Mesopotamian society, but as it highlights the role of adoption in mediating the social needs of some (Naramtum and Migir-Enlil) with the political and economic desires of others (Ur-Pabilsag), this archive also indicates how the institution of adoption could be manipulated to the point where economic motives would be paramount in some situations. Once economic and political ambition on the part of the adoptee became accepted as part of the adoption process, then it is but a short step before economic motivations on the part of (both) adopter and adoptee may form the basis of the transaction. Such a situation will be illustrated in the case study that follows.

Case Study 2: The Mannum-mešu-liṣṣur Archive

This archive, like that of Atta studied by Goetze,[36] documents the acquisition of property, mostly in the form of temple offices, by a single individual in the troubled economic times associated with the eleventh year of Samsuiluna, around 1739 B.C.[37] Without the texts from this archive which are now housed at Cornell University and published below by David I. Owen, the social implications of the activities it represents were not clear. The Cornell texts not only fill in details of Mannum-mešu-liṣṣur's economic activities, but they spotlight the significance of adoption for these activities. In a manner not unlike that of Ur-Pabilsag, Mannum-mešu-liṣṣur, and to a lesser extent, his brother Ninurta-muballiṭ were able to use the institution of adoption to place themselves in a powerful economic position. However, unlike those in the Ur-Pabilsag archive, their adopters had primarily economic, not social, motivations for their acts.

The similarities between the Ur-Pabilsag archive and that of Mannum-mešu-liṣṣur should not be overstressed. The antecedents of the two are quite different. Whereas Ur-Pabilsag was a property owner by birthright, albeit a youngest son, all available evidence suggests that Mannum-mešu-liṣṣur's property ownership was only made possible through adoption. He was born of a property-less, but clearly wealthy, family, and apparently used adoption as a way of turning his family's wealth into an opportunity for social mobility.

Since it was Mannum-mešu-liṣṣur's admission into the Sin-iqišam family (see fig. 2) that allowed him entry into the property-owning group, an examination of that family is in order. The texts from this archive allow the reconstruction of a fairly complete genealogy for the last three generations of the Sin-iqišam family. In addition, four texts which apparently shared a

[36] See A. Goetze, "The Archive of Ātta from Nippur," *Journal of Cuneiform Studies* 18 (1964) 102–13; Stone, *Nippur Neighborhoods*, 291–94.

[37] See Stone, "Economic Crisis."

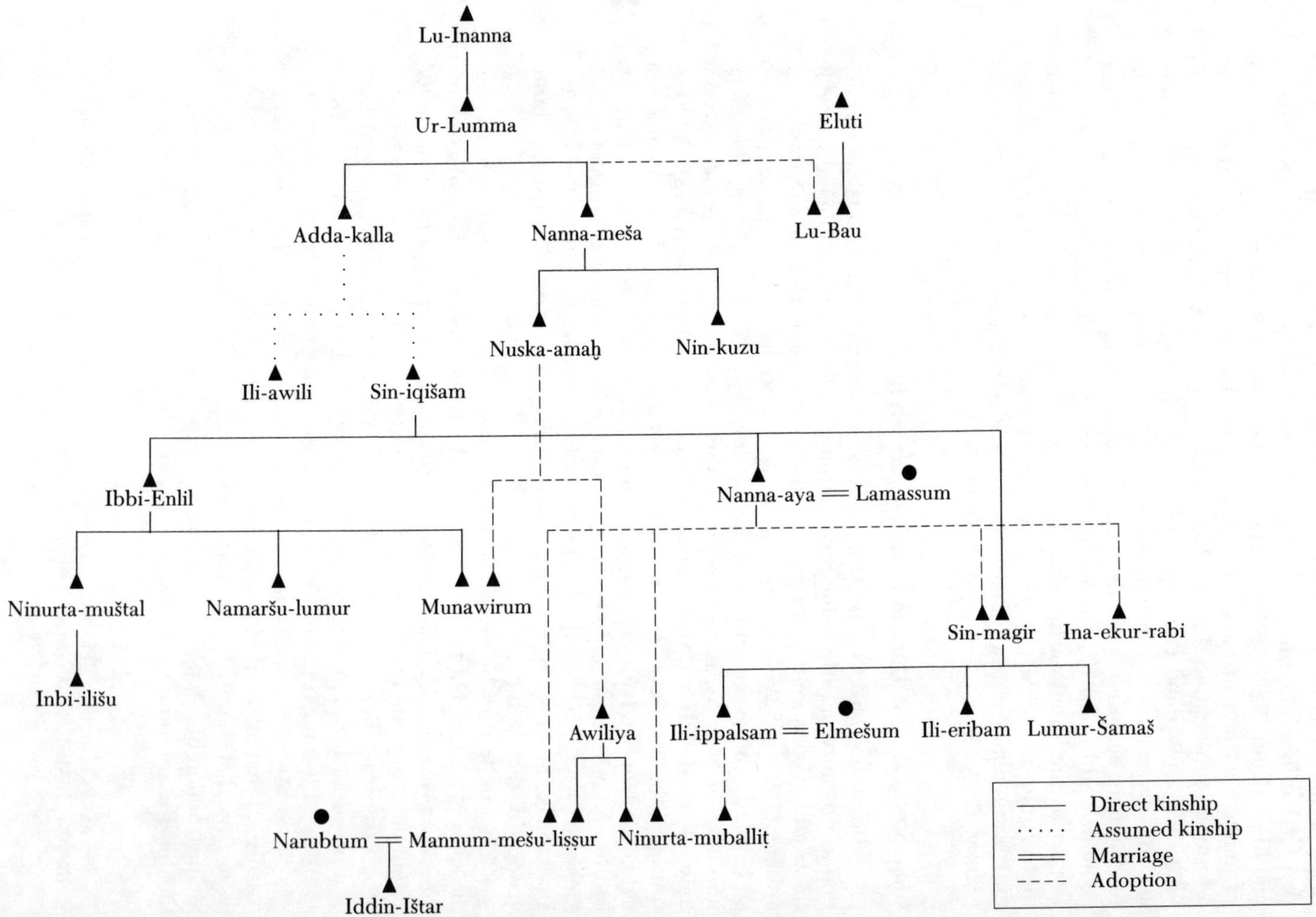

Fig. 2 Genealogy of Mannum-mešu-liṣṣur

findspot with the others (OECT 8 4 [no. 25], OECT 8 17/18 [nos. 24 and 53], and OECT 8 20 [no. 23])[38] describe the activities of Sin-iqišam's ancestors. Regrettably, texts concerning members of the intervening generations are mostly lacking, resulting in a somewhat incompletely reconstructed genealogy.

The evidence suggests that the family had controlled a quite substantial amount of temple-office property from the late Isin–Larsa period onward, as well as more limited amounts of real estate. However, from the beginning there are grounds for suggesting that the family was in economic difficulties. As noted above, OECT 8 20 [no. 23] describes how around 1870 B.C. Ur-Lumma adopted Lu-Bau. This was a type 1 adoption (see table 1) wherein Ur-Lumma made his adoptive son his heir. The consequences of this adoption to the family were not as dire as might have been feared; OECT 8 17/18 [nos. 24 and 53] was written on the death without issue of Lu-Bau, with his property therefore reverting to Adda-kala and Nanna-meša, the natural sons of Ur-Lumma.[39]

It must be assumed that Ur-Lumma adopted Lu-Bau because the inalienability of temple offices at that time gave him no opportunity for obtaining an income large enough for his needs. Lu-Bau must have provided the liquid assets necessary to keep Ur-Lumma afloat, but at the cost of the disinheritance of his natural sons. When these sons eventually inherited from Lu-Bau, this should have left the family finances in a very healthy condition; the property was still intact and the adoption should have brought with it an infusion of cash. However, it appears that this was not the case. Perhaps the estate was too heavily concentrated in minor temple offices to be viable, but only one generation later, adoption was again resorted to. In OECT 8 4 [no. 25], a text whose meaning is largely opaque, Nuska-amaḫ, a grandson of Ur-Lumma, is found in dispute with his sister over an inheritance share. Within the text, both on the seal and on the tablet, is a reference to two heirs of Nuska-amaḫ. Once again the use of the term "heir" (ibila) on both seal and tablet indicates that these men were not the sons of Nuska-amaḫ. One,

[38] These texts were published in the same volume as many of the others (OECT 8) and were apparently part of the same purchase. Although several non-Nippur texts were included in this volume (e.g., nos. 3, 12, 13, 15), texts 4, 17, 18, and 20 are assuredly from Nippur. More importantly, however, the fact that they concern the same types of property as those later texts, much of which is unattested outside this archive, seems to confirm the relationship between the two groups of texts.

[39] Two features of this text indicate that Adda-kala and Nanna-meša were not the sons of Lu-Bau. First, although Nanna-meša is named the eldest son, this is the only inheritance text known from Nippur where a living eldest son is not awarded the customary 10 percent preference portion. The absence of such a preference portion is always an indicator of some irregularity of relationship between testator and heir. The second customary marker of such irregularity is found in the seal. Here Adda-kala and Nuska-meša are described simply as the heirs of Lu-Bau, not as his sons. In all texts where a father-son relationship can be established, this relationship is also reflected in the wording of the seal. Only in those texts where such a direct relationship is not implied is the term for heir substituted. These anomalies and the fact that the two heirs were brothers have led to the interpretation forwarded here.

Munawirum, may have been a grandson,[40] since he was alive some thirty-five years later when the estate was divided (Cornell 23 [no. 51]). Munawirum also occurs as a witness to Cornell 18 [no. 28], where he is described as the son of Nuska-amaḫ. This affiliation is to be expected if he were a grandson of Nuska-amaḫ who had inheritance expectations.[41] The other heir, Awiliya, was dead—with two sons old enough to conduct business for themselves—fifteen or twenty years later and would therefore have been too old when OECT 8 4 [no. 25] was written to have been a grandson. In this case it seems more likely that this individual was an outsider, perhaps an adoptive son who, like Lu-Bau before him, was adopted into the family for financial reasons.[42]

The two eventual heirs of Nuska-amaḫ, Mannum-mešu-liṣṣur the son of Awiliya and Munawirum, also had dealings in OECT 8 16 [no. 30], where they exchange property. Since the house that Mannum-mešu-liṣṣur gives is recorded as an inheritance share, this text may represent the exchange of inheritance expectations, and not the property that they owned at the time.[43]

Nuska-amaḫ's branch of the family was not the only one to adopt members of Awiliya's family. Although the amount of property listed in the inheritance document (Cornell 6 [no. 26]; see tables 6 and 7), in which Sin-iqišam leaves his property to his sons Ibbi-Enlil and Nanna-aya, is considerably less than that recorded in OECT 8 17/18 [nos. 24 and 53], it is nevertheless substantial. Converting all of the property into shekels of silver,[44] this estate can be valued at approximately one half of that recorded in OECT 8 17/18 [nos. 24 and 53] (112 shekels as opposed to 244), but still greater in value than 60 percent of all known estates from Nippur. Nevertheless, shortly after receiving their patrimony,[45] both Ibbi-Enlil and Nanna-aya forge links with outsiders, especially with Mannum-mešu-liṣṣur, son of Awiliya the adoptive son of Nuska-amaḫ.

Cornell 4 [no. 27] provides the context in which these links were made. In this text, Nanna-aya the younger son of Sin-iqišam marries a woman named Lamassum and at the same time adopts four sons, two of whom, Mannum-

[40] Although the name Munawirum is unusual, it seems unlikely that this is the same person as Munawirum son of Ibbi-Enlil. If these two did represent the same person, then in Cornell 18 [no. 28] he would have been witnessing the sale of property by his own father, which was not a common practice at Nippur.

[41] Such extension of kinship terms is well documented in the texts from Nippur.

[42] Since the term for son is frequently used at Nippur to refer to all male descendants on the direct agnatic line, the use of the term "heir" here should probably be taken as an indication that the individual involved did not fall into this category.

[43] This is not without precedent; indeed, in the Ur-Pabilsag archive he and his adoptive sister exchange property, some of which they were later to inherit.

[44] See Stone, "Economic Crisis," for details of the methods used. Field, house, and temple-office property are converted into shekels of silver based on the mean value of each class of property as recorded in sale contracts.

[45] The date on Cornell 6 [no. 26] is broken; all that can be determined is that it was written between 1749 and 1721 B.C., during the reign of Samsuiluna. Since texts dating to 1744 B.C. and later concern the actions of Sin-iqišam's sons acting as heads of households, it must be assumed that the text was written between 1749 and 1745 B.C. The only other chronological indicator is the name of the scribe, Ku-Ninimma, who is otherwise attested on texts ranging in date from 1746 to 1739 B.C.

mešu-liṣṣur and Ninurta-muballiṭ, are known from other sources to be the sons of Awiliya. The origins of the other two adoptees, Sin-magir and Ina-ekur-rabi, are less clear. In Cornell 6 [no. 26], a Sin-magir son of Sin-iqišam is a witness, suggesting that he may have been a brother of Ibbi-Enlil and Nanna-aya who had been excluded from Sin-iqišam's inheritance for some reason.[46] If this Sin-magir were the same as the one adopted by Nanna-aya, it would accord well with his age, since Sin-magir's sons were old enough to conduct transactions of their own a mere five years later. No information is available on the antecedents of Ina-ekur-rabi, the fourth adoptee.

A different interpretation of this text is possible, and is one which superficially would seem to accord better with our understanding of other type 3 adoptions. This interpretation would assume the four adoptees to be the sons of the wife, Lamassum, by a previous marriage (presumably to Awiliya). But such an interpretation is not without difficulties. One lies in the wording of the text itself. In other type 3 adoptions the natural parent of the adoptees is said to give the sons as heirs to their new spouse (nam-ibila-ni-šè in-na-an-sum), but in this text, no connection is drawn between the marriage and the adoption. The second objection is that such an interpretation would not explain the complexities of interrelationship which are evidenced in the later texts. It is possible, therefore, that the connection between Nanna-aya's marriage and adoptions was less direct; the two acts that were recorded on the same tablet may have been linked by undocumented factors about which one can only guess.[47] I would venture that this text is not strictly a type 3 adoption, but is rather a marriage contract and a type 1 or 2 adoption contract combined on one tablet;[48] it represents the establishment of external ties by Nanna-aya, presumably because his financial situation gave him no choice.

46 Such a pattern is not unknown at Nippur. Indeed, in BE 6/2 43 an almost parallel example can be found. There, two grandsons inherit (presumably after their father had died), while their paternal uncle who was excluded from this inheritance acted as one of the witnesses. It seems likely that this act of witnessing represented the acceptance by the excluded son of his disinheritance. In many instances it appears that such excluded sons received their patrimony before their father's death in the form of moveable property. See Elizabeth C. Stone, "Social and Economic Organization of Old Babylonian Nippur" (Ph.D. diss., University of Chicago, 1979).

47 It is possible, for instance, that Nanna-aya's marriage to Lamassum was only made possible through adoption, that the bride-price was provided by the adopters. This, of course, is but one of many possible explanations. See S. Greengus, "Old Babylonian Marriage Ceremonies and Rites," *Journal of Cuneiform Studies* 20 (1966) 55–72; idem, "The Old Babylonian Marriage Contract," *Journal of the American Oriental Society* 89 (1969) 505–32; and G. R. Driver and John C. Miles, *The Babylonian Laws* (Oxford: Clarendon, 1952) for more information on marriage practices.

48 Although this text includes the name of both husband and wife and has neither a detailed description of the property to be received by the adopters nor a clause describing the level of support to be provided to the adopter, it is nevertheless not identical to type 2 adoptions. In the penalty clauses, the wife is in the same category as the adoptive sons, as is found in type 3 adoptions. If we ignore her presence, then the penalty clauses more closely resemble those of type 1 texts. This text, therefore, remains a unique example.

[*text continues on p. 28*]

TABLE 6. *The Mannum-mešu-liṣṣur Archive*

Text No.	*Publication*	*Date*	*Transaction*
23	OECT 8 20	1873–1869/6/-	Ur-Lumma adopts Lu-Bau.
24	OECT 8 17	1837/13/-	Nanna-meša and Adda-kala inherit from Lu-Bau.
25	OECT 8 4	1762/5/-	Court dispute between Nanna-amaḫ and Nin-kuzu over an inheritance share.
26	Cornell 6	1749–1721/5/-	Ibbi-Enlil and Nanna-aya inherit from Sin-iqišam.
27	Cornell 4	1744/6/-	Nanna-aya and Lamassum adopt Mannum-mešu-liṣṣur, Ninurta-muballiṭ, Sin-magir, and Ina-ekur-rabi.
28	Cornell 18	1742/1/14	Mannum-mešu-liṣṣur buys house from Ibbi-Enlil.
29	OECT 8 19	1741/10/25	Ninurta-muštal, Namaršu-lumur, and Munawirum inherit from Ibbi-Enlil.
30	OECT 8 16	1740/3/23	Mannum-mešu-liṣṣur and Munawirum exchange house and temple offices.
31	OECT 8 11	1740/9/3	Mannum-mešu-liṣṣur and the heirs of Ibbi-Enlil settle accounts.
32	OECT 8 21	1739/-/22	Ili-ippalsa adopts Ninurta-muballiṭ.
33	Cornell 12	1739/2/1	Mannum-mešu-liṣṣur buys temple offices from Ninurta-muštal.
34	OECT 8 6	1739/9/16	Mannum-mešu-liṣṣur buys temple offices from Ili-ippalsa.
35	Cornell 8	1739/10/8	Mannum-mešu-liṣṣur buys temple offices from Ninurta-APIN.
36	Cornell 19	1739/11/8	Mannum-mešu-liṣṣur buys temple offices from Ninurta-APIN.
37	Cornell 20	1739/12/-	Mannum-mešu-liṣṣur buys temple offices from Inbi-ilišu.
38	OECT 8 2	1738/3/15	Mannum-mešu-liṣṣur buys fields from Arad-Enlila.
39	OECT 8 5	1738/3/-	Mannum-mešu-liṣṣur buys temple offices from the sons of Sin-magir.
40	BE 6/2 38	1738/4/6	Mannum-mešu-liṣṣur buys temple offices from Ea-iddinam.
41	OECT 8 9	1738/4/21	Mannum-mešu-liṣṣur buys temple offices from Sin-lidiš.
42	OECT 8 1	1738/6/1	Mannum-mešu-liṣṣur buys house from Rimtum and Ali-aḫuya.
43	TIM 4 54	1738/6/-	Mannum-mešu-liṣṣur buys temple offices from Ea-iddinam.
44	Cornell 7	1738/10/20	Mannum-mešu-liṣṣur buys temple offices from Warad-Ištar.
45	OECT 8 10	1738/10/24	Mannum-mešu-liṣṣur buys temple offices from Mar-erṣetim's heirs.

TABLE 6. *The Mannum-mešu-liṣṣur Archive* (CONT'D)

46	Cornell 21	1738/11/11	Ninurta-raḫim-ṣerim buys temple offices from Ninurta-mansum.
47	Cornell 11	?	Mannum-mešu-liṣṣur buys temple offices from the heirs of Ali-waqrum.
48	Cornell 16	?	Mannum-mešu-liṣṣur buys temple offices from Ninurta-raḫim-ṣerim.
49	OECT 8 8	1737/3/5	Mannum-mešu-liṣṣur buys temple offices from Ninurta-mansum.
50	OECT 8 7	1737/12/2	Mannum-mešu-liṣṣur buys temple offices from Ninurta-raḫim-ṣerim.
51	Cornell 23	1727/3/-	Mannum-mešu-liṣṣur and Munawirum inherit from Nuska-amaḫ(?).
52	BE 6/2 64	1721/2/20	Ninurta-muballiṭ, Iddin-Ištar, and Narubtum sell *kislaḫ* to Ninurta-raḫim-ṣerim.
53	OECT 8 18	1837/13/-	See no. 24 above.

Key to Table 7

1. House property, measured in *gín*.
2. Field property in the uz-za plot, measured in *iku*.
3. Field property in the ^{id}gír-ta-bal-e plot, measured in *iku*.
4. Field property in the ká-din-na plot, measured in *iku*.
5. Temple office, ì-du$_8$ ká-sumun ^{d}en-lí-lá, measured in days.
6. Temple office, ì-du$_8$ é-gu-la or ì-du$_8$ ká é-gu-lá, measured in days.
7. Temple office, ì-du$_8$ ká ^{d}nin-gá-gi$_4$-a, measured in days.
8. Temple office, ì-du$_8$ ká é-gal-maḫ or ì-du$_8$ kisal é-gal-maḫ, measured in days.
9. Temple office, ì-du$_8$ ká uš-gíd-da or ì-du$_8$ uš-gíd-gíd-da, measured in days.
10. Temple office, ì-du$_8$ ká-gal or ì-du$_8$ ká-gal ^{d}nin-líl-lá, measured in days.
11. Temple office, ì-du$_8$ ^{giš}-kin-ti, measured in days.
12. Temple office, ì-du$_8$ ká du$_6$-kù, measured in days.
13. Temple office, é-da-di ^{d}en-líl ^{d}nin-líl, measured in days.
14. Temple office, ì-du$_8$ ká kisal ^{d}nin-líl-lá, measured in days.
15. Temple office, en-num alam é-kur-igi-gál, measured in days.
16. Temple office, ká á-sal-a, measured in days.
17. Temple office, ub-šu-ukkin-na, measured in days.
18. Temple office, ì-du$_8$ kisal-lá é-kur-igi-gál, measured in days.
19. Temple office, ì-du$_8$ ká ^{d}lama ^{d}lama šà é-kur-ra, measured in days.
20. Temple office, gudu$_4$ ^{d}en-líl u$_{19}$-ru-maḫ ^{d}utu, measured in days.

TABLE 7. *Property of Mannum-mešu-liṣṣur (represented by bold numbers)*

Text No	*Publication*	1	2	3	4	5	6	7	8
23.	OECT 8 20						45	22.5	
24.	OECT 8 17	1.3 + 1.3	1.6 + 1.6	2 + 2		22.5 + 22.5[a]		11.5 + 11.5	22.5 + 22.5
26.	Cornell 6	8 + 56 + 56	0.16 + 0.72 + 0.72	0.2 + 0.8 + 0.8				2 + 6 + 6	
28.	Cornell 18	**64**							
29.	OECT 8 19							6	
30.	OECT 8 16	12					**10.5**	**5**	
31.	OECT 8 11								
33.	Cornell 12							**6**	
34.	OECT 8 6								
35.	Cornell 8								
36.	Cornell 19								**20**
38.	OECT 8 2				**3**				
39.	OECT 8 5								
40.	BE 6/2 38	**80**							
41.	OECT 8 9								
42.	OECT 8 1	**40**							
43.	TIM 4 54								
44.	Cornell 7								**20**
45.	OECT 8 10								
46.	Cornell 21								
47.	Cornell 11						**7.5**		
48.	Cornell 16						**30**		
49.	OECT 8 8								**20**
50.	OECT 8 7						**30**		
51.	Cornell 23	**1 + x + x**					**2 + 10** + 10	**1 + 5** + 5	**2 + 10** + 10
52.	BE 6/2 64	**80**							
	Total[b]	**265+**			**3**		**90**	**17**	**72**

Notes

a. Since this text has divided all property evenly with the exception of this entry, it is likely that 22½ days were intended, but the scribe made an error.

b. Total represents only the property inherited and acquired by Mannum-mešu-liṣṣur.

TABLE 7. *Property of Mannum-mešu-liṣṣur* (CONT'D.)

Text No.	9	10	11	12	13	14	15	16	17	18	19	20
23.												
24.	22.5 + 22.5	22.5 + 22.5	22.5 + 22.5	22.5 + 22.5	6 + 6							
26.	2.5 + 10 + 10	x + 10 + 10	2.5 + 10 + 10	2.5 + 3.5 + 3.5	x + 81 + 81							
28.												
29.	12.5	12.5	12.5	12	10 + 20 + 20 + 20							
30.		**1.5**										
31.					**30**							
33.	**12**				**20**							
34.					**30**							
35.	**20**	**20**	**50**			**20**						
36.	**20**	**20**	**20**			**20**						
38.												
39.						**6**						
40.												
41.							**15**	**15**	**15**			
42.												
43.					**10**							
44.	**20**		**20**									
45.									**10**	**10**	**10**	
46.							12					
47.						7.5						
48.						**30**						
49.	**20**		**20**			**20**						
50.						**30**						
51.	**2 + 10** + 10	**2 + 10** + 10	**2 + 10** + 10	**2.5 + 10** + 10	**18** + x + x							4 + **18** + ?
52.												
Total	**104**	**53.5**	**122**	**12.5**	**108+**	**133.5**	**15**	**15**	**25**	**10**	**10**	**22**

KEY TO NUMBERS IS ON PAGE 25.

During the next four years, through 1740 B.C., our central character, Mannum-mešu-liṣṣur, may be observed as he takes advantage of his new-found membership in the Sin-iqišam family, and as he begins to exert his power over the other branch of that family, that of Ibbi-Enlil (see fig. 2). Cornell 18 [no. 28], written in 1742 B.C., records the sale of a house plot by Ibbi-Enlil to Mannum-mešu-liṣṣur. The property in question was the entire house that Ibbi-Enlil had received through inheritance.[49] Ibbi-Enlil himself died in the following year, leaving—if OECT 8 19 [no. 29] represents the complete estate[50]—a small amount of temple-office property (and no house property) to be divided among his three sons. This estate was not, however, unencumbered; in the following year the three sons of Ibbi-Enlil had to give away a considerable amount of temple-office property to clear it from debt (OECT 8 11 [no. 31]). Again the recipient of this property was Mannum-mešu-liṣṣur, their adoptive cousin.

An examination of the property recorded in the three major inheritance documents—that of Lu-Bau (OECT 8 17/18 [nos. 24 and 53]), that of Sin-iqišam (Cornell 6 [no. 26]), and that of Nuska-amaḫ (Cornell 23 [no. 51]; see tables 6 and 7)—shows a striking similarity between the types and amounts of property listed in the latter two texts and that received by the two brothers in the earliest text.[51] It may be suggested therefore that the property left by Lu-Bau to Ur-Lumma's two sons Adda-kala and Nanna-meša was passed

[49] Not only is the amount of property identical in Cornell 6 [no. 26] and Cornell 18 [no. 28], but the name of the neighbor, Ubarum, is also the same.

[50] The temple-office property given for exchange by one of Ibbi-Enlil's sons in OECT 8 16 [no. 30] is different from that listed in OECT 8 19 [no. 29], the inheritance document. Unfortunately, Cornell 20 [no. 37] is broken, making the exact identification of the office sold by Ibbi-Enlil's grandson hard to identify, but again it does not seem to be one of those listed in OECT 8 19 [no. 29]. There are two possible explanations: the first is that this was not the complete inheritance text, but perhaps a supplement to it; the second explanation is that the individuals in question were able to acquire property by means other than inheritance. Since the evidence tends to support the latter explanation (see p. 29 below), it seems unnecessary to assume that OECT 8 19 [no. 29] does not represent the entirety of Ibbi-Enlil's estate.

[51] One difficulty exists since in OECT 8 17 [no. 24] the amount of é-da-di office is listed as six days, whereas the later texts deal with much more. However, an examination of the text itself shows that where é-da-di property belonging to Adda-kala is recorded, the sign is unclear and could be read either as u_4 (day) or itu (month). On the reverse, however, in the section describing Nanna-meša's inheritance, the sign clearly seems to be u_4. Nevertheless, I would like to suggest that this was a scribal error (a fairly common occurrence, especially in long inheritance documents like this one) and that the scribe meant to record six (months) of é-da-di office for each heir. The six months would therefore translate into approximately 180 days which would accord well with the amount of this office recorded in Cornell 6 [no. 26]. Cornell 6 [no. 26] has a number of days of this office (the number is broken) given as a preference portion. Assuming that the total number of days of office was 180, and applying the usual preference portion of 10 percent of the whole, then this portion can be reconstructed as 18 days of office. This number subtracted from the assumed total of 180 days would leave 162 days to be divided between the two heirs, or 81 days each, which is precisely what is recorded in the text.

down undivided in Cornell 23 [no. 51] to Sin-iqišam, the direct descendant presumably of Adda-kala, and to Nuska-amaḫ the son of Nanna-meša. It was at the time of these later generations that the family's financial difficulties resurfaced; within two decades almost all of this property had fallen into other hands.

The period from 1744 to 1740 B.C. represents a period of consolidation for Mannum-mešu-liṣṣur. First, with his brother, he was adopted by Nanna-aya. Now a member of the Sin-iqišam family, he apparently became extensively involved financially with the Ibbi-Enlil branch of the family through loans and purchases, at the same time accumulating the property that his position at birth had denied him. In addition, he received the other half of the original estate which had been due to his father through adoption. Mannum-mešu-liṣṣur had already bought his way into property and status, but at the same time it seems that the family with which he was enmeshed had also attained what they needed, the ability to pay their debts while accepting a still moderate amount property loss. However, the economic crisis of 1739 B.C. was to change all that; as it bankrupted many of Nippur's property owners, it allowed Mannum-mešu-liṣṣur, a rare member of the property-owning group who also controlled wealth in the form of silver—as demonstrated by his many purchase texts—to amass a very considerable estate.[52]

Table 6 shows that the majority of the texts of the Mannum-mešu-liṣṣur archive are dated between 1739 B.C., the year in which the economic crisis was first in evidence,[53] and 1737 B.C. During this period it is possible to document Mannum-mešu-liṣṣur's purchase of temple offices and other property in seventeen different instances.[54] In addition to a modest amount of house and field property, Mannum-mešu-liṣṣur's acquisitions concentrated on temple-office property like that which he must already have inherited from Nanna-aya (see table 7). While the types of property that he acquired during this period were similar to those he had received through his association with the Sin-iqišam family, many of those from whom he was purchasing property cannot be shown to belong to that family.

In OECT 8 6 [no. 34] and OECT 8 7 [no. 50] Mannum-mešu-liṣṣur buys temple offices from the sons of Sin-magir, one of his adoptive brothers, while

[52] Calculating the total amount of property known to have been accumulated by Mannum-mešu-liṣṣur shows that he owned a total of 352 shekels worth of property, not including, for example, that which he inherited from Nanna-aya. Even this minimum figure is larger than five-sixths of the estates known from Nippur; with the addition of a mere twenty shekels to its value, which is much less than can be expected from the broken sections of the texts, this estate is greater than 90 percent of all known Nippur estates.

[53] See Stone, "Economic Crisis."

[54] Since our knowledge of the existence of these texts is due entirely to activities of tablet hunters, it is likely that this archive originally contained more tablets, tablets whose poor condition rendered them worthless in the antiquities market. This type of selection is evident in the final disposition of the tablets themselves; those largely intact went to Oxford, while those with slight damage (usually in the form of pick-marks) went to Cornell.

TABLE 8. *Participants in the Mannum-mešu-liṣṣur Archive*

Name *Text No.:*	23	24	25	26	27	28	29	30	31	32	33	34	35	36	37
Lu-Bau son of Eluti	A														
Ur-Lumma son of Lu-Inanna	A	A													
Adda-kala son of Ur-Lumma		A													
Nanna-meša son of Ur-Lumma		A	A												
Nuska-amaḫ son of Nanna-meša			A												
Nin-kuzu son of Nanna-meša			A												
KA-Damu son of Dada-kala		W													
Nanna-aya son of Sin-iqišam				A	A										
Ibbi-Enlil son of Sin-iqišam				A		A	A								
Ninurta-muštal son of Ibbi-Enlil							A		A		A				
Inbi-ilišu son of Ninurta-muštal															A
Namaršu-lumur son of Ibbi-Enlil							A		A						
Munawirum son of Ibbi-Enlil			A		W?		A	A	A						
Awiliya			A												
Mannum-mešu-liṣṣur son of Awiliya					A	A		A	A		A	A	A		A
Ninurta-muballiṭ son of Awiliya					A					A					
Sin-magir (son of Sin-iqišam)				W?	A										
Ili-ippalsa son of Sin-magir										A		A			
Lumurša-Šamaš son of Sin-magir															
Ili-eribam son of Sin-magir															
Ina-ekur-rabi					A										
Ninurta-mansum son of Taribum							W								
Ninurta-raḫim-ṣerim son of Nanna-mansum															
Ili-ḫaziri son of Awiatum									A						
Ninurta-APIN son of Ipqatum													A	W	
Lu-Enlila agrig son of Eluti							W	W	W	W	W				W
Nuska-nišu son of Ninurta-mušallim						W				W	W				
Mar-erṣetim son of Girni-iša												W			W
Riš-Ea son of Zinatum												W			W
Sin-ipturam son of Nabi-Enlil															
Mannum-ḫiršu son of Imgur-Ninurta			W					W							
Adad-tayar son of Ḫumurum															
Ubarum gala?			W		N		N								
Awiliya bur-gul					W	W	W	W		W	W	W			
ḪI.TAR-Adad bur-gul													W		
Nuska-nišu dub-sar						W		W	W	W					
Imgur-Sin dub-sar															
Atta dub-sar															
Lu-Ninurta uku-uš								W		W					
Apil-ilišu dub-sar							W								
Abbatum dub-sar													W	W	W
Ibbi-Ninšubur dub-sar															
Idišum bur-gul															
Ninurta-nišu dub-sar											W				
Ninurta-gamil dub-sar												W			

A = Actor   N = Neighbor   W = Witness

TABLE 8. *Participants in the Mannum-mešu-liṣṣur Archive* (CONT'D.)

Name *Text No.:*	38	39	40	41	42	43	44	45	46	47	48	49	50	51	52
Lu-Bau son of Eluti															
Ur-Lumma son of Lu-Inanna															
Adda-kala son of Ur-Lumma															
Nanna-meša son of Ur-Lumma															
Nuska-amaḫ son of Nanna-meša															
Nin-kuzu son of Nanna-meša															
KA-Damu son of Dada-kala															
Nanna-aya son of Sin-iqišam															
Ibbi-Enlil son of Sin-iqišam															
Ninurta-muštal son of Ibbi-Enlil															
Inbi-ilišu son of Ninurta-muštal															
Namaršu-lumur son of Ibbi-Enlil															
Munawirum son of Ibbi-Enlil															
Awiliya														A	
Mannum-mešu-liṣṣur son of Awiliya	A	A	A	A	A	A	A	A		A	A	A	A	A	
Ninurta-muballiṭ son of Awiliya															
Sin-magir (son of Sin-iqišam)															
Ili-ippalsam son of Sin-magir															
Lumurša-Šamaš son of Sin-magir		A													
Ili-eribam son of Sin-magir		A													
Ina-ekur-rabi															
Ninurta-mansum son of Taribum									A			W			
Ninurta-raḫim-ṣerim son of Nanna-mansum									A		A		A		
Ili-ḫaziri son of Awiatum		W?													
Ninurta-APIN son of Ipqatum															
Lu-Enlila agrig son of Eluti	W		W	W	W		W	W			W	W	W	W	W
Nuska-nišu son of Ninurta-mušallim				W	W										
Mar-erṣetim son of Girni-iša	W				W							W	W		
Riš-Ea son of Zinatum					W										
Sin-ipturam son of Nabi-Enlil									W		W		W		
Mannum-ḫiršu son of Imgur-Ninurta														W?	
Adad-tayar son of Ḫumurum											W		W		
Ubarum gala?															
Awiliya bur-gul			W		W	W					W			W	
ḪI.TAR-Adad bur-gul	W			W			W	W						W	
Nuska-nišu dub-sar															
Imgur-Sin dub-sar							W	W							
Atta dub-sar	W		W												
Lu-Ninurta uku-uš															
Apil-ilišu dub-sar				W				W							
Abbatum dub-sar															
Ibbi-Ninšubur dub-sar									W				W		
Idišum bur-gul										W					W
Ninurta-nišu dub-sar			W											W	
Ninurta-gamil dub-sar		W													

the seller in Cornell 12 [no. 33] is a son of, and in Cornell 20 [no. 37] a grandson of, Ibbi-Enlil. In all other instances, however, the sellers cannot be confidently associated with the Ur-Lumma family. Moreover, instead of using either his natural or his adoptive brothers as witnesses to his texts as was customary, it seems that Mannum-mešu-liṣṣur had a small group of outsiders as his witnesses. Most notable are Lu-Enlila, Nuska-nišu, and Mar-erṣetim (see table 8). His ties with Lu-Enlila were especially strong. Not only did he witness some of Mannum-mešu-liṣṣur's earliest transactions, but he even witnessed the text concerning his property which was written by Mannum-mešu-liṣṣur's widow, brother, and child (BE 6/2 64 [no. 52]).

With the exception of Cornell 23 [no. 51], the text in which Mannum-mešu-liṣṣur divided an estate with Munawirum (see pp. 21–22 above), the only preserved text dated after 1737 B.C. is this 1721 B.C. text which records a transaction following Mannum-mešu-liṣṣur's death. In BE 6/2 64 [no. 52] Mannum-mešu-liṣṣur's brother, son, and widow sell a plot of unbuilt house property, previously purchased in BE 6/2 38 [no. 40] from the sons of Ea-iddinam,[55] to Ninurta-raḫim-ṣerim. This latter individual is known from a number of other texts (BE 6/2 66, BE 6/2 68, OIMA 1 45) as a frequent purchaser of temple offices and other property at about this time. It is less clear, however, whether he was also involved in earlier transactions with Mannum-mešu-liṣṣur.

Cornell 16 [no. 48], Cornell 21 [no. 46], and OECT 8 7 [no. 50] all concern the purchase and sale of temple-office property by Ninurta-raḫim-ṣerim. However, in this instance, the texts all date around 1738 B.C. and the patronymic used is Nanna-mansum,[56] while in the later texts, all dating to around 1721 B.C.,[57] the patronymic is recorded as Ninurta-mansum. Thus it is not clear whether in BE 6/2 64 [no. 52] Mannum-mešu-liṣṣur's survivors are selling property to an old associate of their recently deceased relative, or whether the purchaser is simply an up-and-coming property owner, similar to Mannum-mešu-liṣṣur himself a decade or so earlier.

In conclusion, in spite of the complexities and ambiguities of the texts, it seems possible to view the Mannum-mešu-liṣṣur archive as the record of a moneyed individual who became absorbed into a large propertied family probably through adoption, presumably due to economic necessity on the part of the adopters. Mannum-mešu-liṣṣur was then able to use his position to acquire very large amounts of property, especially in the form of temple offices. This case differs from that of Ur-Pabilsag in that Ur-Pabilsag and his adopters had both social and economic motives for their action, while with Mannum-mešu-liṣṣur economic motives predominate, especially on the part of the adopters. This archive thus illustrates the functioning of what have

[55] At the time of the original purchase, some seventeen years earlier, the plot was described as é-dù-a, indicating that it had a structure on it.

[56] The date is broken on Cornell 16 [no. 48]. In Cornell 21 [no. 46] the patronymic is recorded as Nanna-aya, which is a contraction for any name with Nanna as the initial theocratic element. Ninurta-raḫim-ṣerim is an extremely unusual name at Nippur.

[57] OIMA 1 45 and BE 6/2 66 have the date broken off.

been considered here as economic adoptions, adoptions which lack the social functions usually ascribed to adoption (see pp. 1–2 above). These economic adoptions took place in the context of a period of decline of lineages and traditional social values. Through adoption, new foci of propertied wealth could be created, foci without which the social fabric would have disintegrated.

Conclusions

Although Old Babylonian texts concerning the adoption of children of a previous marriage by the new spouse and the adoption of children (in one case a suckling infant) by childless couples attest to adoptions fulfilling the largely social needs of providing orphans with parents and childless couples with children and heirs, this was not so in all instances. In other texts the economic aspects of adoption came to the fore: adoption provided the adoptee with the chance for upward social mobility that had been denied to him by birth, while the adopter received a measure of security. Indeed, where economic gain is seen as motivation for both adopter and adoptee, the natural sons often lost security; in at least one instance these sons saw their inheritance fall into the hands of a stranger.

Nevertheless, even where property exchange appears to have been the primary motivation for an adoption, the adoptive son gained all of the rights and privileges that were normally accorded to a natural son or to a son adopted for more conventional reasons. Even at Nuzi, where fictive adoption texts are primarily concerned with the exchange of real estate for silver, and where one individual could be "adopted" by well over two hundred people,[58] a new text suggests that the adoptive element in the transaction was still taken seriously.[59]

Thus, while the transformation of a long-established institution, adoption, could be used to bring about needed social change, it still retained at least some vestiges of its traditional attributes.

[58] M. Maidman, "A Socio-Economic Analysis of a Nuzi Family Archive" (Ph.D. diss., University of Pennsylvania, 1976).

[59] Abdulillah Fadhil, "Ein frühes *ṭuppi mārūti* aus Tell al-Faḫḫār/Kurruḫanni," in *Studies on the Civilization and Culture of Nuzi and the Hurrians*, vol. 1: *In Honor of Ernest R. Lacheman* (ed. M. A. Morrison and D. I. Owen; Winona Lake, IN: Eisenbrauns, 1981) 363–76.

Additions to the Old Babylonian Archive of Mannum-mešu-liṣṣur in the Olin Library, Cornell University

David I. Owen

Introduction to the Cornell Tablet Collection

The preliminary study of the Cornell tablet collection was begun shortly after I joined the Cornell University faculty in the fall of 1974. E. V. Leichty informed me of the existence of the collection in the Olin Library and he provided me with a copy of a brief catalog prepared by A. Leo Oppenheim which the latter had made during a visit to the Cornell campus in 1961. The collection was in storage in the Olin Library basement. After searching it out and checking the acquisition records, I came across another catalog of the collection—apparently unknown to Oppenheim—prepared by E. Chiera in approximately 1929 when he had the collection on loan and was preparing it for publication.[1] O. Neugebauer had apparently examined all or part of the collection on a visit to Cornell in 1946 (letter of September 21, 1946, on file in the library archives) and two of the tablets, nos. 31 and 58, were listed in O. Neugebauer and A. Sachs, *Mathematical Cuneiform Texts*.[2] A. Goetze, possibly in the same year, also had access to the collection and copied nine texts (nos. 1, 4, 9, 22, 24, 26, 42, 52, and 116), one of which, Cornell 4 [no. 27], is reproduced here with the addition of the seal inscription and some minor corrections. Goetze's copies will appear in his posthumous volume in the Yale Oriental Series (vol. 15).[3] No other references to the collection or work on

[1] According to the *Cornell Alumni News* 32/30 (1930) 413, "Prof. Edward Chiera, of the Oriental Institute of the University of Chicago, whose excavations near modern Kirkuk have brought to light the remains of an ancient Subaraean civilization . . . is engaged on the publication of Mr. Patten's tablets. . . ." Other than the undated catalog in the Olin Library, no other details as to the progress, if any, of Chiera's work exists here. Perhaps additional information is to be found in the Oriental Institute archives.

[2] O. Neugebauer and A. Sachs, *Mathematical Cuneiform Texts* (American Oriental Series 29; New Haven: American Oriental Society, 1945) 21–22, nos. 78 and 99.4.

[3] Dr. Mark Cohen, who had prepared a preliminary manuscript of YOS 15, was kind enough to send me a copy of his manuscript so that I might collate the Goetze copies against the original tablets at Cornell. It is, perhaps, interesting to note that no record exists at Cornell of a visit by Goetze or to his borrowing of the tablets for copying. Only a single letter from Goetze in 1946 inquiring about a now lost collection of cylinder seals, which was supposed to have been in Cornell Library, provides any clue to his knowledge of the collection. His copies, however, clearly show that he had

individual tablets is otherwise known to me. The tablets themselves were donated to Cornell University in the 1920s (exact date unknown) by Mr. Henry Jay Patten, a distinguished alumnus of Cornell. No information on the source of the collection is recorded.[4]

With both catalogs at hand, it was a relatively easy task to go through the collection and to check the numbers against the respective descriptions, noting those texts and fragments which had escaped notice or which were incorrectly identified due to the sometimes poor state of preservation of some of the tablets. Since it was obvious that the collection was in need of cleaning and baking, I was able, with the financial aid provided by the Olin Library authorities, to deliver the tablets to the University Museum in Philadelphia where they were treated at the Israel Stifle Tablet Laboratory. On the basis of my revised and corrected catalog, the tablets were given permanent numbers so as to avoid any future confusion. The final number of texts and fragments was 195 after some modern joins were separated and envelopes were joined to their respective tablets. Of these, twenty were from the Ur III period. The majority of the texts dates to the Isin-Larsa and Old Babylonian periods and consists primarily of economic documents and the nine letters copied by Goetze.[5] One text, a loan of sheep for seven years, dates to the Middle Babylonian period (reign of Šagarakti-Šuriaš), and a handful of texts dates to the Neo-Babylonian period, one of which is a fragment of a medical commentary.[6] Excluding the texts published below, all but the Neo-Babylonian tablets have been copied by me and Marcel Sigrist and will be published in the near future.[7]

---

access to at least some of the tablets. Marten Stol is preparing an edition of the Cornell letters copied by Goetze, which will be included in the final volume being prepared by me and by M. Sigrist.

[4] With the aid of Ms. Julia Crepeau of Cornell's Department of Manuscripts and University Archives, I was able to obtain some background information on the interesting career and life of Mr. Patten. He graduated from Cornell in 1884 and later became an alumni trustee (1915–20). He was treasurer of Bartlett, Frazier & Co., grain brokers in Chicago, where he lived most of his life. He was particularly interested in archeology and assisted in various excavations in Greece. He was a member of the directing committee of the Princeton Archaeological Expedition in Antioch, a trustee of the American Museum in Corinth, a fellow of the Royal Geographic Society, and vice-president of the Chicago Historical Society. Since he traveled widely in the Near East it is not clear when or, for that matter, where he may have purchased the tablet collection. In a letter in the university archives from the American Consulate in Baghdad written by a Mr. John Randolph (another Cornell alumnus [the consul?] who donated to the university the now missing collection of cylinder seals), it is noted that Mr. Patten was in Baghdad in 1925, at which time he may have acquired the tablets.

[5] During the summer of 1986, Marcel Sigrist of the Ecole Biblique in Jerusalem, under a grant from the National Science Foundation, copied all of the remaining texts of the Isin-Larsa and Old Babylonian periods. He and I will publish all of the Cornell texts, other than those included here, in a separate volume.

[6] Fragment to text 21 in R. Labat, *Traité akkadien de diagnostics et pronostics médicaux* (Paris: Académie Internationale d'Histoire des Sciences, 1951).

[7] For the twenty Ur III texts, see now my *Neo-Sumerian Texts from American Collections* (Materiali per il Vocabolario Neosumerico 15; Roma: Multigrafica Editrice, 1990), nos. 142–61.

During the preparation of the revised catalog and the copying of selected texts, I noted the existence of an interesting Old Babylonian archival group consisting of twelve relatively well-preserved tablets and envelopes which recorded the affairs of Mannum-mešu-liṣṣur. At the time, I made preliminary transliterations and began to copy the texts with the intention of publishing them as a separate article. While researching materials for this article I read Elizabeth Stone's study on "Economic Crisis and Social Upheaval in Old Babylonian Nippur," where she briefly mentioned the significance of the Mannum-mešu-liṣṣur materials.[8] I wrote to Stone shortly thereafter and sent her my notes to the Cornell texts, which were then of some importance to her nearly completed University of Chicago doctoral dissertation.[9] This correspondence set in motion the collaboration that resulted in this monograph. The inclusion of the prosopographic index by J. R. Mitchell developed from a casual remark by Jerrold Cooper, his thesis advisor, who asked me if I knew of any unpublished Old Babylonian texts dealing with prebends. I provided Mitchell with my copies and transliterations and this developed into a three-way consultation between the authors which had a very beneficial effect on the final versions of our respective contributions.

The Archive of Mannum-mešu-liṣṣur

The activities of Mannum-mešu-liṣṣur have been long known from nineteen previously published texts in the collections of Oxford (OECT 8), Philadelphia (BE 6/2), and Baghdad (TIM 4). To these nineteen texts we have now added twelve from the Rare Book Collection in the Olin Library, Cornell University, bringing the total to thirty-one tablets in which Mannum-mešu-liṣṣur plays a significant role (see the concordance of texts on pp. 93–94). The importance of this archive for the understanding of social mobility in Old Babylonian Nippur has now been demonstrated in Stone's essay in this volume. The addition of the Cornell texts to the previously known archive has greatly augmented the available data and has allowed for a more detailed reconstruction both of the career of Mannum-mešu-liṣṣur and of the workings of Nippur society in the Old Babylonian period.

The publication below of the twelve Cornell tablets includes complete transliterations, translations, copies (1:1 scale), and photographs (1:1 scale [except edges are occasionally slightly enlarged], enhanced through the addition of ammonium chloride [NH_4Cl] vapor). In addition, we have provided complete transliterations and translations of all previously published Mannum-mešu-liṣṣur tablets with accompanying photographs, where available. Stone

[8] Elizabeth C. Stone, "Economic Crisis and Social Upheaval in Old Babylonian Nippur," in *Mountains and Lowlands: Essays in the Archaeology of Greater Mesopotamia* (ed. L. D. Levine and T. C. Young, Jr.; Bibliotheca Mesopotamica 7; Malibu, CA: Undena, 1977) 267–89, at 286.

[9] Elizabeth C. Stone, "Social and Economic Organization of Old Babylonian Nippur" (Ph.D. diss., University of Chicago, 1979). She was able to incorporate brief references to the Cornell texts in the final version of her dissertation, pp. 252 n. 3, 253 n. 1.

has collated all of the tablets in Oxford, Philadelphia, and Baghdad, and Mitchell those in Philadelphia. Their collations have been incorporated into the transliterations. I have also collated the Cornell tablets and all other tablets transliterated below which were available to me in photograph. All but two of the photographs were prepared by Paul E. Zimansky and E. Stone. Prints of the Oxford texts were processed by my student, D. Deuel, from negatives kindly provided by E. Stone. The final plates were prepared by me. The index of personal names was undertaken by Mitchell, who added numerous observations on the relationships of the individuals who appear in the archive. The many questions he raised often led to collations and improvements in the readings of the Cornell tablets. His indexes were revised by E. Stone to conform with the final style of the citations used in this volume and certain changes were made in line with our interpretation of the texts. Where significant differences of opinion remain, they are so indicated in the notes. The order of presentation of the texts is chronological within each group of texts: the adoption tablets (nos. 1–22; see table 1, pp. 4–5) and the Mannum-mešu-liṣṣur archive (nos. 23–53; table 6, pp. 24–25), with the exception of no. 53 (OECT 8 18), which is mainly a duplicate of no. 24 (OECT 8 17).

Adoption Texts from Nippur: Transliteration and Translation

Texts 1–53

Transliterations follow the sign list in Rykle Borger, *Assyrisch-babylonische Zeichenliste* (4th ed.; Alter Orient und Altes Testament 33; Neukirchen-Vluyn: Neukirchener Verlag, 1988). We follow Borger in subsuming all of the variants of sam under the reading sa$_{10}$. The divine name ^{d}EN.ZU is transliterated as ^{d}en-zu in all instances. Where 30 is used for the god Sin, it is transliterated as sin. We have attempted to maintain a consistent transliteration style throughout, although some variation may have escaped the editors' eyes.

Where the case/envelope differs from the tablet, the differences are noted in brackets with the transliterations. Restorations based on preserved portions of the cases/envelopes are not otherwise indicated but should be obvious from the accompanying copies and photographs.

Type 1 Adoptions: Texts 1–8

(For OECT 8 20, see text 23 below.)

Other texts from Nippur that may concern adoptions are BE 6/2 5, SAOC 44 40, and the disinheritance texts *ARN* 36, *ARN* 38, OIMA 1 65, and SAOC 44 24.

1. TIM 4 13

1. ^{Id}nanna-á-maḫ dumu ab-a-ab-gub-ba
2. ^{I}*i*-[*pí*]-*iq*-^{d}en-líl dumu *we-e-di*-ra
3. še-ba [ì-b]a ù síg ba
4. mu-á-ta in-na-an-kal
5. gibil-bi-eš-àm ^{I}*i-pí-iq*-^{d}en-líl-e
6. kišib nam-ibila ^{Id}nanna-á-maḫ-ra in-na-an-tak$_{4}$
7. nam-gudu$_{4}$ ^{d}lú-làl mu-a itu-2-àm
8. nam-ugula-é nam-ì-du$_{8}$ nam-kisal-luḫ ù bur-šu-ma
9. ^{I}*i-pí-iq*-^{d}en-líl-e
10. ^{Id}nanna-á-maḫ-ra in-na-an-sum
11. 5 (bán) še-ba ½ sila$_{2}$ ì-giš itu-á 4 ma-na síg mu-⸢a⸣
12. ^{Id}nanna-á-maḫ-e

13. ^{I}*i-pí-iq*-^{d}en-líl-ra in-na-ab-kal-ge
14. u_4 kúr-šè *i-pí-iq*-^{d}en-líl-e
15. ^{Id}nanna-á-maḫ dumu-na-ra
16. dumu-mu nu-me-en ba-na-an-du_{11}
17. nam-$gudu_4$ ù nam-ugula-é-ni-ta
18. ba-e-ri-a-e_{11}-dè
19. ù ⅓ ma-na kù-babbar [ì-lá-e]
20. ù ^{d}nanna-á-maḫ-[e]
21. ^{I}*i-pí-iq*-^{d}en-líl-[ra]
22. ad-da-mu nu-me-en ba-n[a-an-du_{11}]
23. še-ba ì-ba ù síg-ba in-na-a[n-kal]
24. inim nu-um-gá-gá
25. ù ⅓ ma-na kù-babbar ì-lá-e
26. en-na *i-pí-iq*-^{d}en-líl-e al-ti-la-aš
27. nam-$gudu_4$ ù nam-ugula-é-ta(!) al-kú-e
28. igi $geme_2$ é-kur-ri-tum nin-dingir-^{d}lú-làl
29. ù arad-ì-lí-šu dumu-ne-ne-šè
30. ^{I}*i-pí-iq*-^{d}en-líl ad-da ti-la
31. mu lugal-bi in-pà

Nanna-amaḫ son of Abab-guba has provided annual rations of barley, oil, and wool to Ipiq-Enlil the son of Wedi. For a second time Ipiq-Enlil has made out a sealed tablet of adoption to Nanna-amaḫ. Ipiq-Enlil has given to Nanna-amaḫ a gudu-ship of Lulal for 2 months annually, and the offices of ugula-e, i-du, kisal-luḫ, and buršuma. Nanna-amaḫ will provide to Ipiq-Enlil 5 ban of barley and ½ sila of oil monthly, and 4 mina of wool annually. In future (if) Ipiq-Enlil says to Nanna-amaḫ his son, "You are not my son," he will forfeit the gudu-ship and the ugula-e and pay ⅓ mina of silver; and if Nanna-amaḫ says to Ipiq-Enlil "You are not my father," he will not reclaim the rations of grain, oil, and wool which he has already provided and will pay ⅓ mina of silver. While Ipiq-Enlil lives, he will receive the income from the gudu and the ugula-e offices. In the presence of Geme-ekurritum the entu priestess of Lulal and Warad-ilišu his children, Ipiq-Enlil the(ir) father when alive swore in the name of the king.

2. PBS 8/1 16

1. [ ] x ús-a-du ^{d}en-líl-*na-da*
2. [ ] ús-a-du ^{d}en-zu-*ub-lam*

[11 lines largely destroyed]

14. [ ]-gi_4-gi_4
15. [ ]-ni še-ga-ne-ne-ta
16. [giš-šub-ba]-⌜ta⌝ in-ba-eš
17. [u_4 kúr-šè lú-lú]-ù inim nu-um-gá-gá-a
18. [mu lugal-bi] in-pà-dè-eš
19. ^{I}arad-^{d}en-zu ù *nu-úr*-^{d}utu-ke_4

20. ^{I}*a-wi-il-ì-lí* ad-da-ne-ne-ra
21. itu-da 1 (pi) še-ta-àm ⅓ silà ì-giš-ta-àm
22. mu-àm 3 ma-na síg-ta-àm
23. še-ba ì-ba ù ⟨síg⟩-ba in-na-kal-la-ge-dè
24. lú še-ba ì-ba ù síg-ba
25. nu-mu-un-na-ab-kal-la-ge-ne
26. nam-ibila-a-ni nu-mu-un-ak-e
27. mu lugal-bi in-pà-dè-eš

. . . [a field] beside (the field) of Enlil-nada, [a field] beside (the field) of Sin-ublam [an 11-line gap probably containing more items of inheritance]. In mutual agreement they have divided (the property) by casting lots. (In future) neither shall make a claim against the other. Thus have they sworn in the name of the king. Warad-Sin and Nur-Šamaš will each provide to Awil-ili their father a monthly ration of 1 pi of barley and ⅓ sila of oil and an annual ration of 3 mina of wool. (If) either of them fails to provide these rations, he will no longer receive his inheritance. Thus have they sworn in the name of the king.

3. TIM 4 14

1. ^{I}ur-du$_6$-kù-ga dumu *šum-*[*ma*]*-an*
2. ^{I}*šum-ma-an* ad-da-[ni]
3. nam-dumu-ne-šè ba-da-[an-ri]
4. tukun-bi u$_4$ kúr-šè
5. ^{I}ur-du$_6$-kù-ga-ke$_4$
6. ^{I}*šum-ma-an* ad-da-na
7. ad-da-mu nu-me-en ba-an-na-du$_{11}$
8. é a-šà ^{giš}kiri$_6$ ba-ra-è-dè
9. ⅓ ma-na kù-babbar ì-lá-e
10. ù tukun-bi u$_4$ kúr-šè
11. ^{I}*šum-ma-an* ur-du$_6$-kù-ga
12. dumu-na-ra dumu-mu nu-me-en
13. ba-an-na-du$_{11}$
14. é a-šà ^{giš}kiri$_6$ ba-ra-è-dè
15. ⅓ ma-na kù-babbar ì-lá-e
16. ^{I}a-ḫa-sú-nu
17. dumu-munus ur-du$_6$-kù-ga
18. še-ga-ne-ne-ta
19. giš-šub-ba-ta in-ba-eš
20. mu lugal-bi in-pà-dè
    [7 witnesses]
28. 4 (pi) še mu-àm 3 silà ì-giš
29. igi-4-gál kù-babbar síg
30. ^{I}*lu-li-ya*-ra ur-du$_6$-kù-ga
31. in-na-an-sum

Šumman his father has adopted Ur-dukuga son of Šumman as their (*sic*) son. If in future Ur-dukuga says to Šumman his father, "You are not my father," he will forfeit all houses, fields, and orchards and pay 1/3 mina of silver. And if in future Šumman says to Ur-dukuga his son, "You are not my son," he will forfeit all houses, fields, and orchards and pay 1/3 mina of silver. With Aḫassunu the daughter of Ur-dukuga by mutual agreement they have divided it up by casting lots. Thus have they sworn in the name of the king. [7 witnesses.] Ur-dukuga has given to Luliya 4 pi of grain annually, 3 sila of oil, and 1/4 (shekel?) of silver's worth of wool.

4. BE 6/2 28

1. ^{I}[*ip-qú*]-*ša* dumu dingir-[kù-ta]
2. ^{I}é-a-*ta-a-a-ar* dumu kù$^{?}$-x-[ ]
3. nam-ibila-ni-šè ba-an-d[a-ri]
4. u$_4$ nam-ibila-ni-šè ba-an-da-ri-a
5. 4 (gur) še ḫar-ra *ip-qú-ša* ad-da-ni
6. ^{I}é-a-*ta-a-a-ar* in-su
7. gibil-bi-šè-àm *ip-qú-ša* ad-da ti-la-[ ]
8. ^{I}é-a-*tu-ra-am* dumu-nitalam-ni
9. ù é-a-*ta-a-a-ar* dumu šu-ti-⸢x-x-x-x⸣
10. ḫa-la in-ne-en-ba
11. 15 gín é-dù-a da é *ip-qú*-é-a dumu dingir-kù-ta
12. 1 gán a-šà ^{d}en-líl-gar-ra ús-a-du *ip-qú*-é-a
13. níg-gú-na é-a šu-ri-a-bi-šè
14. ḫa-la-ba é-a-*tu-ra-am*
15. 15 gín é-dù-a da é é-a-*tu-ra-am* šeš-a-ni
16. 1 gán a-šà ^{d}en-líl-gar-ra ús-a-du é-a-*tu-ra-am* šeš-a-ni
17. níg-gú-na é-a šu-ri-a-bi-šè
18. ḫa-la-ba é-a-*ta-a-a-ar* šeš-a-ni
19. 2 (gur) 2 (pi) še-gur 3 ma-na síg 3 silà ì-giš
20. á-mu-u$_8$-a-še
21. ⟪2 (gur) 2 (pi) še-gur 3 ma-na síg 3 silà ì-giš⟫
22. ⟪á-mu-u$_8$-a-še⟫
23. ^{I}é-a-*tu-ra-am* ù é-a-*ta-a-a-ar*
24. ^{I}*ip-qú-ša* ad-da-ne-ne-ra
25. in-na-ab-kal-la-ge-ne
26. ibila lú nu-mu-na-ab-kal-la-ge
27. nam-ibila-ni-ta ba-ra-è-dè
28. še-ga-ne-ne-ta mu lugal-bi in-pà-dè-eš

Ipquša son of Dingir-kuta has adopted Ea-tayyar son of KU-[ ] as his heir. On the day of the adoption, Ea-tayyar repaid the 4-gur grain debt of Ipquša his father. During Ipquša's life, Ea-turam the son by his wife and Ea-tayyar the son by adoption have made a new division of inheritance shares. A 15-gin house plot next to that of Ipqu-Ea the son of Dingir-kuta, a 1-*iku* field plot in the Enlil-gara field next to that of Ipqu-Ea, one-half of whatever household property there is—(the above is the inheritance) share of Ea-turam. A 15-gin house plot next to that of Ea-turam his brother, a 1-*iku* field plot in the Enlil-gara field next to that of Ea-turam his brother, one-half of whatever household property there is—(the above is the inheritance) share of Ea-tayyar his brother. Ea-turam and Ea-tayyar will each provide to Ipquša their father 2 gur 2 pi of barley, 3 mina of wool, and 3 sila of oil, paid annually. Whichever heir fails to make this provision for him will lose his heirship. Together they have sworn in the name of the king.

5. PBS 8/2 153

1. ^{Id}nin-šubur-*ta-a-a-ar*-ke$_4$
2. ^{I}*pa-ti-ya*-ra
3. [nam]-dumu-ni-šè ba-da-an-ri-ke$_4$
4. [é a]-sà ^{giš}kiri$_6$ a-na-me-a-bi
5. ^{Id}nin-šubur-*ta-a-a-ar*
6. [^{I}]*pa-ti-ya* dumu-ni-ra
7. in-na-sum tukun-bi
8. [^{I}*pa-ti*]-*ya a-na* ^{d}nin-šubur-ta-a-a-ar
9. [ad]-da-na-ra ad-da-mu nu-me-en
10. [ba]-na-an-du$_{11}$ ⅓ ma-na kù-babbar
11. ì-lá-e ù tukun-[bi]
12. ^{d}nin-šubur-*ta-a-a-ar*
13. ^{I}*pa-ti-ya* dumu-ni-ra
14. [dum]u-mu nu-me-en ba-na-an-du$_{11}$
15. [ma-n]a kù-babbar ì-lá-e
16. é-a ù níg-gú-na
17. ba-na-an-è
18. ^{I}*pa-ti-ya a-na* ^{d}nin-šubur-*ta-a-a*-[*ar*]
19. itu-da gar-ra mu-àm 1 (gur) 1 (pi) še-gur
20. [m]a-na síg 6 silà ì-giš
21. in-na-ab-kal(!)-ge

Ilabrat-tayyar has adopted Patiya as his son. House, field, orchard—all that there is Ilabrat-tayyar has given to Patiya his son. If Patiya says to Ilabrat-tayyar his father, "You are not my father," he will pay ⅓ mina of silver, and if Ilabrat-tayyar says to Patiya his son, "You are not my son," he will pay [⅓+(?)] mina of silver and he will forfeit his house and all his property. Patiya will provide to Ilabrat-tayyar, paid monthly, an annual ration of 1 gur 1 pi of barley, [ ] mina of wool, and 6 sila of oil.

6. SAOC 44 10

1. [ ] dumu ^{d}inanna-[ ]
2. [ ] dumu *zi-ya-tum*

3. [nam-dumu-n]i-šè ba-da-ri
4. [nam-ibila-ni-šè] in-gar
5. [x gán a-šà] šub$_{x}$-še
6. [šà a-šà] egir-sum-lá
7. [ús-a-du ^{d}*da*]-*gán*-ma-an-sum ba-za
8. [*ì*]-*lí-tu-ra-am* gudu$_{4}$
9. [x gán a-šà] šub$_{x}$-še
10. [ ]-1-kam
11. [ ] lú-sin íl$^{?}$-⸢íl$^{?}$⸣
12. [x gán a-šà] šub$_{x}$-še
13. [ ] ⸢ra-aš⸣ ^{d}[ ]
14. [ ] *sin-i-tu-ra-am* [ ]
15. [ ] nag x [ ]
16. [x sar ^{giš}]kiri$_{6}$ giš gub-[ba]
17. [šà a-šà] ú-[sal]

[rest not preserved]

[ ] son of Inanna-[ ] has adopted as his son (or, has been adopted as a son by) [ ] son of Siyatum and has made him his heir (or, and has been made his heir). (This is followed by a damaged list of field property. The rest of the tablet is destroyed.)

7. *ARN* 45

1. ^{I}dingir-*ga-mil* šeš-gal
2. ^{I}*ma*-⸢*ri*⸣-*er-ṣe-tim* šeš-[a-n]i
3. ⸢ù dingir-*šu-ba*⸣-*ni* šeš-a-[n]i
4. [^{I}*da*]-*mi*-⸢*iq*⸣-*ì-lí-šu*-ke$_{4}$
5. dumu *i-din-ya*
6. nam-ibila-ni-šè
7. ba-da-an-ri-eš
8. é a-šà ^{giš}kiri$_{6}$ níg-ga a-na-me-a-bi
9. níg *da-mi-iq-ì-lí-šu*
10. téš-a sì-ga-bi
11. ì-ba-e-ne
12. tukun-bi *da-mi-iq-ì-lí*-[*šu*]
13. ^{I}dingir-*ga-mil* ^{I}*ma-ri-er-ṣe*-[*tim*]
14. ù dingir-šu-ba-ni dumu-ne-n[e-ra]
15. dumu-⸢mu⸣ nu-me-en-dè-[en]
16. ba-an-na-⸢du$_{11}$-x⸣
17. níg-ga ⸢ad-da-ni⸣ [ ]
18. ⸢ba-ra⸣-[è-dè]
19. ⸢tukun-b⸣[i ^{I}dingir-ga-mil]
20. ^{I}*ma-ri-er-ṣe-tim*
21. ù dingir-[*šu-ba-ni*]
22. ^{I}*da-mi-i*[*q-ì-lí-šu* ad-da-ne-ne-ra]

23. ad-da-[mu nu-me-en]
24. ba-an-na-[du$_{11}$-ge-eš]
25. ½ ma-na kù-[babbar in-ne-en-lá]
26. še-ga-ne-n[e-ta]
27. mu lugal-bi [in-pà-dè-eš]

Damiq-ilišu son of Iddinya has adopted Ilum-gamil the eldest brother, Mar-erṣetim his brother, and Ilšu-bani his brother as his heirs. They will divide equally, by casting lots, the house, field, (and) orchard—all that there is of the property of Damiq-ilišu. If Damiq-ilišu says to Ilum-gamil, Mar-erṣetim, and Ilšu-bani his sons, "You are not my sons," he will forfeit the property of his father [ ](?). If Ilum-gamil, Mar-erṣetim, and Ilšu-bani say to Damiq-ilišu [their father], "You are not our father," [they will pay] ½ mina of silver. In mutual agreement they have sworn in the name of the king.

8. *ARN* 65

1. ^{I}dingir-*ga-mil ma-ri-er-ṣe-tim*
2. ù dingir-*šu-ba-ni*
3. ibila ^{d}en-zu-*e-ri-ba-am*-ke$_4$-ne
4. [ki] ^{d}en-zu-*e-ri-ba-am* ad-da-ne-ne-ta
5. [^{I}]*da-mi-iq-ì-lí-šu*
6. dumu *i-din*-^{d}iškur-ke$_4$
7. [n]am-ibila-ni-šè
8. [b]a-da-ri-eš
9. ⸢í⸣ [gá]n ^{giš}kiri$_6$ giš gub-ba ^{giš}kiri$_6$ é-gal
10. šà a-šà ḫi-li-a
11. zag ^{giš}kiri$_6$ ^{d}en-zu-*i-qí-ša-am* dumu *kù-ga-tum*
12. ù zag ^{giš}kiri$_6$ lú-igi šeš-a-ni
13. 2 gán a-šà ú-gu-ub-be
14. šà me-at lú-dingir-ra
15. ^{I}*da-mi-iq-ì-lí-šu* ad-da-ti-⟨la⟩
16. ^{I}dingir-*ga-mil ma-ri-er-ṣe-tim*
17. ù dingir-*šu-ba-ni* dumu-ne-ne-sè
18. in-ne-en-ku$_4$-re
19. u$_4$ kúr-šè tukun-bi
20. ^{I}dingir-*ga-mil* ^{I}*ma-ri-er-ṣe-tim*
21. ù dingir-*šu-ba-ni*
22. [^{I}]*da-mi-iq-ì-lí-šu* ad-da-ne-ne-ra
23. [a]d-⸢da-me⸣ nu-me-en ba-ne-en-du$_{11}$
24. [umbin] ⸢al⸣-ku$_5$-ru-ne kar in-gar-re-eš
25. [ù kù-šè] ba-ab-sum-mu-ne
26. [ù tukun-bi ^{I}*da*]-*mi-iq-ì-lí-šu*
27. [^{I}dingir-*ga-mil* ^{I}*ma*]-*ri-er-ṣe-tim*
28. [ù dingir-*šu-ba*]-*ni* dumu-ne-ne-ra
29. [dumu-mu nu-me-en ba]-ne-en-du$_{11}$

30. [ ] ba-ra-è-dè
31. [ ] kù-babbar ì-lá-e
32. [ ] x šá-ga-ni nu-ub-si-ma
33. [ ] ibila-ni-šè šu la$^{?}$-ba-ti
34. [ ] mu-lugal-bi in-pà-eš

Damiq-ilišu has adopted as his heirs Ilum-gamil, Mar-erṣetim, and Ilšu-bani, the heirs of Sin-eribam, [from] Sin-eribam their father. Damiq-ilišu in his lifetime will turn over to Ilum-gamil, Mar-erṣetim, and Ilšu-bani a 1-*iku* orchard plot with standing plants, a palace orchard in the Ḫilia field next to the orchard of Sin-iqišam son of Kugatum and next to the orchard of Lu-igi his brother, and a 2-*iku* field plot with standing plants in Meat-Lu-dingira. In future if Ilum-gamil, Mar-erṣetim, and Ilšu-bani say to Damiq-ilišu their father, "You are not our father," they will be shaved and slave marks will be placed on them and they will be given for silver, and if Damiq-ilišu says to Ilum-gamil, Mar-erṣetim, and Ilšu-bani his sons, "[You are not my sons]," he will forfeit [ ] and pay [x shekels of silver] (2 unclear lines). Thus have they sworn in the name of the king.

Type 2 Adoptions: Texts 9–13

(For OECT 8 21, see text 32 below.)

9. BE 6/2 24

1. ^{I}*i-lí-i-din-nam* šeš-gal
2. ù *i-lí-um-ma-ti* šeš-a-ni
3. ^{I}é-a-*i-din-nam* dumu *ip-qú-ša*
4. ù *ku-ri-tum* dam-a-ni
5. nam-dumu-ni-šè ba-da-an-ri
6. nam-ibila-a-ni-šè in-gar-[ri-eš]
7. é a-šà níg-ga a-na-me-a-bi
8. šeš-gal síb-ta-na
9. ù-ba-ab-te-gá-en
10. téš-a sì-ga-a-bi ì-ba-e-ne
11. u$_4$ kúr-šè tukun-bi
12. *i-lí-i-*[*din*]*-nam* šeš-gal
13. ù *i-lí-um-ma-ti* šeš-a-ni
14. ^{I}é-a-*i-din-nam* ad-da-na-ra
15. ù *ku-ri-tum* ama-na-ra
16. nu-ad-da-mu nu-ama-mu
17. ba-an-na-du$_{11}$-eš
18. é a-šà níg-ga a-na-me-a-bi
19. ba-ra-è-dè-eš
20. ù kù-šè ba-ab-sum-mu-eš
21. ù tukun-bi é-a-*i-din-nam*

22. ù *ku-ri-tum* dam-a-ni
23. ^{I}*ì-lí-i-din-nam* dumu-na-ra
24. ù *ì-lí-um-ma-ti* šeš-a-ni
25. nu-dumu-me ba-an-ne-du$_{11}$-eš
26. é a-šà níg-ga a-na-me-a-bi
27. ba-ra-è-dè-eš
28. ù 1 ma-na kù-babbar ì-lá-e-ne
29. še-ga-ne-ne-ta
30. mu lugal-bi in-pà-eš

Ea-iddinam son of Ipquša and Kuritum his wife have adopted Ili-iddinam the eldest brother and Ili-ummati his brother as their sons and have made them their heirs. House and field—all that there is—after the eldest son has taken his preference portion, they will divide equally by casting lots. In future if Ili-iddinam the eldest brother and Ili-ummati his brother say to Ea-iddinam their father and to Kuritum their mother, "You are not our father, you are not our mother," they will forfeit house and field—all that there is—and will be given away for silver. And if Ea-iddinam and Kuritum his wife say to Ili-iddinam their son and to Ili-ummati his brother, "You are not our sons," they will forfeit house and field—all that there is—and will pay 1 mina of silver. In mutual agreement they have sworn in the name of the king.

10. SAOC 44 15

1. ^{Id}e[n-líl-*a-bi* dumu ^{d}nin-urta-*a-bi*]
2. ^{Id}⸢utu⸣-[*še-mi* ^{I}*ip-qú-*^{d}*da-mu*]
3. nam-ib[ila-ni-šè]
4. ba-da-[an-ri-eš]
5. ḫa-la-ba [é a-šà níg-ga]
6. a-na-me-[a-bi]
7. ^{Id}utu-*še*-[*mi* šeš-gal síb-ta-ni]
8. šu ba-[ab-te-gá ì-ba-e-ne]
9. tuk[un-bi u$_4$ kúr-šè]
10. ^{Id}[utu-*še-mi* ^{Id}en-líl-*a-bi*]
11. ù [*ip-qú-*^{d}*da-mu* ad-da-ni-ra]
12. ad-da-[mu nu-me-en]
13. ba-an-[du$_{11}$-ge-eš]
14. ⅓ ma-[na kù-babbar ì-lá-e-ne]
15. ù tu[kun-bi u$_4$ kúr-šè]
16. [erasure]
17. ^{Id}utu-*še-mi* ^{Id}en-líl-*a-bi*
18. ù *ta-bi-ya* ama-ni-[ra]
19. ama-mu nu-me-en ba-an-[du$_{11}$-ge-eš]
20. ⅓ ma-na kù-babbar ì-l[á-e-ne]
21. ^{I}*ip-qú-*^{d}*da-mu* ad-d[a-ni]
22. ù ibila-a-ni a-na-me-a-bi
23. še-ga-ne-ne *ṭu-pa-am iš*-[*ṭu-ru*]

[Ipqu-Damu] has adopted [Enlil-abi son of Ninurta-abi, and Šamaš-šemi] as his heirs. They will divide by casting lots the inheritance [of house and field—all that there is—after] Šamaš-šemi has received [his preference portion]. If [Šamaš-šemi] and [Enlil-abi] say to and (*sic*) [Ipqu-Damu, "You are not our] father," [they will pay] 1/3 mina of silver, and if (erasure) Šamaš-šemi and Enlil-abi say to and (*sic*) Tappiya their mother, "You are not our mother," they will pay 1/3 mina of silver. Ipqu-Damu their father and his heirs, however many there may be, have written this tablet in mutual agreement.

Note

The difficulties caused by the breaks in this text are exacerbated by erasures, often a sign of scribal error. In the reconstruction proposed here, it is assumed that the scribe made some errors.

11. BE 6/2 57

1. ^{I}*ṭà-ab-ba-la-ṭù* dumu *e-tel*-pi$_4$-^{d}utu
2. ^{I}*be-el-ti-ya* dam-a-ni
3. ^{I}*ḫa-bil-a-ḫi* nam-dumu-ne-ne-šè ba-an-da-ri
4. é a-sà níg-ga é-a gál-la a-na-me-a-bi
5. ^{Id}nin-urta-*ga-mil* šeš-gal síb-ta-na
6. šu ba-ab-te-gá
7. téš-a sì-ga-bi ì-ba-e-ne
8. *a-na* dub-nam-ibila ^{I}*ap-lum* gala
9. garza a-šà é ù ^{giš}kiri$_6$ ^{I}*ḫa-bil-a-ḫi*
10. ^{Id}nin-urta-*ga-mil* šeš-a-ni
11. inim nu-gá-gá-a
12. tukun-bi *ṭà-ab-ba-la-ṭù*
13. ù *be-el-ti-ya* dam-a-ni
14. ^{I}*ḫa-bil-a-ḫi* dumu-ni-ra
15. dumu nu-me-en ba-e-ne-in-du$_{11}$-uš
16. 1/2 ma-na kù-babbar ì-lá-e-ne
17. ù tukun-bi *ḫa-bil-a-ḫi*
18. ^{I}*ṭà-ab-ba-la-ṭù* ù *be-el-ti-ya*
19. ad-da nu-me-en ama nu-me-en
20. [ba]-ne-en-du$_{11}$-uš
21. umbin al-ku$_5$-ru-ne
22. kar an-ni-íb-dù-e
23. ù kù-šè ba-ab-sum-mu-ne

Ṭab-balaṭu son of Etel-pi-Šamaš and Beltiya his wife have adopted Ḫabil-aḫi as their son. They will divide equally by lots house, field, and household property—all that there is—after Ninurta-gamil the eldest son has taken his preference portion. Ninurta-gamil his brother will not make a claim against the tablet of heirship of Aplum the gala or the temple offices, fields, house, and orchards of Ḫabil-aḫi. If Ṭab-balaṭu and Beltiya his wife say to Ḫabil-aḫi their son, "You are not our son," they will pay ½ mina of silver. And if Ḫabil-aḫi says to Ṭab-balaṭu and Beltiya, "You are not my father, you are not my mother," they will shave him and place a slave mark on him and give him for silver.

12. SAOC 44 30

[several lines missing]
1′. ⸢tukun-bi⸣
2′. [^{Id}en-líl]-*ni-šu* ad-da-ni
3′. [ù] ⸢*a-ḫa*⸣-*tum* ama-a-ni
4′. [^{Id}nin]-⸢urta-*a-bi*⸣ dumu-ni-ra
5′. ⸢dumu⸣-mu ⸢nu⸣-me-en [ba-an-na-du$_{11}$-uš]
6′. ½ ma-na ⸢kù⸣-babbar ⸢ì-lá-e-ne⸣
7′. ù tukun-bi ^{Id}nin-urta-a-[bi]
8′. ^{Id}en-líl-*ni-šu* ad-da-ni
9′. ù ⸢*a-ḫa*⸣-*tum* ama-ni
10′. ad-da-mu nu-me-[en]
11′. [am]a-mu nu-me-en ba-an-na-[du$_{11}$]
12′. [um]bin al-k[u$_5$]-ru-ne [ ]
13′. ⸢^{I}*a-ḫa*⸣-*tum* mu-na-an-[ ]
14′. [ ]
15′. [ ]
16′. [mu lugal-la] ⸢tés-bi in⸣-[pà-dè-eš]

(Several lines missing.) If Enlil-nišu his father and Aḫatum his mother [say] to Ninurta-abi their son, "You are not our son," they will pay ½ mina of silver. And if Ninurta-abi says to Enlil-nišu his father and to Aḫatum his mother, "You are not my father, you are not my [mother]," [they will] shave him [and place a slave mark on him and give him for silver]. Aḫatum annually (two lines missing) [Thus have they sworn in the name of the king].

13. PBS 8/2 107

1. 1 dumu-nita-gaba
2. *ì-lí-a-wi-li* mu-ni-im
3. dumu *a-a-ar-tum*
4. ki *a-a-ar-tum* ama-ni-ta
5. ù *e-ri-iš-tum* dam-a-ni
6. [^{I}*y*]*a-si-ru-um*
7. ù ama-^{d}en-zu
8. nam-dumu-ni-meš
9. [šu] ba-an-t[i]-eš
10. kù nam-bulug$_3$-ga-ni-šè
11. [ ] gín kù-babbar 2 ma-na síg
12. *ya-si-ru-um*

13. ù ama-^{d}en-zu
14. *a-na a-a-ar-tum*
15. ù *e-ri-iš-tum*
16. [i]n-na-an-sum
17. *ya-si-ru-um*
18. ù ama-^{d}en-zu
19. [ki *a-a-ar-tum*]
20. [ù *e*]*-ri-*[*iš-tum* *i-lí*]*-a-wi-li*
21. *i-ṣa-*[*ba-a*]*t-ma i-ta-la-ak*

Yasirum and Ama-Suen have taken as their son a suckling baby called Ili-awili the son of Ayartum, from Ayartum his mother and Erištum her husband. As payment for his upbringing Yasirum and Ama-Suen have given [ ] shekels of silver and 2 mina of wool to Ayartum and Erištum. Yasirum and Ama-Suen [will take] Ili-awili [from Ayartum and Erištum] and will depart.

Type 3 Adoptions: Texts 14–17

(For Cornell 4, see text 27 below.)

14. SAOC 44 1

1. ^{I}sal-kal-la dumu-munus dingir-kù-ta
2. ^{I}*da-mi-iq-ì-lí-šu* dumu *ip-qú-ša*
3. nam-dam-šè in-tuk-àm
4. mu lugal-ka-ni in-pà
5. ^{I}*nu-úr-*⸢kab⸣-ta ^{I}*ì-lí-tu-ra-am*
6. ù *a-lí-a-bu-ša* dumu-me-⸢eš⸣
7. ^{I}sal-kal-la *a-na da-mi-iq-ì-lí-šu*
8. ad-da-na-ra nam-dumu-ni-šè
9. in-na-an-sum
10. tukun-bi *da-mi-iq-ì-lí-šu*
11. [^{I}sal]-kal-la dam-a-na-ra
12. ^{I}*nu-úr-*kab-ta ^{I}*ì-*[*lí-tu-ra-am*]
13. ^{I}*a-lí-a-bu-ša* dumu-na-⸢ra⸣
14. dam-mu nu-me-en dumu-mu nu-me-en
15. ba-na-an-du$_{11}$ ⅓ ma-na kù-babbar ì-lá-e
16. tukun-bi sal-kal-la
17. ^{I}*da-mi-iq-ì-lí-šu* dam-a-na-ra
18. dam-mu nu-me-en ba-na-an-du$_{11}$
19. ù *nu-úr-*kab-ta *ì-lí-tu-ra-am*
20. ^{I}*a-lí-a-bu-ša* ad-da-na-ra
21. ad-da-mu nu-me-en ba-na-an-du$_{11}$
22. kù-šè in-na-an-sum
23. [erased]

Damiq-ilišu son of Ipquša has married Sal-kala daughter of Dingir-kuta and has so sworn in the name of his king. Sal-kala has given her children Nur-Kabta, Ili-turam, and Ali-abuša as children to Damiq-ilišu their father. If Damiq-ilišu says to Sal-kala his wife and to Nur-Kabta, Ili-turam, and Ali-abuša his children, "You are not my wife, you are not my children," he will pay ⅓ mina of silver. If Sal-kala says to Damiq-ilišu her husband, "You are not my husband," and Nur-Kabta, Ili-turam, (and) Ali-abuša say to their father, "You are not our father," he will give them away for silver.

15. *ARN* 37

1. ^{I}arad-^{d}utu [dumu *ib-ni-*^{d}]
2. ^{I}*ir-ṣi-ya* [dumu-munus ur-]
3. sà nibru^{ki} ba-[an-tuk]
4. mu lugal-la-k[a-ni in-pà]
5. [é] a-šà ^{giš}kiri$_6$ [ ]
6. [ ]
7. [ ]
8. igi$^{?}$ [ ]
9. in-[ ]
10. ^{I}arad-^{d}[utu]
11. ki x x [ ]
12. šà nibru^{ki}[ ]
13. ⸢uru-ni-šè šà$^{?}$ x⸣ [ ]
14. u$_4$ kúr-šè [tukun-bi]
15. [^{I}]⸢*ir*⸣-[*ṣi-ya*]
16. ^{I}arad-^{d}utu dam-na-[ra]
17. dam-mu [nu]-⸢me-en⸣ ba-[na-an-du$_{11}$]
18. [é] a-[šà ^{giš}k]iri$_6$ [níg-ga]
19. [a-na-me-a-bi ba-ra]-è-d[è]
20. [ ] ⸢ì-lá-e⸣
21. [ù] tukun-bi ì[r-^{d}utu]
22. ^{I}*ir-ṣi-ya* dam-a-na
23. ^{I}dingir-*šu-ib-ni-šu* dumu-[a-na]
24. ù *a-píl-ì-lí-šu* [dumu-a-na]
25. dam-mu ù dumu-mu [nu-me-en]
26. ba-ne-en-du$_{11}$
27. ½ ma-na kù-babbar ì-[lá-e]
28. še-ga-ne-ne-dub in-na-[an-sar-eš]
29. mu lugal-bi in-pà-d[è-eš]

Ir-Utu [son of Ibni-] has [married] Erṣiya [daughter of Ur-] in Nippur and has so [sworn] in the name of his king. [House], field, orchard—[all that there is]—(several lines too damaged to understand). From Nippur [ ] to his city [ ]. In future [if] Erṣiya says to Ir-Utu her husband, "You are not my husband," [she will forfeit house], fields, [orchards—all of the property]—and will pay [x shekels of silver]. And if Ir-Utu says to Erṣiya his wife and to Ilšu-ibnišu his son and to Apil-ilišu his brother, "You are not my wife and my sons," he will pay ½ mina of silver. In mutual agreement [they wrote the tablet] and swore in the name of the king.

16. BE 6/2 48

1. ^{I}*a-wi-li-ya* dumu arad-^{d}en-zu
2. ^{I}*na-ra-am-tum* dumu-munus ^{d}en-zu-*na-tum*
3. nam-dam-še in-tuk
4. ^{I}i-bi-^{d}en-líl ibila-šeš-gal dingir-*šu-ib-ni-šu* šeš-a-ni
5. ù *ì-lí-ma-a-bi* šeš-a-ne-ne ^{I}*a-wi-li-ya*-ke$_4$
6. ^{I}*na-ra-am-tum* dam-a-ni-ra nam-ibila-ni-šè in-na-an-sum
7. ^{I}*i-bi*-^{d}en-líl ibila-šeš-gal dingir-*šu-ib-ni-šu* šeš-a-ni
8. ù *ì-lí-ma-a-bi* šeš-a-ne-ne
9. é a-šà ^{giš}kiri$_6$ gemé arad$_2$ níg-ga é-a gál-la
10. ^{I}*a-wi-li-ya* ad-da-ne-ne-ke$_4$
11. šeš-gal-e síb-ta-na-šu ba-ab-te-gá-àm
12. téš-a sì-ga-bi ì-ba-e-ne
13. tukun-bi ^{I}*a-wi-li-ya na-ra-am-tum* dam-a-ni-ra
14. dam-mu nu-me-en ba-na-an-du$_{11}$ ½ ma-na kù-babbar ì-lá-e
15. tukun-bi ^{I}*na-ra-am-tum a-wi-li-ya* dam-a-ni-ra
16. dam-mu nu-me-en ba-na-an-du$_{11}$ umbin al-ku$_5$-ru-dè kù-šè bí-ib-sum-mu-uš
17. tukun-bi ^{I}*i-bi*-^{d}en-líl dingir-*šu-ib-ni-šu*
18. ù *ì-lí-ma-a-bi* šeš-a-ne-ne *na-ra-am-tum* ama-ne-ne-ra
19. ama-ma nu-me-en ba-na-an du$_{11}$-uš
20. níg-ga *a-wi-li-ya* ad-da-ne-ne-ke$_4$ ba-ra-è-ne-en-ne-en
21. tukun-bi ^{I}*na-ra-am-tum i-bi*-^{d}en-líl
22. ^{I}dingir-*šu-ib-ni-šu* ù *ì-lí-ma-a-bi* dumu-ne-ne-ra
23. dumu-mu-me nu-me-en ba-na-an-du$_{11}$
24. níg-ga *a-wi-li-ya* dam-a-na-ke$_4$
25. [^{I}*na-ra*]*-am-tum* šag-ga-[ ]
26. [ ] nam-ibila [ ]
27. [mu-a] 2(gur) 2(pi) še-gur 6 m[a-na síg x silà ì]-giš
28. ^{I}i-bi-^{d}en-líl ibila-[šeš-gal dingir-*šu*]*-ib-ni-šu*
29. ù *ì-lí-ma-a-bi* [šeš-a-ne]-ne
30. ^{I}*na-ra-am-tum* ama-ne-ne-ra ⸢in-na⸣-ab-kal-ge-ne
31. ibila še-ba ì-ba ù síg-ba nu-mu-na-ab-kal-ge
32. níg-ga *a-wi-li-ya* ad-da-na-ke$_4$ ba-ra-è-dè
33. še-ga-ne-ne-ta mu lugal-bi in-pà-dè-eš

Awiliya son of Warad-Sin has married Naramtum daughter of Sinatum. Awiliya has given Ibbi-Enlil the heir and eldest son, Ilšu-ibnišu his brother, and Ilima-abi their brother to Naramtum his wife as heirs. To Ibbi-Enlil the heir and eldest son, to Ilšu-ibnišu his brother, and to Ilima-abi their brother, house, field, orchard, male and female slaves, and household goods, Awiliya their father, after the eldest son has taken his preference portion, will divide by lot among them equally. If Awiliya says to Naramtum his wife, "You are not my wife," he will pay ½ mina of silver. If Naramtum says to Awiliya her husband, "You are not my husband," he will shave her and place a slave mark on her and give her for silver. If Ibbi-Enlil, Ilšu-ibnišu, and Ilima-abi his brothers say to Naramtum their mother, "You are not our mother," they will forfeit the property of Awiliya their father. If Naramtum says to Ibbi-Enlil, Ilšu-ibnišu, and Ilima-abi her sons, "You are not my sons," Naramtum will [ ] the property of Awiliya her husband. [ ] heirship [ ]. Ibbi-Enlil [the heir and eldest] son, Ilšu-ibnišu, and Ilima-abi his brothers will provide [an annual ration of] 2 gur 2 pi of barley, 6 mina [of wool, and x sila of] oil to Naramtum their mother. Any heir who fails to provide the barley, wool, and oil rations will forfeit his father's property. In mutual agreement they have sworn in the name of the king.

17. PBS 8/2 155

1. [^{I}dingir-*šu-ba*]-*ni*
2. [^{I}*mu-ḫa-di-tum*] nam-dam-ni-šè in-tuk
3. [^{Id}nin-urta-*mu*]-*ba-lí-iṭ*
4. [^{I}*ṣi-lí*-eš$_4$-dar] ù gìr-ni-ì-ša$_5$
5. [dumu-me] *mu-ḫa-di-tum*
6. [^{I}dingir-*šu*]-*ba-ni*-ke$_4$ *mu-ḫa-di-tum*[ ] ⟨nam-ibila-ni-šè in-gar⟩
7. [x] ⌜sar⌝ é-dù-a da é *ip-qú*-^{d}d[a-mu dumu *n*]*a-ra-am*-^{d}en-zu
8. [ù da é] *ì-lí-i-din-nam* dumu *lu-mu-ur-ì*-[*lí*]
9. [ ] gán a-šà ú-gub ús-a-du *ip-qú*-[*ša* dumu ^{d}en-zu-*ma-g*]*ir*
10. [ ] sar ^{giš}kiri$_6$ giš-gub-ba é-gal šà a-š[à x x]-na
11. [ús]-a-du *i-da-tum* dumu *bur*-^{d}[ ]
12. [ ] 10 sar ^{giš}kiri$_6$ giš gub-ba šà ^{id}2x-[ ]
13. [ús]-a-du *ì-lí-ip-pa-al-sà* dumu ^{I}[ ]
14. [ù] *ip-qú-ša* dumu ^{d}en-zu-*ma-gir*
15. [x] sar ^{giš}kiri$_6$ igi a-gàr-ri-[ ]
16. šà a-šà nanga ús-a-du *ì-lí-i*[*p-pa-al-sà*]
17. ù ús-a-du *ip-qú-ša* dumu ^{d}en-[zu-*ma-gir*]
18. ^{I}*mu-ḫa-di-tum*-ra dam-a-ni
19. ^{Id}nin-urta-*mu-ba-lí-iṭ*
20. ^{I}*ṣi-lí*-eš$_4$-dar ù gìr-ni-ì-ša$_5$
21. [in]-na-an-ni-in-ku$_4$
22. [^{I}]^{d}nin-urta-*mu-ba-lí-iṭ* šeš-gal-la
23. síb-ta-na šu ba-ab-ti-gá
24. téš-a sì-ga-bi ì-ba-e-ne-eš
25. [tuku]n-bi ^{I}*mu-ḫa-di-tum*
26. [^{I}dingir-*š*]*u-ba-ni*-ra dam-a-n[i]
27. [^{Id}]nin-urta-*mu-ba-lí-iṭ* d[umu-ni]
28. [^{I}*ṣi-lí*-eš$_4$-dar] ù gìr-ni-ì-ša$_5$
29. [dam-mu] nu-me-en ad-da-mu nu-me-[en]

30. [ba-na-an]-du$_{11}$ é a-šà ^{giš}kiri$_6$
31. [ba-an]-è-dè-eš
32. [ù tukun]-bi ^{I}dingir-*šu-ba-ni*
33. [^{I}*mu-ḫa-di-tum*] dam-a-ni [^{d}]nin-ur[ta-*mu-ba-lí-iṭ*]
34. [*ṣi-lí*-eš$_4$-dar] ù gìr-ni-ì-ša$_5$
35. [dam-mu nu-me-en dumu-mu] nu-me-en ba-na-an-du$_{11}$-eš
36. [é a-šà ^{giš}kiri$_6$ ba]-an-è-dè-eš
37. [še-ga-ne-ne-ta] mu lugal-téš-bi in-pà-dè-eš

Ilšu-bani has married Muḫadditum. Ilšu-bani has (taken) from Muḫadditum (as his heirs/sons) Ninurta-muballiṭ, Ṣilli-Ištar, and Girni-iša, the sons of Muḫadditum. An x-sar house plot next to the house of Ipqu-Damu son of Naram-Sin and next to the house of Ili-iddinam son of Lumur-ili; an x-*iku* field plot with standing plants, beside (the plot of) Ipquša son of Sin-magir; an x-sar orchard plot with standing trees, (property of) the palace, in the [ ]-na irrigation district, beside (the plot of) Iddatum son of Bur-[ ]; [an x-*iku*] 10-sar orchard plot with trees standing, by the canal [ ], beside (the plot of) Ili-ippalsa son of [ ] and beside (the plot of) Ipquša son of Sin-magir; an x-sar orchard plot in front of the meadow, in the Nanga irrigation district, beside (the plot of) Ili-ippalsa and beside (the plot of) Ipquša son of Sin-magir—(all this) he has turned over to Muḫadditum his wife, Ninurta-muballiṭ, Ṣilli-Ištar, and Girni-iša. After Ninurta-muballiṭ the eldest brother has taken his preference portion, they will divide it equally by casting lots. If Muḫadditum says to Ilšu-bani her husband and (if) Ninurta-muballiṭ her son, Ṣilli-Ištar, and Girni-iša say, "You are not my husband, you are not my father," they will forfeit house, field, and orchard property. And if Ilšu-bani says to [Muḫadditum] his wife and to Ninurta-muballiṭ, [Ṣilli-Ištar], and Girni-iša, "You are not (my wife), you are not [my sons]," he will forfeit [house, field, and orchard property. In mutual agreement] they have sworn in the name of the king.

Type 4 Adoptions: Texts 18–22

18. *ARN* 9

1. [^{I}a-ka]-a-a dumu-munus [gub-ba-ni-dùg]
   [rest of obverse and much of reverse destroyed]

Akaya daughter of [Gubbani-dug]. . . . (Most of the rest of the text destroyed.)

19. SAOC 44 62

1. [ ] *la-ma-sà-tu*[*m*]
2. dumu-munus níg-ba-[^{d}nin-urta]
3. ^{I}lú-⌜^{d}nuska⌝ [ ]
4. nam-dumu-[ni-šè ba-da-an-ri]
   [rest destroyed]

[Sealed tablet:] Lamassatum daughter of Nigba-Ninurta has adopted as a son (or, has been adopted as a daughter by) Lu-Nuska [son of]. (Rest of text destroyed.)

20. BE 6/2 4

1. ^{I}*a-pi-ir-tum* dumu-munus *ḫu-pa-tum*
2. ki *ḫu-pa-tum* ad-da-ni
3. ù *ru-ba-tum* ama-ni-ta
4. ^{I}*ša-lu-ur-tum* dam ka-^{d}nanna-ke$_4$
5. nam-dumu-munus-a-ni-šè
6. ba-da-an-ri
7. 1 $\frac{1}{3}$ gín kù-babbar
8. kù nam-á-è-a-ni-šè
9. ^{I}*ša-lu-ur-tum*-ke$_4$
10. ^{I}*ḫu-pa-tum*-ra
11. in-na-an-lá
12. ^{I}*a-pi-ir-tum*-ke$_4$
13. kar-kid al-dù-ni-*ma*
14. ^{I}*ša-lu-ur-tum* ama-a-ni
15. ninda an-né-ib-kú-a
16. tukun-bi ^{I}*a-wi-ir-tum*-ke$_4$
17. ^{I}*ša-lu-ur-tum* ama-a-ni
18. ama-mu nu-me-en ba-na-an-du$_{11}$
19. kù-šè sum-mu-dam
20. ù tukun-bi
21. ^{I}*ša-lu-ur-tum*-ke$_4$
22. ^{I}*a-wi-ir-tum* dumu-munus-a-ni-ra
23. dumu-munus-mu nu-me-en ba-na-an-du$_{11}$
24. 10 gín kù-babbar ì-lá-e
25. ù kù nam-á-è-a-ni-šè
26. ba-ra-è-dè
27. [mu lugal-bi] in-pà

Šallurtum wife of Ka-Nanna has adopted Apirtum daughter of Ḫupatum, from Ḫupatum her father and from Ribatum her mother. Šallurtum will pay to Ḫupatum $1\frac{1}{3}$ shekels of silver as an upbringing payment. Apirtum will be made a prostitute and Šallurtum her mother will take the income. If Apirtum says to Šallurtum her mother, "You are not my mother," she will be given away for silver, and if Šallurtum says to Apirtum her daughter, "You are not my daughter," she will pay 10 shekels of silver and will forfeit the adoption payment. Thus has she sworn in the name of the king.

21. BE 6/2 46

1. kišib [nam-dumu-šè]
2. ^{I}*la-ma-*[*sum* lukur ^{d}nin]-urta

3. dumu-mu[nus ^{d}en-líl-ma]-an-sum
4. ^{I}*ša*-[*at*-^{d}]utu
5. dam [ ]-*e-ri-ba-am*
6. nam-dumu-[munus]-a-ni-šè
7. ba-da-⸢an⸣-ri-a

Sealed document [of adoption]: Lamassum *nadītu* of Ninurta daughter of Enlil-mansum has adopted as a daughter (or, has been adopted as a daughter by) Šat-Šamaš wife of [ ]-eribam. . . .

22. *ARN* 100

1. ^{I}*be-el-ta-ni* lukur ^{d}n[in-urta]
2. ù *il-ta-ni* lukur ^{d}nin-ur[ta]
3. dumu ^{d}utu-*ki-ma-ì-lí-šu*
4. ^{Id}nin-urta-*mu-ša-lim* ⸢x⸣ [ ]
5. dumu ^{d}nanna-ma-an-sum
6. ù ^{d}ašnan-a-⸢x⸣ [ ]
7. dumu ^{d}utu-*ga-mil*
8. nam-ibila-ne-ne-[šè]
[rest of obverse destroyed]

Beltani *nadītu* of Ninurta and Iltani *nadītu* of Ninurta, daughter(s) of Šamaš-kima-ilišu, [have adopted] as heirs (or, have been adopted as heirs by) Ninurta-mušallim, [ ] son of Nanna-mansum [ ], and Ašnan-a-[ ] son of Šamaš-gamil-. . . . (Rest of the obverse destroyed.)

Mannum-mešu-liṣṣur Archive: Texts 23–53

23. OECT 8 20 [collated by Stone]; photo: pls. 61–62

1. ^{I}ur-^{d}lum-ma
2. dumu lu-^{d}inanna agrig
3. ^{I}lú-^{d}ba-ú
4. dumu é-lú-ti
5. nam-ibila-ni-šè
6. ba-an-re-e
7. nam-ì-du$_8$ ká é-gu-⟨la⟩ ^{d}en-líl-lá
8. mu-àm iti 1-kam u$_4$ 15-kam
9. nam-ì-du$_8$ ká ^{d}nin-gá-gi$_4$-a
10. mu-àm u$_4$ 22½-kam
11. nam-gudu$_4$ ^{d}a-ba-^{d}en-lil-gím
12. [ ] ù bur-šu-ma
13. [x x]-*da-ka*
14. [é] a-šà ù nì-gur$_{11}$ a-na-me-a-bi

reverse
15. ur-^{d}lum-ma-ke$_4$ ^{I}lú-^{d}ba-[ú-ra]
16. [in]-na-an-sum
17. [en-na] ur-^{d}lum-ma na-an-ga-til-la
18. [iti]-da 40 silà še-ta 4 ⟨silà⟩ ì-giš-ta-a
19. [mu]-àm 4 ma-na sìg-ta-a
20. in-na-ab-kal-la-ge-ne
21. u$_4$ kúr-šè ur-^{d}lum-ma ù ibila-a-ni
22. a-na-me-a-bi inim nu-um-gá-gá-a
23. mu lugal-bi in-pà
24. igi kù-^{d}nanna dumu inim-^{d}en-líl
25. igi inim-^{d}da-mu ni-da-kal$^{?}$-la
26. igi lú-ì-si-in^{ki}-na dumu ^{d}utu-ḫé-gál
27. igi *na-bi*-^{d}en-líl dumu en-na
28. igi arad-^{d}nanna dumu lugal-iti-da
29. igi ur-^{d}sa-dàr-nun-na dub-sar
30. iti kin-^{d}inanna
31. mu ús-sa ^{d}*li-pí-iṭ*-^{d}en-líl [lugal-e]
32. ^{d}en-líl-ka á-daḫ-a-ni
33. ^{d}en-líl-ra mu-na-dím

SEAL
ur-^{d}lum-ma
dumu lú-^{d}inanna

Ur-Lumma son of Lu-Inanna the farmer has adopted Lu-Bau son of Eluti as his heir. Ur-Lumma has given to Lu-Bau the custodianship of the Egula gate of Enlil for 1 month and 15 days, the custodianship of the Ningagia gate for $22\frac{1}{2}$ days, the gudu-ship of Aba-Enlil-gim, the [ ] and buršuma of [ ], house, field, and movable property—all that there is. Now, as long as he is indeed alive he (i.e., Lu-Bau) shall provide him (i.e., Ur-Lumma) each month with 40 liters of barley, 4 (liters) of oil, and each year with 4 minas of wool. In future, Ur-Lumma and his heirs, however many there are, will not raise a claim for all these things. Thus has he sworn in the name of the king.

Note

line 33: For this year-name, see the comments of M. Sigrist, "èš-ta-gur-ra," *Revue d'Assyriologie* 71 (1977) 121ff.

24. OECT 8 17 [collated by Stone]; photo: pls. 54–56

1. $1\frac{1}{3}$ sar é-dù-a da é ka-kù-ga
2. ki-è-bi e-sír-ra
3. 3 sar kislaḫ da é mu-ni-ki-en-gi$_4$-šè
4. 4 sar kislaḫ da é lú-^{d}en-zu-na
5. 1 ^{giš}ig mi-rí-za šà kisal-lá$^{!}$ gub-ba
6. 1 ^{giš}ig dib-ba é-pa-paḫ gub-ba

7. 1 ^{giš}ig zé-na
8. 1 gán a-šà uz-za ús-a-du lugal-a-ma-ru
9. ½ gán 10 sar a-šà uz-za ki-duru$_5$ ús-a-du ama$^{!}$-da-kal-la
10. 2 gán a-šà íd-gìr-ta-bal-e ús-a-du é-lú-ti š[u-ḫa-a]
11. nam-ì-du$_8$ ká-sumun ^{d}en-líl-lá mu-àm u$_4$ 22½-kam
12. nam-ì-du$_8$ ká é-gal-maḫ mu-àm u$_4$ 22½-kam
13. nam-ì-du$_8$ ká ús-gíd-da mu-àm u$_4$ 22½-kam
14. nam-ì-du$_8$ ká-gal ^{d}nin-líl-lá mu-àm u$_4$ 22½-kam
15. nam-ì-du$_8$ ká ^{giš}kin-ti mu-àm u$_4$ 22½-kam
16. nam-ì-du$_8$ ká ^{d}nin-gá-gi$_4$-a mu-àm u$_4$ 11½-kam
17. nam-ì-du$_8$ ká du$_6$-kù mu-àm u$_4$ 22½-kam
18. nam-é-da-di ^{d}en-líl ^{d}nin-líl mu-àm u$_4$ 6-kam
19. šà ^{giš}kiri$_6$ pe-ru-ru-tum ḫa-la-ba ur-^{d}lum-ma
20. šu-ri-a-bi in-ba-e-eš
21. 1 naga$_4$-esir 1 ^{giš}gag-maš mar-gíd-da
22. 2 ^{giš}u$_4$-sakar ^{giš}mar-gíd-da
23. ḫa-la-ba ^{d}nanna-me-ša$_4$ šeš-gal
24. 1⅓ sar é-dù-a ki-tuš da é nin-du$_{10}$-[ga]
25. 3 sar kislaḫ da é ^{d}nanna-me-ša$_4$
26. 4 sar kislaḫ da é lú-^{d}en-zu-na
27. 1 ^{giš}ig mi-rí-za ki-tuš gub-ba

reverse

28. 1 ^{giš}ig dib-ba ki-tuš gub-ba
29. 1 ^{giš}ig zé-na
30. [1] gán a-šà uz-za ús-a-du ^{d}nanna-me-ša$_4$
31. ½ gán 10 sar a-šà uz-za ki-duru$_5$ ús-a-du ^{d}nanna-me-ša$_4$
32. 2 gán a-šà ^{íd}gìr-ta-bal-e ús-a-du ^{d}nanna-[me-ša$_4$]
33. nam-ì-du$_8$ ká-sumun ^{d}en-líl-lá šu-ri-a-bi
34. nam-ì-du$_8$ ká é-gal-maḫ mu-àm u$_4$ 22½-kam
35. nam-ì-du$_8$ ká ús-gíd-da mu-àm u$_4$ 22½-kam
36. nam-ì-du$_8$ ká-gal ^{d}nin-líl-lá mu-àm u$_4$ 22½-kam
37. nam-ì-du$_8$ ká ^{giš}kin-ti mu-àm u$_4$ 22½-kam
38. nam-ì-du$_8$ ká ^{d}nin-gá-gi$_4$-a mu-àm u$_4$ 11½-kam
39. nam-ì-du$_8$ ká du$_6$-kù mu-àm u$_4$ 22½-kam
40. nam-é-da-di ^{d}en-líl ^{d}nin-líl mu-àm u$_4$ 6-kam
41. šà ^{giš}kiri$_6$ *pe-ru-ru-tum* ḫa-la-ba ur-^{d}lum-ma
42. šu-ri-a-bi in-ba-e-eš
43. 2 ^{giš}umbin mar-gíd-da 2 ^{giš}u$_4$-sakar mar-gíd-da
44. 1 ^{giš}gu-za
45. ḫa-la-ba ad-da-kal-la
46. še-ga-ne-ne-ta giš-šub-ba-ta in-ba-e-eš
47. u$_4$ kúr-šè lú-lú-ù-ra inim nu-um-gá-gá-a
48. mu lugal-bi téš-bi in-pà-dè-eš
49. igi nì-gur$_{11}$-^{d}nanna gudu$_4$ dumu ^{d}en-líl-gú-gal
50. igi ^{d}nanna-ma-an-sum dumu *a-wi-il-ili*

51. igi inim-^{d}da-mu dumu da-da-kal-la
52. igi ^{d}en-zu-*li-di-iš* dumu$^{!}$ lú-si-gar
53. igi arad-^{d}en-líl-lá dumu inim-^{d}en-líl-lá
54. igi *im-gur*-^{d}en-zu dub-sar
55. iti še-gur$_{10}$-ku$_{5}$ mu ^{d}en-zu-*i-qí-ša-am* lugal
56. alam guškin alam kù-babbar
57. ^{d}utu-ra mu-un-na-an-ku$_{4}$

SEAL
^{d}nanna-me-ša$_{4}$
ad-da-kal-la
ibila lú-^{d}ba-ú

A 1⅓-sar house plot next to the house of Kakuga(ni), its exit to the street; a 3-sar plot of unimproved residential property next to the house of Muni-kiengi; a 4-sar plot of unimproved residential property next to the house of Lu-Suen; 1 door of small boards in the courtyard; 1 door of boards in the shrine; 1 door of date wood; a 1-*iku* field plot (in the) Uzza (irrigation district), beside (the field of) Lugal-amaru; a 1-*iku* field plot (in the) Uzza (irrigation district), wet land, beside (the field of) Amada-kala; a 2-*iku* field plot (in the) Girtabale canal (irrigation district), beside (the field of) Eluti the fisherman; the custodianship of the old gate of Enlila for 22½ days annually; the custodianship of the Egalmaḫ gate for 22½ days annually; the custodianship of the Usgida gate for 22½ days annually; the custodianship of the great gate of Ninlil for 22½ days annually; the custodianship of the Craftsmen's gate for 22½ days annually; the custodianship of the Ningagia gate for 11½ days annually; the custodianship of the Duku gate for 22½ days annually; the edadiship of Enlil and Ninlil for 6 days annually; they divided up into lots the rest of Ur-Lumma's share in the orchard of Perurutum; 1 bitumen mortar, 1 x of a wagon wheel, 1 wagon wheel, 2 halves of a wagon wheel—(the above is the inheritance) share of Nanna-meša, the eldest son.

A 1⅓-sar house plot, the bedroom, next to the house of Nin-duga; a 3-sar plot of unimproved residential property next to the house of Nanna-meša; a 4-sar plot of unimproved residential property next to the house of Lu-Suen; 1 door of small boards in the bedroom; 1 door of boards in the bedroom; 1 door of date wood; a (1)-*iku* field plot (in the) Uzza (irrigation district), beside the field of Nanna-meša; a ½-*iku* 10-sar field plot (in the) Uzza (irrigation district), wet lands, beside (the field) of Nanna-meša; a 2-*iku* field plot (in the) Girtabale canal (irrigation district), beside (the field) of Nanna-meša; the remainder of the custodianship of the old gate of Enlila; the custodianship of the Egalmaḫ gate for 22½ days annually; the custodianship of the Usgida gate for 22½ days annually; the custodianship of the great gate of Ninlil for 22½ days annually; the custodianship of the Craftsmen's gate for 22½ days annually; the custodianship of the Ningagia gate for 11½ days annually; the custodianship of the Duku gate for 22½ days annually; the edadiship of Enlil and Ninlil for 6 days annually; they divided up into lots the rest of Ur-Lumma's share in the orchard of Perurutum; 2 wagon wheels, 1 wheel hubs on a wagon, 1 chair—(the whole the inheritance) share of Adda-kala.

Together they have agreed to the division. In future each will not make a claim against the other. Thus have they sworn in the name of the king.

Note

line 57: On this year-name, see the remarks of M. Stoll, *Studies in Old Babylonian History* (Leiden: Nederlands Historisch-Archaeologisch Instituut te Istanbul, 1976) 25.

25. OECT 8 4 [collated by Stone]; photo: pls. 32–33

1. mu 5 gín kù-babbar sa$_{10}$ 15 gín é-dù-a
2. ^{Id}nanna-me-ša$_{4}$ ad-da til-la
3. ^{I}nin-kù-zu dumu-munus-na-ra
4. in-sum-ma-àm
5. šà-mul é ad-da-na
6. ^{I}*a-ḫa-mar-si* dumu *sí-ya-tum*
7. ^{I}*ip-qú-er-ṣe-tim* dumu illat-ti
8. ^{I}*i-na-ša-me-e-wu-súm*
9. ù ^{d}nuska-á-maḫ-ke$_{4}$-ne
10. ^{Id}nuska-á-maḫ dumu ^{d}nanna-me-ša$_{4}$-ra
11. in-lá-lá-e-eš-àm
12. u$_{4}$ kúr-šè *a-wi-li-ya*
13. ù *mu-na-wi-ru-um*-ke$_{4}$
14. ibila ^{d}nuska-á-maḫ-ke$_{4}$-ne
15. 15 gín é-dù-a
16. da é ^{d}da-mu-a-zu
17. nì ^{d}nanna-me-ša$_{4}$ ad-da-ti-la-ke$_{4}$
18. ^{I}nin-kù-zu dumu-munus-na-ra
19. in-sum-ma-àm
20. inim nu-um-gá-gá-ne-a

reverse

21. mu lugal-bi in-pà-dè-eš
22. ù mu ^{d}en-líl-u$_{19}$-ru-maḫ-^{d}utu$^{!}$
23. mu-a u$_{4}$ 10-kam
24. 5/6 gín 10 še kù-babbar ^{I}*a-ḫa-mar-si*-ke$_{4}$
25. ^{I}*ip-qú-er-ṣe-tim a-wi-li-ya*
26. ù *mu-na-wi-ru-um* šeš-a-na-ra
27. in-ne-en-búr
28. u$_{4}$ kúr-šè *ip-qú-er-ṣe-tim* ^{I}*a-wi-li-ya*
29. ù *mu-na-wi-ru-um* kù nam-búr-ra
30. 5/6 gín 10 še kù-babbar inim nu-um-gá-gá-ne-a
31. mu lugal-bi in-pà-dè-eš
32. igi ^{d}en-líl-gal-zu dumu a-gu-ú-a
33. igi ^{d}nin-urta-*mu-ša-lim* šeš-a-ni
34. igi *ma-nu-um-ma-ḫir-šu* dumu *im-gu-ru-um*
35. igi *u-bar-ru-um* gala

36. igi ^{d}da-mu-*i-din-na-am* dub-sar
37. igi *ta-ri-ba-tum* bur-gul
38. iti ne-ne-gar mu ^{d}*ḫa-am-mu-ra-pí* lugal-e
39. ma-da *e-mu-ut-ba-lum*^{ki}
40. ù lugal-e su-ni
41. šà bí-in-du$_{11}$-ga

SEAL

a-wi-li-ya
mu-na-wi-ru-um
ibi[la] ^{d}nuska-á-m[aḫ]

Concerning the 5 shekels of silver, price of a 15-gin house plot which Nanna-meša the living patriarch gave to Nin-kuzu his daughter from the assets of the house of his/her father, (and which) Aḫamarši son of Siyatum, Ipqu-erṣetim son of Illati, Inšame-wusum, and Nuska-amaḫ paid to Nuska-amaḫ son of Nanna-meša. In future Awiliya and Munawirum, heirs of Nuska-amaḫ, will raise no claim against the 15-gin house plot next to the house of Damu-azu which Nanna-meša the living patriarch had given to Nin-kuzu his daughter. Thus have they sworn in the name of the king. And concerning the Enlil-urumaḫ-Utu office for 10 days annually, Aḫamarši has delivered it (for) ⅚ gín 10 še of silver to Ipqu-erṣetim, Awiliya, and Munawirum his brothers. In future Ipqu-erṣetim, Awiliya, and Munawirum will make no claim on the delivery money, ⅚ gín 10 še of silver. In the name of the king they have sworn.

Note

line 22: For additional references to ^{d}en-líl-u$_{19}$-ru-maḫ-^{d}utu, see note to text 51, line 36.

26. Cornell 6; copy: pp. 60–63; photo: pls. 3–5

Column I

1. [nam-é-da-di mu-a]
2. [u$_{4}$ x-kam]
3. [nam-ì-du$_{8}$ ká-gal mu-a]
4. [u$_{4}$ x-kam]
5. [nam-ì-d]u$_{8}$ ká ús-gíd-gíd-da
6. mu-a u$_{4}$ 2½-kam
7. [n]am-i-du$_{8}$ ká ^{giš}kin-ti
8. mu-a u$_{4}$ 2½-kam
9. nam-ì-du$_{8}$ ká ^{d}nin-gá-gi$_{4}$-a
10. mu-a u$_{4}$ 2-kam
11. 8 gín é-dù-a
12. da é dumu-me *u-bar-rum*
13. 16 sar a-šà uz-za
14. ús-a-du dumu-me *i-din*-^{d}en-zu

15. 20 sar a-šà ^{id}gìr-ta-bal-e
16. síb-ta nam-šeš-gal-la-šè
17. nam-é-da-di mu-a
18. iti 2 u$_4$ 21-kam
19. nam-ì-du$_8$ ká-gal mu-a
20. u$_4$ 10-kam
21. nam-ì-du$_8$ ká ús-gíd-gíd-da
22. ù ká-gal ^{d}nin-líl-lá
23. mu-a u$_4$ 10-kam
24. nam-ì-du$_8$ ká ^{giš}kin-ti
25. mu-a u$_4$ 10-[kam]

Column II

1. [nam-ì-du$_8$ ká du$_6$-kù-ga]
2. [mu-a u$_4$ 3½-kam]
3. [nam-ì-du$_8$ ká ^{d}nin-gá-gi$_4$-a]
4. mu-a u$_4$ 6-kam
5. ½ sar 6 gín é-dù-a
6. da é síb-ta-na
7. ½ gán 22 sar šà a-šà uz-za
8. ús-a-du síb-ta-na
9. ½ gán 30 sar šà a-šà ^{id}gìr-ta-bal-e
10. ḫa-la-ba *i-bi*-^{d}en-líl šeš-gal
11. nam-é-da-di mu-a
12. iti 2 u$_4$ 21-kam
13. nam-ì-du$_8$ ká-[gal] mu-a
14. u$_4$ 10-kam
15. nam-ì-du$_8$ ká ús-gíd-gíd-da
16. ù ká-gal ^{d}nin-líl-lá
17. mu-a u$_4$ 10-kam
18. nam-ì-du$_8$ ká ^{giš}kin-ti
19. mu-a u$_4$ 10-kam
20. nam-ì-du$_8$ ká du$_6$-kù-ga
21. mu-a u$_4$ 3½-kam
22. nam-ì-du$_8$ ká ^{d}nin-gá-gi$_4$-a
23. mu-a u$_4$ 6-kam

Column III

1. [½ sar] 6 gín é-dù-[a]
2. [d]a é šeš-a-ni
3. [½] gán 22 sar [šà a-šà uz-za]
4. ús-a-du še[š-a-ni]
5. ½ gán 30 sar šà [a-šà ^{id}gìr-ta-bal-e]
6. ḫa-la-ba ^{d}nanna-a-a šeš-a-ni
7. [ib]ila ^{d}en-zu-*i-qí*-[*ša*]-*am* ad$^{!?}$-da$^{!}$
8. *i-lí-a-wi-li*
9. šeš ad-da-ne-ne

10. ḫa-la-ba in-ne-en-ba
11. u$_4$ kúr-šè *i-bi*-^{d}en-líl
12. ù ^{d}nanna-a-a
13. nam-ibila *ì-lí-a-wi-li-šè*
14. inim nu-um-gá-gá-dè-e
15. mu lugal-bi in-pà-dè-eš
16. kišib ḫa-la-ba kišib sag-ta
17. nì-nam *ì-lí-a-wi-li*
18. ù nì-nam ^{d}en-zu-*še-mi*-ke$_4$
19. téš-a síg-ga-bi in-ba-eš-a
20. [ ]x-x

Column IV
1. [ ]
2. igi ^{d}nin-urta-ma-an-[sum]
3. ugula ⟨dag$_4$⟩-gi$_4$-a
4. igi ^{d}en-zu-*ma-gir*
5. dumu ^{d}en-zu-*i-qí-šam*
6. igi arad-^{d}imin-bi lú-túg
7. igi ^{d}nin-urt[a-ma-an]-sum
8. šagin
9. igi dingir-ma-an-sum
10. dumu *be-el-šu-nu*
11. igi kù-^{d}nin-immà dub-sar
12. igi *a-wi-il-ya* bur-gul
13. [iti] ne-ne-gar
14. [mu *sa*]-*am-su-i-lu-na* lugal
15. [ ]x

SEAL
i-bi-^{d}en-líl
^{d}nanna-a-a
ibila ^{d}en-zu-*i-qí-ša-am*

The edadi-ship for [x] days annually; the custodianship of the great gate for [x] days annually; the custodianship of the Usgida gate for 2½ days annually; the custodianship of the Craftsmen's gate for 2½ days annually; the custodianship of the Ningagia gate for 2 days annually; an 8-gin house plot next to that of the sons of Ubarum; a 16-sar field plot (in the) Uzza (irrigation district), beside (the field) of the sons of Iddin-Sin; a 20-sar field plot (in the) Girtabale canal (irrigation district)—(the above) form the portion allotted to the eldest son. The edadi-ship for 22 months and 21 days annually; the custodianship of the great gate for 3½ days annually; the custodianship of the Usgida gate and the great gate of Ninlila for 10 days annually; the custodianship of the craftsman's gate for 10 days annually; the custodianship of Dukuga gate for 3½ days annually; the custodianship of the Ningagia gate for 6 days annually; ½ sar and 6 gin of a house plot next to that of his allotted house; ½ *iku* 30 sar of field plot (in the) Girtabale canal (irrigation district)—(all the above being the inheritance) portion of Ibbi-Enlil the eldest brother. The edadi-ship for 2 months and 21 days annually; the custodianship of the great gate for 10 days annually; the custodianship of the Usgida gate and of the great gate of Ninlila for 10 days annually; the custodianship of the Craftsmen's gate for 10 days annually; the custodianship of the Dukuga gate for 10 days annually; the custodianship of the Ningagia gate for 6 days annually; ½ sar 6 gin of a house plot next to that of his brother; ½ *iku* 22 sar of a field plot (in the) Uzza (irrigation district) adjacent to that of his brother; ½ *iku* 30 sar of a field plot (in the) Girtabale canal (irrigation district)—(all of the above being the inheritance) portion of Nanna-aya his brother. The heir of Sin-iqišam the father being Ili-awili, the brother of their father has been given (his) inheritance portion. So that in future neither Ibbi-Enlil nor Nanna-aya shall raise a claim against the heirship of Ili-awili, in the name of the king they swore. According to the sealed tablet of the division (of inheritance), the items of Ili-awili and the items of Sin-šemi will be divided equally by lot.

Notes

column III, line 20: Traces of two, possibly three, signs are preserved here. Mitchell suggests the possibility of reading tag$_4$ but Owen is not sure that the preserved portions will substantiate such a reading. See the photographs on plate 4.

column IV, line 3: Restored according to the suggestion of M. Stol, *Studies in Old Babylonian History* (Leiden: Nederlands Historisch-Archaeologisch Instituut te Istanbul, 1976) 80 n. 47.

27. Cornell 4; copy by A. Goetze: pp. 63–64 [collated by Owen]; photo: pls. 1–2

1. ^{I}*la-ma-súm* dumu-munus *ip-qú*-é-a
2. ^{Id}nanna-a-a dumu ^{d}en-zu-*i-qí-ša-am*
3. nam-dam-šè in-tuk
4. ^{I}*ma-an-nu-um-me-šu-li-ṣur*
5. ^{Id}nin-urta-*mu-ba-al-lí-iṭ*
6. ^{Id}en-zu-*ma-gir*
7. ù *i-na*-é-kur-*ra-bi*
8. nam-ibila-a-ni-šè ba-an-da-g[ub]
9. é a-šà ^{giš}kiri$_6$ garza
10. ù nì-gur$_{11}$ gál-la a-na-me-a-bi
11. inim-dub ḫa-la-ba
12. i-in-sar-ri-me-[eš]
13. ^{I}*la-ma-súm* 〈*dam*〉 ^{Id}nanna-a-[a]
14. ^{I}*ma-an-nu-um-me-šu-l*[*i-ṣur*]
15. ^{Id}nin-urta-*mu-ba-l*[*í-iṭ*]
16. ^{Id}en-zu-*ma-*[*gir*]
17. ù *i-na*-é-kur-[*ra-bi*]
18. ^{Id}nanna-a-a a[d-da-ne-ne-ke$_4$]
19. 10 gín kù-[babbar]
20. [ ]

reverse

1′. [ ]
2′. tuk[un-bi]
3′. ^{I}*la-ma-*[*súm* dam-a-ni]
4′. ^{I}*ma-an-nu-um-me-*[*šu-li-ṣur* dumu-ni]
5′. ^{Id}nin-urta-*mu-*[*ba-lí-iṭ*]
6′. ^{Id}en-zu-*ma-g*[*ir* ù *i-na-*é-kur-*ra-bi*]
7′. dam-mu nu-me-en [ad-da-mu nu-me-en]
8′. ba-an-na-du$_{11}$ é [a-šà]
9′. ba-ra-e$_{11}$-[ne-en]
10′. ù ½ ma-na kù-[babbar in-ne-en-lá]
11′. igi *ì-lí-a-wi-li* dumu [ ]
12′. igi *ib*$^{!}$*-ni* dumu *i-*[ ]
13′. igi ^{d}en-zu-*ma-gir* dumu x[ ]
14′. igi *mu-na-wi-rum* dumu [^{d}nuska]
15′. igi ^{d}nuska-*ni-šu* [dumu ^{d}nin-urta-*mu-ša-lim*]
16′. igi ^{d}en-zu-*še-mi* dumu [ ]
17′. igi *a-wi-li-ya* bur-gul
18′. igi ^{d}nuska-*ni-šu* dub-sar
19′. itu du$_{6}$-kù mu *sa-am-su-i-lu-na* lugal-e
20′. urudu-alam-sub-bí ^{d}lama guškin dil-dil-bi-ta

SEAL

la-ma-súm dumu-munus *ip-qú-*é-a
^{d}nanna-a-a dam-a-ni (*sic*)
ma-an-nu-u[*m-me-šu-li-ṣur*]
^{d}nin-urta-*mu-ba-al-lí-iṭ*
^{d}en-zu-*ma-gir*
ù *i-na-*é-kur-*ra-bi*
ibila ^{d}nanna-a-a

Lamassum the daughter of Ipqu-Ea has been taken in marriage by Nanna-aya. He established Mannum-mešu-liṣṣur, Ninurta-muballiṭ, Sin-magir, and Ina-ekur-rabi as his heirs. House, field, orchard, temple office, and all the moveable property that there is—their division has been written according to the tablet. (To) Lamassum ⟨the wife of⟩ Nanna-aya, Mannum-mešu-liṣṣur, Ninurta-muballiṭ, Sin-magir, and Ina-ekur-rabi, Nanna-aya their father, 10 shekels of silver [ ]. If Mannum-mešu-liṣṣur, Ninurta-muballiṭ, Sin-magir, and Ina-ekur-rabi say to Lamassum his (i.e., Nanna-aya's) wife, "You are not my (i.e., his) wife," then they shall forfeit house, field, [ ], and they shall pay ½ mina of silver.

28. Cornell 18; copy: p. 64–65; photo: pls. 20–21

1. ⅔ sar 4 gín é-dù-a
2. ús-a-du *u-bar-ru-um*
3. é i-bi-^{d}en-líl

4. dumu ^{d}en-zu-*i-qí-ša-am*
5. [ki *i*]-*bi*-^{d}en-líl-ta
6. [^{I}*ma-an*]-*nu-um-me-šu-li-ṣur*
7. [dumu *a*]-*wi-li-ya*-ke_4
8. [in-ši-i]n-sa_{10}
9. [sa_{10}]-til-[la]-a-bi-šè
10. ⅓ ma-na kù-babbar
11. in-na-an-lá

reverse

12. [u_4 kúr-šè *i-bi*-^{d}en-líl]
13. [ù ibila-a-ni a-na-me-a-bi]
14. ⅔ sar 4 gín é-[dù-a]
15. inim nu-um-gá-gá-[a]
16. mu lugal-bi in-pà
17. igi ^{d}nuska-*ni-šu* dumu ^{d}nin-urta-*mu-ša-lim*
18. igi *mu-na-wi-rum* dumu ^{d}nuska-á-maḫ
19. igi lú-nibru^{ki} dumu ur-du_6-kù-ga
20. igi *a-wi-li-ya* bur-gul
21. igi *a-píl-ì-lí-šu* dub-sar
22. iti bará-zà-gar u_4 14-kam
23. mu *sa-am-su-i-lu-na* lugal-e
24. ki-lugal-gub-ba ḫur-sag ^{íd}dil-dil
25. kisal-maḫ é-tùr-kalam-
26. ma u_6-di mu-un-ge-en

SEAL

i-bi-^{d}en-líl
dumu ^{d}en-zu-*i-qí-ša-am*

Mannum-mešu-liṣṣur son of Awiliya has purchased from Ibbi-Enlil a ⅔-sar 4-gin house plot next to (the house of?) Ubarum (and?) the house of Ibbi-Enlil son of Sin-iqišam. He paid ⅓ mina of silver as its full purchase price. In future, Ibbi-Enlil and his heirs, however many there are, will not raise a claim for the ⅔-sar 4-gin house plot. Thus has he sworn in the name of the king.

Notes

line 2: One expects da é *u-ba-ru-um* here rather than ús-a-du *u-bar-ru-um*.

line 26: The complete preservation of the year-name here confirms the reconstruction proposed by F. R. Kraus, "Ein Edikt des Königs Samsu-iluna von Babylon," *Studies in Honor of Benno Landsberger on His Seventy-fifth Birthday* (Assyriological Studies 16; Chicago: Oriental Institute, University of Chicago, 1965) 226.

29. OECT 8 19 [collated by Stone]; photo: pls. 59–60

1. é-da-di ^{d}en-líl ^{d}nin-líl-lá
2. mu-àm u_4 10-kam

3. ká ^{d}nin-gá-gi$_4$-a
4. mu-àm u$_4$ 6-kam
5. síb-ta garzá a-na-me-a-bi
6. é-da-di mu-àm u$_4$ 20-kam é ús-gíd-da u$_{19}$-ru-maḫ
7. ká ^{d}nin-líl-lá mu-àm u$_4$ 12½-kam
8. ḫa-la-ba ^{d}nin-urta-*mu-uš-ta-al*
9. é-da-di ^{d}en-líl ^{d}nin-líl-lá
10. mu-àm u$_4$ 20-a-kam
11. ká ^{giš}kin-ti mu-àm u$_4$ 12½-kam
12. mu garzá-garzá sá nu-ub-du$_4$-ga-aš
13. [ká du$_6$-kù] mu-àm u$_4$ 12-kam
14. [ḫa-l]a-ba *na-ma-ar-šu-lu-mu-ur*

reverse
15. [é]-da-di ^{d}en-líl ^{d}nin-líl-lá
16. [m]u-àm u$_4$ 20-kam
17. [ká]-gal mu-àm u$_4$ 12½-kam
18. ḫa-la-ba *mu-na-wi-rum*
19. ibila [*ib*]-*ni*-^{d}en-líl-ke$_4$-ne
20. še-ga-ne-ne-ta giš-sub-ba-ta in-ba-e-eš
21. igi lú-^{d}en-líl-lá dumu é-lú-ti
22. igi ^{d}nin-urta-ma-an-sum dumu *ta-ri-bu-um*
23. igi *ta-ri-ba-tum* dumu *ma-ri-er-ṣe-tim*
24. Igi lú-^{d}nin-urta-ma-an-sum aga-ús
25. igi *a-wi-li-ya* bur-gul
26. igi ^{d}nuska-*ni-šu* dub-sar
27. iti ab-è u$_4$ 25-kam
28. mu *ri-im*-^{d}en-zu lugal-e
29. ^{d}nin-maḫ-e é-kèš^{ki}
30. temen an-ki-bi-da-ta

SEAL
^{d}nin-urta-*mu-uš-ta-al*
na-ma-ar-šu-lu-mu-ur
mu-na-wi-ru-[*um*]
ibila-*šu*

The edadi-ship of Enlil and Ninlil for 10 days annually; (the custodianship) of the Ningagia gate for 6 days annually—(this is) the preference portion of whatever temple offices there are—the edadi-ship for 20 days annually (in the) temple of Usgida Urumaḫ; (the custodianship) of the Ninlila gate for 12½ days annually—(the above is the inheritance) share of Ninurta-muštal. The edadi-ship of Enlil and Ninlil for 20 days annually; (the custodianship) of the Craftsmen's gate for 12½ days annually; because the temple offices were not sufficient, (the custodianship) of the Duku gate for 12 days annually (was added)—(the above is the inheritance) share of Namaršu-lumur. The edadi-ship of Enlil and Ninlil for 20 days annually; (the custodianship) of the great gate for 12½ days annually—(the above is the inheritance) share of Munawirum. The heirs of Ibbi-Enlil are in mutual agreement and have divided (the inheritance) up by casting lots.

30. OECT 8 16 [collated by Stone]; photo: pls. 52–53

1. 12 gín é-dù-a
2. ḫa-la-ba ù síb-ta-na
3. ḫa-la-ba *ma-an-nu-um-me-šu-li-ṣur*
4. nam-ì-du$_8$ ká-gu-la
5. mu-àm u$_4$ 10½-kam
6. nam-ì-du$_8$ ká ^{d}nin-gá-gi$_4$-a
7. mu-àm u$_4$ 5-kam
8. nam-ì-du$_8$ ká ^{d}nin-líl-lá
9. mu-àm u$_4$ 1½-kam
10. bal-gub-ba *mu-na-wi-ru-um*
11. ki-ba-gar-ra-bi-šè
12. garza é-e-gim

reverse

13. lú-lú-ù-ra in-gar
14. u$_4$ kúr-šè lú-lú-ù-ra
15. inim nu-um-gá-gá-a
16. mu lugal téš-bi in-pà-dè-eš
17. igi lú-^{d}en-líl-lá agrig
18. igi *nu-ra-bi* gudu$_4$ ^{d}nin-líl-lá
19. igi *ma-an-nu-um-ma-ḫir-šu*
20. dumu *im-gur*-^{d}nin-urta
21. igi *a-wi-li-ya* bur-gul
22. igi ^{d}nuska-*ni-šu* dub-sar
23. iti sig$_4$-a u$_4$ 23-kam
24. mu *sa*-[*am*]-*su-i-lu-na* lugal
25. bal [traces]
26. [ug]nim *e-da-ma-ra-az*[^{ki}]

SEAL	SEAL
mu-na-wi-ru-um	*ma-an-nu-um-me*-[*šu-li-ṣur*]
dumu [*i-bi*-^{d}en-zu]	dumu *a-wi-li-ya*

Mannum-mešu-liṣṣur has exchanged his inheritance of a 12-gin house plot, both his inheritance and his preference portion, with Munawirum for the custodianship of the Gula gate for 10½ days annually, the custodianship of the Ningagia gate for 5 days annually, and the custodianship of the Ninlil gate for 1½ days annually. They have exchanged the house for the offices. In future neither will make a claim against the other. Thus have they sworn in the name of the king.

Note

line 26: The readings of the traces in line 25 of this year-name are still inconclusive, even after collation. See the remarks of M. Stol, *Studies in Old Babylonian History* (Leiden: Nederlands Historisch-Archaeologisch Instituut te Istanbul, 1976) 50, where he is unable to offer any interpretation of the traces preserved in this year-name.

31. OECT 8 11 [collated by Stone]; photo: pls. 50–51

1. ^{I}*ma-an-nu-um-m*[*e*]*-šu-li-ṣur*
2. dumu *a-wi-li-ya*
3. *ki-a-am iq-bi um-ma šu-ú-ma*
4. ^{I}*i-bi*-^{d}en-líl ad-da-ne-ne-ra
5. 2 še gur ù nì-gu$_7$ mu 1-a-kam
6. *gi-im-ru-ú-a iq-bi*
7. dub *gi-im-ri-šu i-mu-ru-ma*
8. še-ga-ne-ne-ta
9. ^{Id}nin-urta-*mu-uš-ta-al*
10. ^{I}*na-ma-ar-šu-lu-mu-ur*
11. ù *mu-na-wi-ru-um*
12. ibila *i-bi*-^{d}en-líl-ke$_4$-ne
13. é-da-di ^{d}en-líl ^{d}nin-líl
14. mu-àm iti 1-a-kam *ma-an-nu-um-me-šu-li-ṣur-ra*
15. in-ne-en-sum-mu-uš
16. u$_4$ kúr-šè ^{d}nin-urta-*mu-uš-ta-al*

reverse

17. ^{I}*na-ma-ar-šu-lu-mu*-[*ur*]
18. ù *mu-na-wi-ru*-[*um*]
19. ibila *i-bi*-^{d}en-líl-ke$_4$-ne
20. mu-àm iti 1-a-kam é-da-di
21. ^{d}en-líl ^{d}nin-líl inim nu-um-gá-gá-a
22. mu lugal téš-bi in-pà-dè-eš
23. igi lú-^{d}en-líl-lá agrig
24. igi ^{d}nin-urta-ma-an-sum dumu *ta-ri-bu-um*
25. igi lú-^{d}nin-urta ukuš
26. igi *a-wi-li-ya* bur-gul
27. igi ^{d}nuska-*ni-šu* dub-sar
28. iti gan-gan-è u$_4$ 3-kam
29. mu ^{d}*sa-am-su-i-lu-na* lugal
30. ugnim *i-da-ma-ra-az*^{ki}
31. *ya-mu-ut-ba-lum*
32. ^{giš}gaz bí-in-ak-a

SEAL

^{d}nin-urta-*mu-uš-ta-al*

na-ma-ar-šu-lu-mu-ur

ù *mu-na-wi-ru-um*
dumu-me *i-bi*-^{d}en-zu

Mannum-mešu-liṣṣur son of Awiliya spoke thus: "2 gur of grain and food for 1 year are my expenses for Ibbi-Enlil their father." They read the tablet of the expenses. Together Ninurta-muštal, Namaršu-lumur, and Munawirum the heirs of Ibbi-Enlil shall give to Mannum-mešu-liṣṣur, from among their portions, the edadi-ship of Enlil and Ninlil for 1 month annually. In future Ninurta-muštal, Namaršu-lumur, and Munawirum the heirs of Ibbi-Enlil will not claim the edadi-ship of Enlil and Ninlil for 1 month annually. Thus have they each sworn in the name of the king.

32. OECT 8 21 [collated by Stone]; photo: pl. 63

1. ^{I}*ì-lí-ip-pa-al-sà-am* dumu ^{d}en-zu-*ma-gir*
2. ù *el-me-šum* dam-a-ni
3. ^{Id}nin-urta-*mu-ba-al-lí-iṭ* dumu *a-wi-li-ya*
4. nam-ibila-a-ni-šè ba-da-re-eš
5. é a-šà ^{giš}kiri$_6$ garzá nì-gur$_{11}$ é-a gál-la
6. ^{Id}nin-urta-*mu-ba-lí-iṭ* dumu-[na]-ra
7. in-[na]-an-ku$_4$-re-[eš]
8. ù ^{d}nin-urta-*mu-ba-lí-iṭ* [dumu]-ni
9. ^{I}*ì-lí-ip-pa-al-sà-am* ad-da-ni-ra
10. ù *el-me-šum* ama-ni-ra
11. 2 gín kù-babbar in-na-an-ku$_4$-re-eš
12. tukun-bi *ì-lí-ip-pa-al-sà-am*
13. ù *el-me-šum* dam-a-ni
14. dumu-mu nu-me-en ba-na-an-du$_{11}$

reverse

15. é a-šà ^{giš}kiri$_6$ garzá nì-gur$_{11}$ é-a gál-l[a]
16. ba-ra-e$_{11}$-dè
17. ù ½ ma-na kù-babbar in-na-an-lá
18. ù tukun-bi ^{d}nin-urta-*mu-ba-lí-iṭ*
19. ^{I}*ì-lí-ip-pa-al-sà-am* ad-da-ni-ra
20. ù *el-me-šum* ama-ni-ra
21. ad-da-mu nu-me-en ù ama-mu nu-me-en
22. ba-na-an-du$_{11}$
23. é a-šà ^{giš}kiri$_6$ garzá nì-gur$_{11}$ é-a gál-la
24. ba-ra-e$_{11}$-ne
25. ù ½ ma-na kù-babbar in-na-an-lá
26. igi lú-^{d}en-líl-lá agrig
27. igi ^{d}nuska-*ni-šu* dumu ^{d}nin-urta-*mu-ša-lim*
28. igi *ì-lí-ip-pa-al-sà-am* šeš-a-ni
29. igi *ḫu-píl*-[dumu]-*na-tum*
30. [igi bur]-gul

31. iti [ ] u_4 22-kam
32. [mu] *sa-am-su-i-lu-na* lugal
33. bàd urí^{ki}-ma unu^{ki}-g[a]

SEAL

ì-lí-ip-pa-al-sà-am

dumu ^{d}en-zu-*ma-gir*

Ili-ippalsa son of Sin-magir and his wife Elmešum took Ninurta-muballiṭ son of Awiliya as their heir. They have turned over house, field, orchard, temple-office property, (and) whatever household property there is to Ninurta-muballiṭ. And Ninurta-muballiṭ their son has turned over 2 shekels of silver to Ili-ippalsa his father and Elmešum his mother. If Ili-ippalsa and Elmešum his wife say (to Ninurta-muballiṭ), "You are not my son," they will forfeit house, field, orchard, temple-office property, whatever household property there is, and they will pay (him) ½ mina of silver. And if Ninurta-muballiṭ says to Ili-ippalsa his father and to Elmešum his mother, "You are not my father and you are not my mother," he will forfeit house, field, orchard, temple-office property, whatever household property there is, and he will pay (them) ½ mina of silver.

33. Cornell 12; copy: pp. 70–71; photo: pls. 14–17

1. nam-é-da-di ^{d}en-líl ^{d}nin-líl
2. mu-àm u_4 20-a-kam
3. ká ús-gíd-da kisal é-maḫ
4. ká ^{d}nin-líl-lá
5. mu-àm u_4 12-a-kam [*case*: 12½-kam]
6. ká ^{d}nin-gá-gi_4-a
7. mu-àm [u_4 6-a-kam]
8. bal-gub-[ba ^{d}nin-urta-*mu-uš-ta-al*]
9. ki ^{d}[nin-urta-*mu-uš-ta-al*]
10. dumu i-[bi-^{d}en-líl-ta]
11. ^{I}*ma-an*-[*nu-um-me-šu-li-ṣur*]

reverse

12. i[n-ši-in-sa_{10}]
13. sa_{10}-til-la-a-b[i-šè]
14. 3½ gín kù-babbar in-[na-an]-lá
15. u_4 kúr-šè ^{d}nin-urta-*mu-uš-ta-al*
16. ù ibila-a-ni a-na-me-a-bi
17. nam-é-da-di kisal é-gal-maḫ
18. nam-é-ús-gíd-da ká ^{d}nin-líl-lá
19. u_4 ká ^{d}nin-gá-gi_4-a a-na-me-a-bi
20. inim nu-um-gá-gá-a
21. mu lugal-bi in-pà
22. igi lú-^{d}en-líl-lá agrig
23. igi ^{d}nuska-*ni-šu* dumu ^{d}nin-urta-*mu-ša-lim*

24. igi ^{d}nin-urta-*mu-uš-ta-al*
25. dumu ^{d}en-zu-*ma-gir*
26. igi ^{d}nin-urta-*ni-šu* dub-sar
27. igi *a-wi-li-ya* bur-gul
28. [iti] gu$_4$-si-su u$_4$ 1-kam [*case*: 1-a-kam]
29. mu *sa-am-su-i-lu-na* lugal
30. bàd urí^{ki} unu^{ki}-ga
31. mu-gul-la

SEAL
^{d}nin-urta-*mu-uš-ta-al*
dumu *i-bi*-^{d}en-líl

Mannum-mešu-liṣṣur has purchased the edadi-ship of Enlil and Ninlil for 20 days annually, (the custodianship of) the Usgida gate of the Kisal-egalmaḫ and the Ninlila gate for 12[½] days annually, (the custodianship of) the Ningagia gate for 6 days annually, the prebend of Ninurta-muštal, from Ninurta-muštal son of Ibbi-Enlil. He paid 3½ shekels of silver as its full purchase price. In future Ninurta-muštal and his heirs, however many there are, will raise no claim for either the edadi-ship of the Kisal-egalmaḫ, or the (custodian)ships of the Ninlila and Ningagia gates. Thus did he swear in the name of the king.

34. OECT 8 6 [collated by Stone]; photo: pl. 36

1. é-da-di ^{d}en-líl ^{d}nin-líl-lá
2. mu-a iti 1-kam
3. bal-gub-ba *ì-lí-ip-pa-al-sà-am*
4. dumu ^{d}en-zu-*ma-gir*
5. ki *ì-lí-ip-pa-al-sà-am* dumu ^{d}en-zu-*ma-gir*
6. ^{I}*ma-an-nu-um-me-šu-li-ṣur*
7. dumu *a-wi-li-ya*-ke$_4$
8. in-ši-in-sa$_{10}$
9. sa$_{10}$-til-la-bi-šè
10. 3½ gín kù-babbar
11. in-na-an-lá
12. u$_4$ kúr-šè *ì-lí-ip-pa-*[*al-sà-am*]
13. ù ibila-a-ni a-[na-me-a-bi]

reverse
14. é-da-di ^{d}en-líl [^{d}nin-líl-lá]
15. mu-a iti 1-[kam]
16. inim nu-um-gá-gá-[a]
17. mu lugal-bi in-pà
18. igi *ma-ri-er-ṣe-tim* dumu gìr-né-ì-sà
19. igi *ri-iš*-é-a dumu *sí-na-tum*
20. igi ḪI.TAR-^{d}iškur bur-gul

21. igi ^{d}nin-urta-*ga-mil* dub-sar
22. iti gan-gan-è u_4 16-kam
23. mu *sa-am-su-i-lu-na* lugal
24. bàd urí^{ki} unu^{ki}-ga
25. mu-un-gul-la

SEAL
ì-lí-ip-pa-al-sà-⟨am⟩
dumu ^{d}en-zu-*ma-gir*

Mannum-mešu-liṣṣur has purchased the edadi-ship of Enlil and Ninlil for one month annually, the prebend of Ili-ippalsa son of Sin-magir from Ili-ippalsa son of Sin-magir. He paid 3½ shekels of silver as its full purchase price. In future Ili-ippalsa and his heirs, however many there are, agree to bring no claim against the edadi-ship of Enlil and Ninlil for 1 month annually. Thus has he sworn in the name of the king.

Note
line 20: The sign ḫi in the name ḪI.TAR-^{d}iškur is clear here and in the other texts where it occurs. The expected reading, di-ku_5, cannot be substantiated.

35. Cornell 8; copy: pp. 72–73; photo: pls. 9–11

1. [nam]-ì-du_8 ká kisal ^{d}nin-líl é-gu-la
2. [k]á gíd-da-gíd-da kisal é-gal-maḫ-a
3. [ ] ká-gal ^{d}nin-líl-lá
4. [mu]-a iti u_4 20-kam
5. [n]am-ì-du_8 ká ^{giš}kin-ti
6. mu-a [*case*: mu-àm] iti 1 u_4 20-kam
7. [bal-gub-b]a ^{d}nin-urta-uru_4 dumu ip-qá-tum
8. [ki ^{d}nin]-urta-uru_4 dumu *ip-qá-tum-⟨ta⟩*
9. [^{I}*ma-an*]-*nu-um-me-šu-li-*[*ṣur*]
10. [dumu] *a-wi-li-ya*-ke_4
11. [in-ši]-in-sa_{10}
12. [sa_{10}-til]-la-bi-šè
13. [4½ gín kù-babbar] in-na-an-lá

reverse
14. [u_4 kúr]-šè ^{d}nin-urta-uru_4
15. ù ibila-a-ni a-na-me-a-bi
16. garza-bi-šè inim nu-um-gá-gá-a
17. [m]u lugal-bi in-pà
18. [igi ^{d}d]a-mu-*e-ri-ba-am* $gudu_4$ ^{d}nin-líl-lá
19. [igi lú-^{d}e]n-líl-lá agrig
20. [igi lugal-a]-ma-ru $gudu_4$ ^{d}nin-líl-lá
21. [igi]-*nu* dumu ^{d}en-zu-*be-li* dub-sar
22. [ig]i [lú]-^{d}nanna dub-sar

23. [ig]i *a-ab-ba-tum* bur-gul
24. iti ab-è u_4 2-kam
25. mu *sa-am-su-i-lu-na* lugal
26. bàd urí[ki] unu[ki]-ga
27. [mu]-un-gul-la

SEAL
[d]nin-urta-uru_4
dumu *ip-qá-tum*

Mannum-mešu-liṣṣur son of Awiliya has purchased the custodianship(s) of the Kisal Ningal Egula gate, the Kisal-egalmaḫ long gate, and the Ninlila great gate for (1) month 20 days annually, and the custodianship of the Craftsmen's gate for 1 month 20 days annually, the prebend of Ninurta-eriš from Ninurta-eriš son of Ipqatum. He paid 4½ shekels of silver as its full purchase price. In future Ninurta-eriš and his heirs, however many there are, will not raise any claim to these temple offices. Thus did he swear in the name of the king.

Note
line 20: Restoration based on the suggestion of Mitchell.

36. Cornell 19; copy: pp. 73–74; photo: pls. 22–23

1. nam-ì-du_8 kisal [d]nin-líl-lá
2. nam-ì-du_8 é ús-gíd-da-gíd-da
3. nam-ì-du_8 ká-gal [d]nin-líl-lá
4. nam-ì-du_8 kisal é-gal-maḫ
5. mu-a u_4 20-kam
6. nam-ì-du_8 [giš]kin-ti
7. [mu]-a u_4 20-kam
8. [šà]-en-bi [dug]ti-x[= gig?]-dù i-giš
9. [bal-gub-b]a [d]nin-urta-uru_4 dumu *a-lí-a-bu-ša*
10. [ki [d]nin]-urta-api[n dumu *la-lu-ú-um*-ta]
11. [ù *a*]-*lí*-[*a-bu-ša* ama-a-ni-ta]
[remainder of obverse destroyed]

reverse
1′. [igi]-*e-ri-ba-am* dumu *i*-[ ]
2′. [igi *na*?]-*bi*-[d]en-líl dumu *ì-lí-iš-na-d*[*i*]
3′. igi *i-da-tum* dumu [d]en-zu-*ma-gir*
4′. igi [d]nin-urta-uru_4 dumu *ip-qá-tum*
5′. igi [d]pa-bil-sag-ma-an-sum dub-sar
6′. igi *a-ab-ba-tum* bur-gul
7′. iti áš-a u_4 8-kam
8′. mu *sa-am-su-i-lu-na* lugal-e
9′. bàd urí[ki] ù unu[ki]-ga
10′. mu-un-gul-la

SEAL
^{d}nin-urta-uru$_4$
dumu *la-lu-ú-um*

(Mannum-mešu-liṣṣur has purchased) from Ninurta-eriš son of Lalum and Ali-abuša his mother the custodianship of the Kisal Ninlila, the custodianship of the Usgidagida temple, the custodianship of the Ninlila great gate, the custodianship of the Kisal-egalmaḫ—all for 20 days annually—its rations, a bowl of sesame oil—all this being the prebend of Ninurta-eriš son of Ali-abuša. (Rest destroyed.)

37. Cornell 20; copy: p. 74; photo: pls. 24–25

1′. [bal-gub-ba *in*]-*bi-ì*-[*lí-šu*]
2′. [dumu ^{d}n]in-urta-*mu-uš-ta-al*
3′. [ki] *in-bi-ì-lí-šu*
4′. ù *la-ma-sà-tum* ama-a-ni-ta
5′. ^{I}*ma-an-nu-um-me-šu*$^{!}$*-li-ṣur*
6′. dumu *a-wi-li-ya*-ke$_4$
7′. in-ši-in-sa$_{10}$
8′. sa$_{10}$-til-la-bi-šè
9′. 2 gín kù-babbar
10′. in-na-an-lá

reverse
11′. u$_4$ kúr-šè *in-bi-ì-lí-šu*
12′. ^{I}*la-ma-sà-tum* ama-a-ni
13′. ù ibila-ne-ne a-na-me-a-bi
14′. é ^{d}en-ki-bi-šè inim nu-um-gá-gá-a
15′. mu lugal-bi in-pà-dè-eš
16′. igi lú-^{d}en-líl-lá agrig
17′. igi *ma-ri-er-ṣe-tim* dumu gìr-né-ì-sa$_6$
18′. igi lú-^{d}nanna dub-sar
19′. igi *ri-iš*-é-a dumu ^{d}en-zu-*na-tum*
20′. igi *a-ab-ba-tum* bur-gul
21′. [iti] še-gur$_{10}$-ku$_5$ mu *sa*-[*am-su-i-lu-na* lugal-e]
22′. [b]àd urí^{ki} unu[^{ki}-ga]
23′. [mu]-un-gul-[la]

SEAL
in-bi-ì-lí-šu
dumu ^{d}nin-urta-*mu-uš-ta-al*

Mannum-mešu-liṣṣur son of Awiliya has purchased the prebend of Inbi-ilišu son of Ninurta-muštal from Inbi-ilišu and his mother Lamassatum. He paid 2 shekels of silver as its full purchase price. In future Inbi-ilišu and his heirs, however many there are, will not raise a claim (for the prebend) to the temple of Enki. Thus did he swear in the name of the king.

38. OECT 8 2 [collated by Stone]; photo: pls. 30–31

1. 3 gán a-šà gug$_4$-še
2. šà a-šà ká-din-na
3. ús-a-du *ma-ri-er-ṣe-tim*
4. dumu agrig-^{d}en-líl-lá
5. a-šà arad-^{d}en-líl-lá
6. dumu *i-bi*-^{d}en-líl
7. ki arad-^{d}en-líl-lá-ta
8. ^{I}*ma-an-nu-um-me-šu-li-ṣur*
9. dumu *a-wi-li-ya*
10. in-ši-in-sa$_{10}$
11. sa$_{10}$-til-la-bi-šè
12. 3½ gín k[ù-bab]bar

reverse

13. in-na-an-lá
14. u$_4$ kúr-šè arad-^{d}en-líl-lá
15. ù ibila-a-ni a-na-me-a-bi
16. 3 gán a-šà gug$_4$-še
17. inim nu-um-gá-gá-a
18. mu lugal-bi in-pà
19. igi lú-^{d}en-líl-lá agrig ^{d}en-líl-lá
20. igi *ma-ri-er-ṣe-tim*
21. dumu gìr-né-ì-sa$_6$
22. igi *ì-lí-i-din-nam* dumu *i-bi*-^{d}en-líl
23. igi ḪI.TAR-^{d}iškur bur-gul
24. igi *a-ta-a* dub-sar
25. iti sig$_4$-a u$_4$ 15-kam
26. mu *sa-am-su-i-lu-na* lugal
27. kur gú-si-a an-ga-àm
28. [mu]-da-bal-eš-[a]

SEAL

arad-^{d}en-líl-lá
dumu *i-bi*-^{d}en-líl

Mannum-mešu-liṣṣur son of Awiliya has purchased from Arad-Enlila a 3-*iku* stubble field plot in the Kadinna irrigation district, beside (the field of) Mar-erṣetim son of Agrig-Enlila, the field of Arad-Enlila son of Ibbi-Enlil. He paid 3½ shekels of silver as its full purchase price. In future Arad-Enlila and his heirs, however many there are, will bring no claim against the 3-*iku* stubble field plot. Thus has he sworn in the name of the king.

39. OECT 8 5 [collated by Stone]; photo: pls. 34–35

1. nam-ì-du$_8$ kisal-lá ^{d}nin-líl é-gu-la
2. mu-a u$_4$ 6-kam

3. bal-gub-ba *lu-mur-*[*ša-*^{d}utu]
4. ù *ì-lí-e-ri-ba-am* šeš-a-ni
5. dumu-me ^{d}en-zu-*ma-gir*
6. ki *lu-mur-ša-*^{d}utu ù *ì-lí-e-ri-ba-am*
7. dumu-me ^{d}en-zu-*ma-gir*-ta
8. ^{I}*ma-an-nu-um-me-šu-li-ṣur* dumu *a-wi-li-ya*-ke$_{4}$
9. in-ši-in-sa$_{10}$
10. sa$_{10}$-til-la-bi-šè
11. 2 gín kù-babbar in-na-an-lá-e-eš
12. u$_{4}$ kúr-šè *lu-mur-ša-*^{d}utu
13. ù *ì-lí-e-ri-ba-am* šeš-a-ni

reverse

14. dumu ^{d}en-zu-*ma-gir*
15. ù ibila-ne-ne a-na-me-a-bi
16. nam-ì-du$_{8}$ kisal-lá ^{d}nin-líl é-gu-la
17. mu-a u$_{4}$ 6-kam
18. inim nu-um-gá-gá-ne-a
19. mu lugal-la téš-bi in-pà-dè-eš
20. igi *ì-lí-ḫa-zi-ri* dumu *a-wi-ya-tum*
21. igi ^{d}iškur-*ib-ni-šu* dumu arad-^{d}en-líl-lá
22. igi *li-pí-it*-eš$_{4}$-dar dumu ^{d}en-líl-ma-an-sum
23. igi *a-wi-li-ya* bur-gul
24. igi ^{d}nin-urta-*ga-mil* dub-sar
25. iti sig$_{4}$-a mu *sa-am-su-i-lu-na* lugal
26. kur gú-si-a an-ga-am
27. mu-un-da-bal-e

SEAL

lu-mur-ša-^{d}utu
ù *ì-lí-e-ri-ba-am*
dumu ^{d}en-zu-*ma-gir*

Mannum-mešu-liṣṣur son of Awiliya has purchased from Lumurša-Šamaš and Ili-eribam his brother, (both) sons of Sin-magir, the custodianship of the Kisala Ninlil Egula for 6 days annually, prebend of Lumurša-Šamaš and Ili-eribam his brother, sons of Sin-magir. He has paid 2 shekels of silver as its full purchase price. In future Lumurša-Šamaš, Ili-eribam, and their heirs, however many there are, will make no claim against the custodianship of the Kisala Ninlil Egula for 6 days annually. Thus have they sworn in the name of the king.

40. BE 6/2 38 [collated by Stone and Mitchell]

1. 1⅓ sar é-dù-a
2. da é ^{d}en-líl-gal-zu
3. dumu *da-mi-iq-ì-lí-šu*
4. é lugal-ḫé-gál

5. ù ^{d}nin-urta-*e-mu-qá-a*
6. dumu-me é-a-*i-din-nam*
7. ki lugal-ḫ̮é-gál
8. ù ^{d}nin-urta-*e-mu-qá-a*
9. ^{I}*ma-an-nu-um-me-šu-*[*li-ṣur*]
10. dumu *a-wi-li-ya*
11. in-ši-in-sa_{10}
12. sa_{10}-[til-la-bi-šè]
13. 3(?) [gín kù-babbar]
14. in-na-[an-lá]

reverse

15. u_4 kúr-šè [lugal-ḫ̮é-gál]
16. ù ^{d}[nin-urta-*e-mu-qá-a*]
17. 1⅓ sar é-[dù-a]
18. inim nu-um-gá-gá-[a]
19. mu lugal-bi in-pà
20. igi lú-^{d}en-líl-lá agrig
21. igi *ib-ni*-é-a dumu i[m]
22. igi *a-wi-li-ya* bur-[gul]
23. igi *a-ta-a* dub-[sar]
24. iti šu-numun-a u_4 6-kam
25. mu *sa-am-su-i-lu-na* lugal
26. kur gú-si-a an-ga-àm
27. mu-da-bal-eš

SEAL

lugal-ḫ̮é-gál
ù ^{d}nin-urta-*e-mu-*[*qá-a*]

Mannum-mešu-liṣṣur son of Awiliya has purchased from Lugal-ḫ̮egal and Ninurta-emuqa a 1⅓-sar house plot next to the house of Enlil-gal-zu son of Damiq-ilišu, a house belonging to Lugal-ḫ̮egal and Ninurta-emuqa sons of Ea-iddinam. He paid 3(?) shekels of silver as its full purchase price. In future Lugal-ḫ̮egal and Ninurta-emuqa will make no claim against the 1⅓ sar house plot. Thus have they sworn in the name of the king.

Note
line 16: Restoration based on the collation of Mitchell.

41. OECT 8 9 [collated by Stone]; photo: pls. 43–46

1. nam-en-nu-un alam é-kur-igi-gál mu-a u_4 15-kam
2. ká á-sal-a ub-šu-ukkin-na mu-àm u_4 15-kam
3. mu-àm u_4 15-kam
4. bal-gub-ba ^{d}en-zu-*li-di-iš*
5. dumu *ì-lí-i-din-nam*
6. ki ^{d}en-zu-*li-di-iš*-ta

7. ^{I}*ma-an-nu-um-me-šu-li-ṣur*
8. dumu *a-wi-li-ya*-ke_4
9. in-ši-in-sa_{10}
10. sa_{10}-til-la-bi-šè
11. 2 gín kù-babbar in-na-an-lá
12. u_4 kúr-šè ^{d}en-zu-*li-di-iš*
13. dumu *ì-lí-i-din-nam*

reverse
14. ù ibila-a-ni a-na-me-a-bi
15. nam-en-nu-un alam é-kur-igi-gál
16. ká á-sal-a ub-šu-ukkin-na
17. inim nu-um-gá-gá-a
18. mu lugal-bi in-pà
19. igi lú-^{d}en-líl-lá agrig ^{d}en-líl-lá
20. igi ^{d}nuska-*ni-šu* dumu ^{d}nin-urta-*mu-ša-lim*
21. igi *ì-lí-ip-pa-al-sà-am* šeš-a-ni
22. igi ḪI.TAR-^{d}iškur bur-gul
23. igi *a-píl-ì-lí-šu* dub-sar
24. iti šu-numun-a u_4 21-kam
25. mu *sa-am-su-i-lu-na* lugal
26. kur gú-si-a an-ga-àm
27. mu-da-bal-eš-am

SEAL
^{d}en-zu-*li-di-iš*
dumu *ì-lí-i-din-nam*

Mannum-mešu-liṣṣur has purchased from Sin-lidiš the guardianship of the statue of the Ekur-igigal for 15 days annually (and the custodianship of the) Asala Ubšu-ukkina gate for 15 days annually ⟪for 15 days annually⟫, prebend of Sin-lidiš son of Ili-iddinam. He paid 2 shekels of silver as its full purchase price. In future Sin-lidiš and his heirs, however many there are, will raise no claim against and guardianship of the statue of the Ekur-igigal (and the custodianship of the) Asala Ubšu-ukkina gate. Thus has he sworn in the name of the king.

Note
line 2: This reading follows the case.

42. OECT 8 1 [collated by Stone]; photo: pl. 29

1. ⅔ sar é-dù-a
2. ^{giš}ig ù ^{giš}sag-kul gub-ba
3. da é *ri-iš*-é-a dumu *sí-na-tum*
4. é *ri-im-tum* dumu-munus *a-ḫa-mar-ši*
5. ù *a-lí-a-ḫu*$^{!}$-*ú-a* ama-ni
6. ki *ri-im-tum* ù *a-lí-a-ḫu-ú-a* ama-ni

7. ^{I}*ma-an-nu-um-me-šu-li-ṣur*
8. dumu *a-wi-li-ya*-ke$_4$
9. in-ši-in-sa$_{10}$
10. sa$_{10}$-til-la-bi-šè
11. 3 gín kù-babbar
12. [i]n-na-an-lá

reverse

13. u$_4$ kúr-šè [*ri-im-tum a-lí-a-ḫu*]*-ú-a*
14. ù ib[ila-ne-ne a-na-me-a-bi]
15. ⅔ s[ar é-dù-a ^{giš}ig ù ^{giš}sag-kul gub-ba-(šè)]
16. inim nu-[um-gá-g]á-a
17. mu lug[al-bi i]n-pà-dè-eš
18. igi lú-^{d}en-líl-lá dumu é-lú-ti
19. igi ^{d}nuska-*ni-šu* dumu ^{d}nin-urta-*mu-ša-lim*
20. igi dumu-ki dumu gìr-né-ì-sa$_6$
21. igi *a-wi-li-ya* bur-gul
22. igi ^{d}nin-urta-*ni-š*[*u* du]b-sar
23. iti kin-^{d}inanna u$_4$ 1-kam
24. mu *sa-am-su-i-lu-na* lugal
25. kur gú-si-a an-ga-àm
26. mu-da-bal-e-eš-a

SEAL

ri-im-tum
dumu-munus *a-ḫa-am-ar-ši*
a-lí-a-ḫu-ú-a ama-[ni]

Mannum-mešu-liṣṣur son of Awiliya has purchased from Rimtum and her mother Ali-aḫuya a ⅔-sar house plot with door and lock next to the house of Riš-Ea son of Aḫamarši, property of Rimtum daughter of Aḫamarši and of Ali-aḫuya her mother. He paid 3 shekels of silver as its full purchase price. In future Rimtum, Ali-aḫuya, and their heirs, however many there are, will make no claim against the ⅔-sar house plot with door and lock. Thus have they sworn in the name of the king.

43. TIM 4 54 [collated by Stone]

1. nam-é-da-di [ ]
2. mu-àm iti 1-ka[m u$_4$ 10-kam]
3. bal-gub-ba ^{I}é-a-*i-din-n*[*am*]
4. ki é-a-*i-din-na*[*m*]
5. ^{I}*ma-an-nu-um-me-šu-li-*[*ṣur*]
6. dumu *a-wi-li-ya*-ke$_4$
7. in-ši-in-sa$_{10}$
8. sa$_{10}$-til-la-bi-šè
9. 3⅓ gín kù-babbar
10. in-na-an-lá

reverse
11. u$_4$ kúr-šè é-a-*i-din-nam*
12. ù ibila-a-ni a-na-me-a-bi
13. iti 1-kam u$_4$ 10-kam é-da-di [*case*: adds bi-šè]
14. inim nu-um-gá-gá-a
15. mu lugal-bi in-pà
16. igi ^{d}nanna-a-ra-mu-un-ge-en
17. dumu ^{d}inanna-ma-an-sum
18. igi *li-pí-it*-eš$_4$-dar dumu *el-li-tum*
19. igi *a-wi-li-ya* bur-gul
20. igi *a-at-ta-a* dub-sar
21. iti kin-^{d}inanna [u$_4$ x-kam]
22. mu *sa*-[*am-su-i-lu-na* lugal-e]
23. kur gú-si-a [an-ga-àm]
24. á-kal-maḫ [^{d}amar-utu-ka-ke$_4$]
25. mu-un-[na-an-sum-ma]

SEAL
é-a-*i-din-nam*
dumu *ma-re-er-ṣe-tim*

Mannum-mešu-liṣṣur son of Awiliya has purchased from Ea-iddinam the edadi-ship of x for 1 month 10 days annually, prebend of Ea-iddinam. He has paid 3$\frac{1}{3}$ shekels of silver as its full purchase price. In future Ea-iddinam and his heirs, however many there are, will raise no claim against the temple office. Thus has he sworn in the name of the king.

44. Cornell 7; copy: pp. 80–81; photo: pls. 6–8

1. nam-ì-du$_8$ ká úš-gíd-da
2. nam-ì-du$_8$ kisal é-gal-maḫ
3. mu-àm u$_4$ 20-kam
4. nam-ì-du$_8$ ká ^{giš}kin-ti
5. ù ki-dé-dé-bi
6. mu-àm u$_4$ 20-kam
7. bal-gub-ba *warad-ištar* dumu *la-a-lum*
8. ki *warad-ištar* [*case adds*: dumu *la-a-lum*$^{!}$-ta]
9. [^{I}*ma-an-nu*]-*um-me-šu-li-ṣur*
10. [dumu *a-wi*]-*li-ya*-ke$_4$
11. [in-ši-i]n-sa$_{10}$
12. [sa$_{10}$-til-la]-bi-šè
13. [x gín kù-babbar] in-na-lá [*case*: in-na-an-lá]

reverse
14. [u$_4$ kúr-šè *warad-ištar* dumu *la*]-*a-lum*
15. [ù ibila-a-ni a-na-me-a-bi]
16. [garza-bi-šè inim nu-um-gá-gá-a]
17. [mu lugal-bi in]-pà

18. igi lú-^{d}en-líl-lá agrig ^{d}en-líl-lá
19. igi *ta-ri-ba-tum* dumu *u-bar-*^{d}utu
20. igi *li-pí-it-*eš$_{4}$-dar dumu *na-ra-am-*^{d}iškur
21. igi ḪI.TAR-^{d}iškur bur-gul
22. igi *im-gur-*^{d}en-zu dub-sar
23. iti ab-è u$_{4}$ 20-kam
24. mu *sa-am-su-i-lu-na* lugal
25. kur gú-si-a an-ga-àm
26. mu-un-da-bal-eš-am

SEAL
arad-eš$_{4}$-dar
dumu *la-a-lum*

Mannum-mešu-liṣṣur son of Awiliya has purchased from Warad-Ištar (son of Lalum) the custodianship of the Usgida gate, the custodianship of the Kisal-egalmaḫ, (both) for 20 days annually, and the custodianship of the Craftsmen's gate and its "ritual place(?)" for 20 days annually, prebend of Warad-Ištar son of Lalum. He paid x shekels of silver as its full purchase price. In future Warad-Ištar and his heirs, however many there are, will raise no claim to these temple offices. Thus has he sworn in the name of the king.

Note
line 5: ki-dé-dé is possibly a phonetic writing for ki-$\genfrac{}{}{0pt}{}{\text{du-du}}{\text{du-du}}$ in Cornell 21 [no. 46]: 16.

45. OECT 8 10 [collated by Stone]; photo: pls. 47–49

1. nam-ì-du$_{8}$ kisal-lá šà é-kur-igi-gál
2. ká á-sal-a ub-šu-ukkin-na
3. ká ^{d}lama-lama šà é-kur-ra
4. ù dil-dil-bi
5. mu-àm u$_{4}$ 10-kam
6. bal-gub-ba *ma-a-ri-er-ṣe-tim*
7. dumu šeš-du$_{10}$-ga
8. ki ^{d}utu-^{d}en-líl-lá
9. ^{d}*li-pí-it-*^{d}en-líl
10. ^{Id}nin-urta-*ni-šu* [*case*: adds dumu *ma-a-ri-er-ṣe-tim*]
11. ù *ri-ba-tum* ama-ni
12. ^{I}*ma-an-nu-um-me-šu-li-ṣur*
13. dumu *a-wi-li-ya*

reverse
14. in-ši-in-sa$_{10}$
15. sa$_{10}$-til-la-bi-šè
16. $1\frac{5}{6}$ gín kù-babbar in-na-an-lá-lá-eš
17. u$_{4}$ kúr-šè ^{d}utu-^{d}en-líl-lá
18. ^{I}*li-pí-it-*^{d}en-líl

19. ù ^{d}nin-urta-ni-šu
20. ù ibila-ne-ne [*case*: ibila-a-ni] a-na-me-a-bi
21. nam-ì-du$_8$ kisal-lá [*case*: adds gárza-bi-šè] inim nu-um-gá-gá-a
22. mu lugal-bi [*case*: adds téš-bi] in-pà-dè-eš
23. igi lú-^{d}en-líl-lá agrig ^{d}en-líl-lá
[23a. *case*: adds igi ^{d}en-líl-ma-an-sum gudu$_4$]
24. igi *a-píl-ì-lí-šu* aga-uš
25. igi ḪI.TAR-^{d}iškur dub-sar (*sic*) [*case*: bur-gul]
26. igi *im-gur*-^{d}en-zu dub-sar
27. iti ab-è u$_4$ 24-kam
[27a. *case*: adds mu ^{d}*sa-am-su-i-lu-na* lu[gal]]
28. kur gú-si-a an-ga-[àm]
[28a. *case*: adds á-kal-maḫ ^{d}[amar-utu]]
29. mu-da-bal-eš

SEAL
^{d}utu-^{d}en-líl-[lá]
li-pí-it-⟨^{d}⟩en-lil
^{d}nin-urta-*ni-šu*
ù *ri-ba-tum* ama-ni
ibila *ma-ri-er-ṣe-tim*

Mannum-mešu-liṣṣur son of Awiliya has purchased from Ninurta-nišu son of Mar-erṣetim and Ribatum his mother the custodianship of the Kisala in the Ekur-igigal, (the custodianship of the) Asala Ubšu-ukkina gate, (the custodianship of the) Lama-Lama gate in the Ekur, etc. for 10 days annually, prebend of Mar-erṣetim son of Šeš-duga. He paid 1⅚ shekels of silver as its full purchase price. In future Utu-Enlila, Lipit-Enlil, and Ninurta-nišu, and their heirs, however many there are, will make no claim against the custodianship of the Kisala. Thus have they sworn in the name of the king.

46. Cornell 21; copy: pp. 82–83; photo: pl. 26

1. nam-ì-d[u$_8$ kisal]
2. en-nu-un ala[m]
3. mu-a u$_4$ 12$^{?}$-[kam]
4. bal-gub-ba ^{d}nin-urta-[ma-an-sum]
5. ki ^{d}nin-urta-ma-an-sum d[umu *ta-ri-bu-um*-ta]
6. ^{Id}nin-urta-*ra-ḫi-im-ṣe-r*[*i*]
7. dumu ^{d}nanna-a-[a-ke$_4$]
8. in-ši-in-sa$_{10}$
9. sa$_{10}$-til-la-bi-šè
10. 4½ gín kù-[babbar]
11. in-na-an-[lá]
12. u$_4$ kúr-šè ^{d}nin-[urta-ma-an-sum]
13. dumu *ta*-[*ri-bu-um*]

reverse
14. ù ibila-a-ni [a-na-me-a-bi]
15. nam-ì-du$_{8}$ kisal [ ]
16. ki ki-du-du-bi [ ]
17. inim nu-um-gá-gá-[a]
18. mu lugal-bi in-[pà]
19. igi ^{d}en-zu-*e-ri-ba-*[*am*]
20. igi ^{d}en-zu-*ip-ṭù-ra-a*[*m*]
21. igi *a-wi-li-ya* bur-gu[l]
22. igi *i-bi-*^{d}nin-šubur dub-sar
23. iti áš-a u$_{4}$ 11-kam
24. mu *sa-am-su-i-lu-na* lugal
25. kur gú-si-a an-ga-àm
26. mu-un-da-[bal-eš-àm]

SEAL
^{d}nin-urta-ma-an-sum
dumu *ta-ri-bu-um*

Ninurta-raḫim-ṣerim son of Nanna-aya has purchased from Ninurta-mansum son of Taribum the custodianship of the Kisal-[ ] and statue [ ] for 12 days annually, the prebend of Ninurta-mansum. He paid 4½ shekels of silver as its full purchase price. In future Ninurta-mansum son of Taribum and his heirs, however many there are, will raise no claim against the custodianship of the Kisal-[ ] and the "place for cultic rites(?)." Thus has he sworn in the name of the king.

Note

line 16: ki-du-du is possibly related to ki-dé-dé in Cornell 7 [no. 44]: 5. Mitchell suggests that we might read ki-dé-dé as $\frac{\text{du-du}}{\text{du-du}}$ ki-du-du. The two signs are not clearly written; see the photograph on plate 26.

47. Cornell 11; copy: pp. 83–84; photo: pls. 12–13

1. nam-ì-du$_{8}$ kisal-lá šà ^{d}[nin-líl-gu-la]
2. é-gu-la
3. mu-a u$_{4}$ 7½-kam
4. bal-gub-ba *ì-lí-ḫa-zi-ri* dumu *a-w*[*i-ya-tum*]
5. ù *a-píl-*^{d}en-zu dumu *a-lí-wa-aq-rum*
6. ki *ì-lí-ḫa-zi-ri* ù *a-píl-*^{d}en-zu-ta
7. ^{I}*ma-an-nu-um-me-e-šu-li-ṣur*
8. dumu *a-wi-li-ya*-ke$_{4}$
9. in-ši-in-sa$_{10}$
10. sa$_{10}$-til-la-bi-šè

reverse
11. 2 gín igi-6-gál kù-babbar
12. in-ne-en-lá
13. u_4 kúr-šè *ì-lí-ḫa-zi-⟨ri⟩* ù *a-píl-sin*(30)
14. ù ibila-ne-ne a-na-me-a-bi
15. nam-ì-du_8 kisal-lá šà ^{d}nin-líl-gu-la
16. mu-a u_4 7½-kam
17. inim nu-um-gá-gá-ne-a
18. mu lu[gal-bi in-pà-dè-eš]
19. igi [ ]
20. igi [ ]
[remainder destroyed]

SEAL	SEAL
ì-lí-ḫa-zi-ri	*a-píl*-^{d}en-zu
dumu *a-wi-ya-tum*	dumu *a-lí-wa-aq-rum*

Mannum-mešu-liṣṣur son of Awiliya has purchased from Ili-ḫaziri and Apil-Sin the custodianship of the Kisala of Ninlil-gula of Egula for 7½ days annually, the prebend of Ili-ḫaziri son of Awiyatum and Apil-Sin son of Ali-waqrum. He paid 2⅒ shekels of silver as its full purchase price. In future Ili-ḫaziri, Apil-Sin, and their heirs, however many there are, will not raise a claim to the custodianship of the Kisala of Ninlil-gula for 7½ days annually. Thus have they sworn in the name of the king.

48. Cornell 16; copy: pp. 84–85; photo: pls. 18–19

1. nam-ì-[du_8 kisal]
2. é-^{d}nin-[líl é-gu-la]
3. mu-a iti 1-[kam]
4. bal-gub-ba ^{d}nin-urta-[*ra-ḫi*]*-im-ṣe-ri-im*
5. dumu ^{d}nanna-[ma-an-sum]
6. ki ^{d}nin-urta-*ra-ḫi-im-ṣe-ri-im*-ta
7. ^{I}*ma-an-nu-um-me-šu-li-ṣur*
8. dumu *a-wi-li-ya*-ke_4
9. in-ši-in-sa_{10}
10. sa_{10}-til-la-bi-šè
11. 8½ gín kù-babbar
12. in-na-an-lá

reverse
13. u_4 kúr-šè ^{d}nin-urta-*ra-ḫi-im-ṣe-ri-im*
14. ù ibila-a-ni
15. a-na-me-a-bi
16. nam-ì-du_8 kisal-bi
17. inim nu-um-gá-gá-a
18. mu lugal-bi in-pà

19. igi lú-^{d}en-líl-lá agrig
20. igi ^{d}en-zu-*ip-ṭù-ra-am*
21. dumu *na-bi*-^{d}en-líl
22. igi *dam-qí-ì-lí-šu*
23. dumu ^{d}nin-urta-ma-an-sum
24. igi ^{d}iškur-*ta-a-a-ar*
25. [year-name destroyed]

SEAL
^{d}nin-urta-*ra-ḫi-/ṣe-ri-im*
dumu ^{d}nanna-ma-an-sum

Mannum-mešu-liṣṣur son of Awiliya has purchased from Ninurta-raḫim-ṣerim the custodianship of the Kisal of the Ninlil Egula temple for 1 month annually. He paid 8½ shekels of silver as its full purchase price. In future Ninurta-raḫim-ṣerim and his heirs, however many there are, will raise no claim against the custodianship of the Kisal. Thus has he sworn in the name of the king.

Note
See note to text 50.

49. OECT 8 8 [collated by Stone]; photo: pls. 40–42

1. nam-ì-du$_8$ ká ^{d}nin-líl-lá
2. nam-ì-du$_8$ ká ús-gíd-da
3. nam-ì-du$_8$ ká é-gal-maḫ
4. mu-àm u$_4$ 20-kam
5. nam-ì-du$_8$ ká ^{giš}kin-ti
6. mu-àm u$_4$ 20-kam
7. bal-gub-ba ^{d}nin-urta-ma-an-sum
8. dumu *ta-ri-bu-um*
[8a. *case*: adds [kù] sa$_{10}$ ^{d}nin-š[ubur-ma-an-su]m]
[8b. *case*: adds [^{d}ni]n-urta-ma⟨-an⟩-sum [i]n-sa$_{10}$]
9. [ki] ^{d}nin-urta-ma-an-sum-ta
10. [^{I}*m*]*a-an-nu-um-me-šu-li-ṣur*
11. dumu *a-wi-li-ya*-ke$_4$
12. [in]-ši-in-sa$_{10}$ sa$_{10}$-til-la-bi-šè
13. [x] gín kù-babbar in-na-an-lá

reverse
14. u$_4$ kúr-šè ^{d}nin-urta-ma-an-sum
15. ù ibila-a-ni a-na-me-a-bi
16. iti 1 u$_4$ 10-kam garza-bi-šè
17. inim nu-um-gá-gá-a
18. mu lugal-bi in-pà
19. igi lú-^{d}en-líl-lá agrig ^{d}en-líl-lá
20. igi *ma-ri-er-ṣe-tim* [*case*: dumu-ki]

21. dumu gìr-né-ì-sa$_{6}$
22. igi *i-di-šum* bur-gul
23. igi *im-gur-*^{d}en-zu dub-sar
24. iti sig$_{4}$-a-ka u$_{4}$ 5-kam
25. mu *sa-am-su-i-lu-na* lugal
26. ki-sur-ra^{ki} *sa-bu-um*
27. da-ke$_{4}$

SEAL
^{d}nin-urta-ma-an-[sum]
dumu *ta-ri-bu-um*

Mannum-mešu-liṣṣur son of Awiliya has purchased from Ninurta-mansum the custodianship of the Ninlil gate, the custodianship of the Usgida gate, the custodianship of the Egalmaḫ gate for 20 days annually, (and) the custodianship of the House of the Craftsmen for 20 days annually, the prebend of Ninurta-mansum son of Taribum, which Ninurta-mansum had bought with silver from Ninšubur-mansum. He paid x shekels of silver as its full purchase price. In future Ninurta-mansum and his heirs, however many there are, will make no claim against the 1 month and 10 days of temple offices. Thus has he sworn in the name of the king.

50. OECT 8 7 [collated by Stone]; photo: pls. 37–39

1. nam-ì-du$_{8}$ kisal é ^{d}nin-líl-ka é-gu-la
2. mu-a iti 1-kam
3. bal-gub-ba ^{d}nin-urta-*ra-ḫi-im-ṣe-ri*
4. dumu ^{d}nanna-ma-an-sum
5. ki ^{d}nin-urta-*ra-ḫi-im-ṣe-ri* [*case*: adds -ta]
6. dumu ^{d}nanna-⟨ki-⟩min-ta [*case*: omits this line]
7. ^{I}*ma-an-nu-um-me-šu-li-ṣur*
8. dumu *a-wi-li-ya*-ke$_{4}$
9. in-ši-in-sa$_{10}$
10. sa$_{10}$-til-la-bi-šè
11. 9 gín igi-4-gál kù-babbar
12. in-na-an-lá

reverse
13. [u$_{4}$ kúr-šè] ^{d}nin-urta-*ra-ḫi-im-ṣe-ri*
14. [ù ibi]la-a-ni
15. [a-na]-me-a-bi
16. nam-ì-du$_{8}$ kisal-bi
17. inim nu-um-gá-gá-a
18. [mu] lugal-bi in-pà
19. igi lú-^{d}en-líl-lá agrig
20. igi ^{d}en-zu-*ip-ṭù-ra-am*
21. dumu *na-bi-*^{d}en-líl
22. igi *ma-ri-er-ṣe-tim*

23. dumu gìr-né-ì-šà
24. igi ^{d}iškur-*ta-a-a-ar* [*case*: adds dumu *ḫu-mu-rum*]
25. igi *i-bi*-^{d}en-líl simug
26. igi ḪI.TAR-^{d}iškur bur-gul
27. igi *i-bi*-^{d}nin-šubur dub-sar
28. iti še-gur$_{10}$-ku$_{5}$ u$_{4}$ 2-kam
29. mu ki-sur-ra [*case*: adds ^{ki}] *sa-bu-um*
30. bi-da-ke$_{4}$
31. [ki-si-il-lá] bi-i[n-tur-ra]

SEAL

^{d}nin-urta-*ra-ḫi-im-ṣe-*[*ri-/im*]
dumu ^{d}nanna-ma-an-[sum]

Mannum-mešu-liṣṣur son of Awiliya has purchased from Ninurta-raḫim-ṣerim son of Nanna-mansum the custodianship of the Kisal of the Ninlil Egula temple for 1 month annually, prebend of Ninurta-raḫim-ṣerim. He paid 9 shekels of silver as its full purchase price. In future Ninurta-raḫim-ṣerim and his heirs will make no claim against the custodianship of the Kisal. Thus has he sworn in the name of the king.

Note

The small fragment pictured below the reverse of the case in plate 37 actually belongs with Cornell 16 [no. 48] although it resides in Oxford. It clearly shows that the tablets came from the same lot before they were sold to different buyers.

51. Cornell 23; copy: pp. 87–89; photo: pls. 27–28

1. 1 gín é-dù-a da é *i*[*m-gur*-^{d}nin-urta]
2. nam-ì-du$_{8}$ ká gu-la mu-a [u$_{4}$ 2-kam]
3. nam-ì-du$_{8}$ ká é-gal-maḫ mu-a [u$_{4}$ 2-kam]
4. nam-ì-du$_{8}$ ká ús-gíd-da mu-a [u$_{4}$ 2-kam]
5. nam-ì-du$_{8}$ ká-gal ^{d}nin-líl-lá mu-a [u$_{4}$ 2-kam]
6. nam-ì-du$_{8}$ é ^{giš}kin-ti mu-a u$_{4}$ 2-kam
7. nam-ì-du$_{8}$ ká ^{d}nin-gá-gi$_{4}$-a u$_{4}$ 1-kam
8. [nam]-ì-du$_{8}$ ká du$_{6}$-kù mu-a u$_{4}$ 2½-kam
9. [nam é-da]-di ^{d}en-líl ^{d}nin-líl mu-a u$_{4}$ 18-kam
10. [ ] ^{d}en-líl-u$_{19}$-ru-maḫ-^{d}utu mu-a u$_{4}$ 4-kam
11. [1 ^{giš}ba]nšur zà-gu-la síb-ta nam-šeš-gal
12. [x gín] é-dù-a da é *im-gur*-^{d}nin-urta
13. [nam-ì-d]u$_{8}$ ká gu-la mu-a u$_{4}$ 10-kam
14. [nam-ì-du$_{8}$ ká] é-gal-maḫ mu-a u$_{4}$ 10-kam
15. [nam-ì-du$_{8}$ ka] ús-gíd-da mu-a u$_{4}$ 10-kam
16. [nam-ì-du$_{8}$ ká-gal ^{d}nin]-líl-lá mu-a u$_{4}$ 10-kam
17. [nam-ì-du$_{8}$ é giš-kin]-ti mu-a u$_{4}$ 10-kam
18. [nam-ì-du$_{8}$ ká ^{d}nin-gá-g]i$_{4}$-a mu-a u$_{4}$ 5-kam

19. [nam-ì-du$_8$ ká du$_6$]-kù mu-a u$_4$ 10-kam
20. [nam-é-da-di ^{d}en-líl ^{d}ni]n-líl mu-a u$_4$ 1-kam xx
21. [*l*]*a-ma-sà-tum* mu-a u$_4$ 2½-kam
22. [ ] ^{d}en-líl ^{d}nin-líl-ke$_4$

upper edge
23. mu-a u$_4$ 21-kam
24. [n]am-gudu$_4$ ^{d}en-líl-u$_{19}$-ru-maḫ-^{d}utu
25. mu-àm u$_4$ 18-kam

reverse
26. nam-ì-du$_8$ ká nì-ur$_5$-ra mu-a u$_4$ 12-kam
27. [ḫa]-la-ba *ma-an-nu-um-me-šu-li-ṣur*
28. [x gín] é-dù-a da é šeš-a-ni
29. [nam-ì-d]u$_8$ ká gu-la mu-a u$_4$ 10-kam
30. [nam-ì-du$_8$ ká] é-gal-maḫ mu-a [u$_4$ 10]-kam
31. [nam-ì]-du$_8$ [ká ús-gíd]-da mu-a u$_4$ 10-kam
32. [nam-ì]-du$_8$ [ká-gal ^{d}nin-líl]-lá mu-a u$_4$ 10-kam
33. [nam]-ì-du$_8$ [é giš-kin]-ti mu-a u$_4$ 10-kam
34. nam-ì-du$_8$ ká [^{d}nin-gá-g]i$_4$-a mu-a u$_4$ 5-kam
35. nam-ì-[du$_8$] ká du$_6$-kù mu-a u$_4$ 18-kam
36. nam-gudu$_4$ [^{d}en-líl-u$_{19}$-r]u-maḫ-^{d}utu mu-a u$_4$ 18-kam
37. na[m é-da-di ^{d}en-líl ^{d}n]in-líl mu-a u$_4$ igi-6-gál
38. na[m *la-ma*]-*sà-tu*[*m* mu-a u]$_4$ 2½-kam
39. nam-[mu-a u$_4$ x-kam]
40. nam-[mu-a] u$_4$ 21-kam
41. nam-[----x] mu-àm u$_4$ 10-kam
42. ḫa-[la-ba *mu-na*]-*wi-ru-um*
43. ibila [^{d}nuska-á-ma]ḫ-ke$_4$-ne
44. še-ga-ne-ne-ta giš-šub-ba-[ta in-ba]-eš
45. igi lú-^{d}en-líl-[lá agrig dumu é-lú-ti]
46. igi *nu-ra-tum* [dumu]
47. igi *ma-an-nu-um-ma-ḫir-šu* d[umu]
48. igi ^{d}nuska-*ni-šu* [dub-sar]

lower edge
49. igi *a-wi-li-ya* [bur-gul]
50. iti sig$_4$-a mu *sa-am-su-*[*i-lu-na* lugal]
51. á-kal ḫuš-r[a]

SEAL
ma-an-nu-um-me-šu-li-ṣur
dumu *a-wi-li-ya*
mu-na-wi-[*ru-um*]
dumu ^{d}nuska-[á-maḫ]
[ ]

A 1-gin house property next to the house of Imgur-Ninurta; the custodianship of the Gula gate for 2 days annually; the custodianship of the Egalmaḫ gate for 2 days annually; the custodianship of the Usgida gate for 2 days annually;

the custodianship of the great gate of Ninlil for 2 days annually; the custodianship of the House of the Craftsmen for 2 days annually; the custodianship of the Ningagia gate for 1 day annually; the edadi-ship of Enlil and Ninlil for 18 days annually; (the gudu-ship?) of Enlil (and?) the urumaḫ of Utu for 4 days annually; (and) 1 ceremonial family table (is) the preference portion of the eldest brother. X gin of house property next to the house of Imgur-Ninurta; the custodianship of the Gula gate for 10 days annually; the custodianship of the Egalmaḫ gate for 10 days annually; the custodianship of the Usgida gate for 10 days annually; the custodianship of the great gate of Ninlil for 10 days annually; the custodianship of the House of the Craftsmen for 10 days annually; the custodianship of the Ningagia gate for 5 days annually; the custodianship of the Dukug(a) gate for 10 days annually; the edadi-ship of Enlil and Ninlil for 1 day annually; x x (the x) of Lamassatum for 2½ days annually; (the x) of Enlil and Ninlil for 21 days annually; the gudu-ship of Enlil (and?) the urumaḫ of Utu for 18 days annually; the custodianship of the Niura gate for 12 days annually—the (above being the inheritance) portion of Mannum-mešu-liṣṣur.

X shekels of house plot next to the house of his brother; the custodianship of the Gula gate for 10 days annually; the custodianship of the Egalmaḫ gate for 10 days annually; the custodianship of the Usgida gate for 10 days annually; the custodianship of the great gate of Ninlil for 10 days annually; the custodianship of the House of the Craftsmen for 10 days annually; the custodianship of the Ningagia gate for 5 days annually; the custodianship of the Dukug(a) gate for 18 days annually; the gudu-ship of Enlil of the urumaḫ of Utu for 18 days annually; the edadi-ship of Enlil and Ninlil for ⅙? day annually; the x-ship of Lamassatum for 2½ days annually; the x-ship for x days annually; the x-ship for 21 days annually; the x-ship for 10 days annually—the (above being the inheritance) portion of Munawirum. The heirs of Nuskaamaḫ have divided their shares according to their agreement.

Notes

line 20: Despite repeated attempts to read the two signs at the end of this line, we are unable to suggest their possible interpretation. See the photograph of the edge of the tablet on plate 27.

line 36: References to ^{d}en-líl-u_{19}-ru-maḫ-^{d}utu other than here and in lines 10 and 24 above occur in OECT 8 4 [no. 25]: 22, OECT 8 19 [no. 29]: 6 (only u_{19}-ru-maḫ), and the unpublished economic text CBS 7075: 6 (Samsuiluna 27–28) (the last reference from M. Stol, in a letter to Mitchell, 6.13.88).

52. BE 6/2 64 [collated by Stone and Mitchell]

1. 1⅓ sar é-kislaḫ
2. da é ^{d}nin-urta-*ra-ḫi-im-ṣe-ri-im*
3. dumu ^{d}nin-urta-ma-an-sum
4. kù-ta sa_{10} ki dumu-me é-a-*i-din-nam*-ta
5. ^{I}*ma-an-nu-um-me-šu-li-ṣur* dumu *a-wi-li-ya*-ke_4

6. kù-šè in-sa$_{10}$-a
7. ki ^{d}nin-urta-*mu-ba-lí-iṭ* dumu *a-wi-li-ya*
8. ^{I}*i-din*-eš$_{4}$-dar dumu *ma-an-nu-um-me-šu-li-ṣur*
9. ù *na-ru-ub-tum* ama-ni-ta
10. ^{Id}nin-urta-*ra-ḫi-im-ṣe-ri-im*
11. dumu ^{d}nin-urta-ma-an-sum-ke$_{4}$
12. é ad-da-na in-du$_{8}$

reverse
13. sa$_{10}$-til-la-bi-šè
14. 6½ gín kù-babbar in-ne-en-lá
15. u$_{4}$ kúr-šè ^{d}nin-urta-mu-ba-lí-iṭ
16. ^{I}*i-din*-eš$_{4}$-dar ^{I}*na-ru-ub-tum* ama-ni
17. ù ibila-ne-ne a-na-me-a-bi
18. 1⅓ sar é-kislaḫ-bi-šè inim nu-gá-gá-a
19. mu lugal-bi in-pà-dè-eš
20. igi *a-píl-ì-lí-šu* ugula é-^{d}maḫ
21. igi lú-^{d}en-líl-lá agrig dumu é-lú-ti
22. igi ^{d}en-zu-*ma-gir* dumu arad-^{d}nanna
23. igi ^{d}en-zu-*a-ḫu-um* dumu dumu-*er-ṣe-tim*
24. igi *i-di-šum* bur-gul
25. igi ^{d}en-líl-*mu-ba-lí-iṭ* dub-sar
26. iti gú-si-su u$_{4}$ 20-kam
27. mu ús-sa *sa-am-su-i-lu-na* lugal-e
28. *ya-di-ḫa-bu* ù *mu-ti-ḫu-ur-ša*-na
29. šita ḫuš-a-na ^{giš}ḫaš-a bí-in-ak-a

SEAL
^{d}nin-urta-*mu-ba-lí-iṭ*
dumu *a-wi-li-ya*
i-din-eš$_{4}$-dar
dumu *ma-an-nu-um-me-šu-li*-[*ṣur*]
[ù *na-ru-ub-tum* ama-ni]

Ninurta-raḫim-ṣerim has returned to the house of his father from Ninurta-muballiṭ son of Awiliya, Iddin-Ištar son of Mannum-mešu-liṣṣur, and his mother Narubtum a 1⅓-sar plot of unimproved residential property, next to the house of Ninurta-raḫim-ṣerim son of Ninurta-mansum, which Mannum-mešu-liṣṣur son of Awiliya had bought for silver from Ea-iddinam. He paid 6½ shekels of silver as its full purchase price. In future Ninurta-muballiṭ, Iddin-Ištar, Narubtum his mother, and their heirs, however many there are, will make no claim against the 1⅓-sar of unimproved residential property. Thus have they sworn in the name of the king.

53. OECT 8 18 [collated by Stone]; photo: pls. 57–58

1. 1⅓ sar é-dù-a ús-a-⟨du⟩ ka-kù-ga
2. ki-è-bi é-sír-ra

3. 3 sar kislaḫ da é mu-ni-ki-en-gi-šè
4. 4 sar kislaḫ da é lú-^{d}en-zu šu-ri-a-bi
5. 1 ^{giš}ig mi-rí-za šà kisal-lá gub-ba
6. 1 ^{giš}ig dib pa-paḫ gub-ba
7. 1 ^{giš}ig zé-na
8. 1 gán a-šà uz-za ús-a-du lugal-a-ma-ru
9. ½ gán 10 sar ki-duru$_5$ a-šà uz-za úš-a-du ama-da-kal-la
10. 2 gán a-šà íd-gìr-ta-bal-e
11. ús-a-du é-lú-ti šu-ḫa-a
12. nam-ì-du$_8$ ká sumun-^{d}en-líl-lá šu-ri-a-bi
13. nam-ì-du$_8$ ^{d}nin-líl-lá ^{giš}kin-ti
14. ká ^{d}nin-gá-gi$_4$-a ká-gal ^{d}nin-líl-lá
15. ù nam-ì$^{!}$-du$_8$ ká du$_6$-kù-ga šu-ri-a-bi
16. šà ^{giš}kiri$_6$ *wa-ru-ru-tum* ḫa-la-ba ur-^{d}lum-ma
17. šu-ri-a-bi in-ba-e-eš
18. 1 naga$_3$-esir 1 ^{giš}gag-maš mar-gíd-da
19. 2 ^{giš}u$_4$-kar mar-gíd-da
20. ḫa-la-ba ^{d}nanna-me-ša$_4$ šeš-gal
21. 1⅓ sar é-dù-a ki-tuš
22. ki-è-bi da é nin-du$_{10}$-ga
23. 3 sar kislaḫ da é ^{d}nanna-me-ša$_4$ šeš-a-ni
24. 4 sar kislaḫ da lú-^{d}en-zu šu-ri-a-bi

reverse

25. 1 ^{giš}ig mi-rí-za šà ki-tuš gub-ba
26. 1 ^{giš}ig dib-⟨ba⟩ ki-tuš gub-ba
27. 1 ^{giš}ig zé-na
28. 1 gán a-šà uz-za ús-a-du ^{d}nanna-me-ša$_4$
29. ½ gán 10 sar ki-duru$_5$ a-šà uz-za
30. ús-a-du ^{d}nanna-me-ša$_4$ šeš-a-ni
31. 2 gán a-šà íd-gìr-ta-bal-e ús-a-du ^{d}nanna-me-ša$_4$
32. 2 ^{giš}umbin mar-gíd-da
33. 1 ^{giš}gu-za 2 ^{giš}u$_4$-sar ^{giš}mar-gíd-da
34. nam-ì-du$_8$ ká til-^{d}en-líl-lá ká ^{giš}kin-ti
35. nam-ì-du$_8$ ^{d}nin-líl-lá ká ^{giš}kin-ti
36. ká ^{d}nin-gá-gi$_4$-a ká-gal ^{d}nin-líl-lá
37. ù nam-ì-du$_8$ ká du$_6$-kù-ga šu-ri-a-bi
38. šà ^{giš}kiri$_6$ *wa-ru-ru-tum* ḫa-la-ba ur-^{d}lum-ma
39. šu-ri-a-bi in-ba-e-eš
40. ḫa-la-ba ad-da-kal-la šeš-a-ni
41. 5 gín kù-babbar mu ki-tuš ad-da-kal-la šu ba-an-ti
42. nam-á kuš-a-g[á]-lá-šè ad-da-kal-la
43. ^{Id}nanna-me-[ša$_4$]-ra in-na-an-búr
44. še-ga-ne-ne-ta giš-šub-ba-ta in-ba-e-eš
45. u$_4$ kúr-šè lú-lú ù inim nu-um-gá-gá-a
46. mu lugal-la téš-bi in-pà-dè-eš
47. igi nì-gur$_{11}$-^{d}nanna gudu$_4$ dumu ^{d}en-líl-gú-gal

48. igi ^{d}nanna-ma-an-sum dumu a-wi-il-ilum
49. igi inim-^{d}da-mu dumu da-da-kal-la
50. igi ^{d}en-zu-*li-di-iš* dumu lú-si-gar
51. igi arad-^{d}en-líl-lá dumu inim-^{d}en-líl-lá
52. igi *im-gur*-^{d}en-zu dub-sar
53. iti še-gur$_{10}$-ku$_{5}$ mu ^{d}en-zu-*i-qí-ša-am* lugal
54. alam guškin alam kù-babbar ^{d}utu-ra
55. mu-na-a[n-ku$_{4}$]

SEAL
^{d}nanna-me-ša$_{4}$
dumu lú-^{d}ba-ú

SEAL
ad-da-kal-la
dumu lú-^{d}ba-ú

See text 24 for translation.

Notes

The photograph and accompanying transliteration of OECT 8 18 are included because of its relationship to the Mannum-mešu-liṣṣur archive. The tablet comes from Nippur (see p. 37 above), and duplicates OECT 8 17 [no. 24].

line 42: The reading and interpretation of the first part of this line remain uncertain.

line 55: On this year-name, see note to text 24, line 57.

Concordance of Texts

Publication	*Text No.*	*Transliteration*	*Copy*	*Photo*
ARN 9	18	p. 53		
ARN 37	15	pp. 50–51		
ARN 45	7	pp. 43–44		
ARN 65	8	pp. 44–45		
ARN 100	22	p. 55		
BE 6/2 4	20	p. 54		
BE 6/2 24	9	pp. 45–46		
BE 6/2 28	4	pp. 41–42		
BE 6/2 38	40	pp. 76–77		
BE 6/2 46	21	pp. 54–55		
BE 6/2 48	16	pp. 51–52		
BE 6/2 57	11	pp. 47–48		
BE 6/2 64	52	pp. 89–90		
Cornell 4	27	pp. 63–64	pp. 126–27	pls. 1–2
Cornell 6	26	pp. 60–63	pp. 128–29	pls. 3–5
Cornell 7	44	pp. 80–81	pp. 130–31	pls. 6–8
Cornell 8	35	pp. 72–73	pp. 132–33	pls. 9–11
Cornell 11	47	pp. 83–84	pp. 134–35	pls. 12–13
Cornell 12	33	pp. 70–71	pp. 136–37	pls. 14–17
Cornell 16	48	pp. 84–85	pp. 138–39	pls. 18–19
Cornell 18	28	pp. 64–65	pp. 140–41	pls. 20–21
Cornell 19	36	pp. 73–74	pp. 142–43	pls. 22–23
Cornell 20	37	p. 74	pp. 144–45	pls. 24–25
Cornell 21	46	pp. 82–83	pp. 146–47	pl. 26
Cornell 23	51	pp. 87–89	pp. 148–49	pls. 27–28
OECT 8 1	42	pp. 78–79		pl. 29
OECT 8 2	38	p. 75		pls. 30–31
OECT 8 4	25	pp. 59–60		pls. 32–33
OECT 8 5	39	pp. 75–76		pls. 34–35
OECT 8 6	34	pp. 71–72		pl. 36
OECT 8 7	50	pp. 86–87		pls. 37–39
OECT 8 8	49	pp. 85–86		pls. 40–42
OECT 8 9	41	pp. 77–78		pls. 43–46
OECT 8 10	45	pp. 81–82		pls. 47–49
OECT 8 11	31	pp. 68–69		pls. 50–51

Publication	*Text No.*	*Transliteration*	*Copy*	*Photo*
OECT 8 16	30	pp. 67–68		pls. 52–53
OECT 8 17	24	pp. 56–59		pls. 54–56
OECT 8 18	53	pp. 90–92		pls. 57–58
OECT 8 19	29	pp. 65–67		pls. 59–60
OECT 8 20	23	pp. 55–56		pls. 61–62
OECT 8 21	32	pp. 69–70		pl. 63
PBS 8/1 16	2	pp. 39–40		
PBS 8/2 107	13	pp. 48–49		
PBS 8/2 153	5	p. 42		
PBS 8/2 155	17	pp. 52–53		
SAOC 44 1	14	pp. 49–50		
SAOC 44 10	6	pp. 42–43		
SAOC 44 15	10	pp. 46–47		
SAOC 44 30	12	p. 48		
SAOC 44 62	19	pp. 53–54		
TIM 4 13	1	pp. 38–39		
TIM 4 14	3	pp. 40–41		
TIM 4 54	43	pp. 79–80		

Prosopographic Index to the Mannum-mešu-liṣṣur Archive

John R. Mitchell

The index which follows is intended as a guide to the activities of Mannum-mešu-liṣṣur, his relatives, and business acquaintances. Prosopographical entries are provided for all persons attested in the thirty(-one) tablets assembled by Elizabeth C. Stone as the Mannum-mešu-liṣṣur archive. Exhaustive references to these individuals inside and outside the archive are given.

This index was prepared as part of my Johns Hopkins University dissertation research on Old Babylonian temple offices at Nippur; this work has been most generously assisted by Elizabeth C. Stone, David I. Owen, and Åke Sjöberg. Stone graciously put at my disposal a copy of her dissertation, "The Social and Economic Organization of Old Babylonian Nippur." Her extensive prosopography served as a starting point for and an invaluable check on the present index. All texts published in SAOC 44 which are in the University Museum were collated; for access to these collections I thank Å. Sjöberg, who introduced me to Sumerian studies. References to Cornell texts are based on my reading of copies provided by D. I. Owen. For the sake of consistency, the index has been edited by E. C. Stone so that it conforms to her interpretations of the texts indexed here. In the cases for which I postulate different relationships, my view appears in the notes.

Royal Chronology

Lipit-Enlil	1873–1869 (cf. Sigrist, *RA* 71 [1977] 121–22)
Sin-iqišam	1840–1836
Rim-Sin	1822–1763
Ḫammurapi	1792–1750
Samsuiluna	1749–1712
Rim-Sin II	1740
Ili-ma-AN	ca. 1720

Other Abbreviations

DN	divine name
dup.	duplicate of
n.d.	no date preserved or none given

NI	no family or professional information
PfN	profession
PN	personal name

a-ab-ba-tum (cf. a-ap-pa-(a)-tum)
bur-gul

Samsuiluna 11	Witness: BE 6/2 37: 19′ (dup. PBS 8/2 131: rev. 12); Cornell 8 [no. 35]: 23; Cornell 19 [no. 36]: rev. 6′; Cornell 20 [no. 37]: 20′.

a-ap-pa-(a)-tum (cf. a-ab-ba-tum)
bur-gul

Samsuiluna 11	Witness: BE 6/2 35: 21; OIMA 1 18: 28; OIMA 1 19: 22 (case N1119: 4′); SAOC 44 75: rev. 10.

a-at-ta-a (cf. a-ta-a)
dub-sar

Samsuiluna 11	Witness: *ARN* 86: rev. 9′.
Samsuiluna 12	Witness: TIM 4 54 [no. 43]: 20.
Samsuiluna 27	Witness: *ARN* 104: 10.

^{d}adad-ib-ni-šu
son of arad-^{d}en-líl-lá

Samsuiluna 12	Witness: OECT 8 5 [no. 39]: 21.

^{d}adad-ta-a-a-ar
nu-banda$_{3}$, son of ḫu-(um)-mu-ru-um

Samsuiluna 11	Buyer of temple offices from ^{d}sin-im-gur-an-ni and ta-ri-ba-tum: SAOC 44 73: tablet obv. 9′, case obv. 9.
Samsuiluna 13	Witness: OECT 8 7 [no. 50]: 24 (dup.$^{?}$ Cornell 16 [no. 48]: 24).
Samsuiluna 26	Witness giving testimony on the sonship of ^{d}nin-urta-ra-ḫi-im-ze-ri-im: PBS 5 100: iii 31, iv 25.

ad-da-kal-la*
son of ur-^{d}lum-ma$^{?}$, younger brother of ^{d}nanna-me-ša$_{4}$

Sin-iqišam 4	Division, with his brother, of lú-^{d}ba-ú's share of ur-^{d}lum-ma's property: OECT 8 17 [no. 24]: 45, seal (dup. OECT 8 18 [no. 53]: 41f.).

* An alternate explanation of the relationship of ^{d}nanna-me-ša$_{4}$ and ad-da-kal-la to ur-^{d}lum-ma and lú-^{d}ba-ú may be offered. Perhaps the former two were sons of lú-^{d}ba-ú, the adopted son of ur-^{d}lum-ma. If lú-^{d}ba-ú predeceased ur-^{d}lum-ma, the heirs to the latter's estate would become lú-^{d}ba-ú's sons, in the way described in OECT 8 17 [no. 24] (dup. OECT 8 18 [no. 53]).

a-gu-ú-a

father of ^{d}en-líl-gal-zu and ^{d}nin-urta-mu-ša-lim

Rim-Sin 48	*ARN* 36: 23.
Ḫammurapi 31	OECT 8 4 [no. 25]: 32.

a-ḫa-mar-ši (also written a-ḫa-am-ar-ši)

son of sí-ia-tum

Ḫammurapi 31	Buyer of temple office from ip-qú-er-ṣe-tim, a-wi-li-ia, and mu-na-wi-ru-um and co-payee of silver as šà-mul to ^{d}nuska-á-maḫ: OECT 8 4 [no. 25]: 6, 24.

father of ri-im-tum, husband of a-lí-a-ḫu-ú-a

Samsuiluna 12	OECT 8 1 [no. 42]: 4, seal.

a-lí-a-bu-ša

mother of ^{d}nin-urta-īriš, wife of la-lu-ú-um

Samsuiluna 11	Cornell 19 [no. 36]: 9, to be restored in line 11.

a-lí-a-ḫu-ú-a

mother of ri-im-tum, wife of a-ḫa-mar-ši

Samsuiluna 12	Co-seller of house property, with her daughter, to ma-an-nu-um-me-šu-li-ṣur: OECT 8 1 [no. 42]: 5, 6, 13 (partially restored), seal.

a-lí-wa-aq-rum

father of a-píl-^{d}sin

n.d.	Cornell 11 [no. 47]: 5, seal.

ama-da-kal-lá

NI

Sin-iqišam 4	Neighbor (field property) of ^{d}nanna-me-ša$_4$: OECT 8 18 [no. 53]: 9 (dup. OECT 8 17 [no. 24]: 9, written ⟨ama⟩-da-kala).

a-píl-ì-lí-šu

dub-sar, son of ^{d}nuska-ni-šu

Samsuiluna 8	Witness: Cornell 18 [no. 28]: 21.
Samsuiluna 12	Witness: OECT 8 9 [no. 41]: 23; OIMA 1 22: 17.
Samsuiluna 13	Witness: BE 6/2 41: 22.

aga-uš

Samsuiluna 12	Witness: OECT 8 10 [no. 45]: 24.

ugula-é-^{d}maḫ

Samsuiluna 8	Witness: SAOC 44 42: rev. 8.
Samsuiluna 11	Witness: BE 6/2 30: 1; SAOC 44 75: tablet rev. 5 (partially restored).

Samsuiluna 13	Witness: BE 6/2 42: 16; PBS 8/2 133: 28.
Samsuiluna 16	Witness: SAOC 44 44: tablet rev. 5′, case rev. 5′.
Samsuiluna 18	Witness: SAOC 44 47: tablet rev. 3.
Samsuiluna 29	BE 6/2 64 [no. 52]: 20.
n.d.	Witness: SAOC 44 24: rev. 4; SAOC 44 89: rev. 6.

a-píl-^{d}sin (written both ^{d}EN.ZU and 30)

son of a-lí-wa-aq-rum

n.d.	Co-seller of temple office, with ì-lí-ḫa-zi-ri, to ma-an-nu-um-me-e-šu-li-ṣur: Cornell 11 [no. 47]: 5, 6, 13, seal.

arad-^{d}en-líl-lá

son of i-bi-^{d}en-líl

Samsuiluna 12	Seller of field property to ma-an-nu-um-me-šu-li-ṣur: OECT 8 2 [no. 38]: 5, 7, 14, seal.

son of KA-^{d}en-líl-lá

Sin-iqišam 4	Witness: OECT 8 17 [no. 24]: 53 (dup. OECT 8 18 [no. 53]: 51).

father of ^{d}adad-ib-ni-šu

Samsuiluna 12	OECT 8 5 [no. 39]: 21.

arad-^{d}imin-bi

lú-túg

Samsuiluna x	Witness: Cornell 6 [no. 26]: iv 6.

arad-^{d}nanna

son of lugal-iti-da

Lipit-Enlil 5	Witness: OECT 8 20 [no. 23]: 28.

father of ^{d}sin-ma-gir

Samsuiluna 29	BE 6/2 64 [no. 52]: 22.

a-ta-a (cf. a-at-ta-a)

dub-sar

Samsuiluna 4	Witness: *ARN* 80: rev. 3′ (partially restored).
Samsuiluna 12	Witness: BE 6/2 38 [no. 40]: 23; OECT 8 2 [no. 38]: 24.
Samsuiluna 26	Witness: BE 6/2 63: 13.

a-wi-ia-tum

father of ì-lí-ḫa-zi-ri

Samsuiluna 12	OECT 8 5 [no. 39]: 20.
n.d.	Cornell 11 [no. 47]: 4 (partially restored), seal; PBS 8/1 94: i 12.

a-wi-il-ili(AN)

father of ^{d}nanna-ma-an-sum

Sin-iqišam 4	OECT 8 17 [no. 24]: 50 (dup. OECT 8 18 [no. 53]: 48.

a-wi-li-ia (also written a-wi-il-ia, a-wi-il-li-ia, and a-wi-lí-ia)

heir of ^{d}nuska-á-maḫ

Ḫammurapi 31	Co-swearer of oath, with mu-na-wi-rum, not to contest house property; co-seller of temple office, with mu-na-wi-rum, to a-ḫa-mar-ši: OECT 8 4 [no. 25]: 12, 25, 28, seal.

bur-gul, son of ur-^{d}ba-ú

Rim-Sin 50	Witness: PBS 8/2 116: 32.
Ḫammurapi 33	Witness: BE 6/2 10: 48; PBS 13 67: 23.
Ḫammurapi 38	Witness: *ARN* 70: 25.
Ḫammurapi 41	Witness: *ARN* 72: rev. 5′ (partially restored).
Samsuiluna 4	Witness: *ARN* 78: 23; BE 6/2 23: 34; BE 6/2 24 [no. 9]: 36.
Samsuiluna 5	Witness: OIMA 1 13: 30; PBS 8/2 129: 37.
Samsuiluna 6	Witness: Cornell 4 [no. 27]: rev. 17′.
Samsuiluna 7	Witness: SAOC 44 13: rev. 4.
Samsuiluna 8	Witness: Cornell 18 [no. 28]: 20; SAOC 44 42: rev. 15.
Rim-Sin IIb	Witness: OECT 8 19 [no. 29]: 25.
Samsuiluna 10	Witness: Cornell 21 [no. 46]: 21; OECT 8 11 [no. 31]: 26; OECT 8 16 [no. 30]: 21; SAOC 44 31: rev. 15; SAOC 44 71: tablet rev. 8, case rev. 6′; SAOC 44 72: tablet rev. 9, case rev. 10
Samsuiluna 11	Witness: *ARN* 92: 17 (partially restored); *ARN* 95: 17; *ARN* 97: 20 (partially restored); BE 6/2 32: 30; BE 6/2 33: 21; BE 6/2 34: 20; Cornell 12 [no. 33]: 27; SAOC 44 74: tablet rev. 12, case rev. 14′.
Samsuiluna 12	Witness: S. Landgon, "Miscellanea Assyriaca II," *Babyloniaca* 7 (1913/23) 71: rev. 6′; BE 6/2 38 [no. 40]: 22; Cornell 21 [no. 46]: 21; OECT 8 1 [no. 42]: 21; OECT 8 5 [no. 39]: 23; OIMA 1 21: 20; OIMA 1 22: 18; PBS 8/2 135: 22; SAOC 44 43: rev. 7; SAOC 44 78: tablet rev. 7′, case rev. 9; SAOC 44 79: tablet rev. 10, case rev. 10′; TIM 4 25: 20; TIM 4 54 [no. 43]: 19.
Samsuiluna 13	Witness: BE 6/2 40: 30; BE 6/2 41: 22; BE 6/2 43: 35.
Samsuiluna 14	Witness: BE 6/2 44: 27.
Samsuiluna 16	Witness: SAOC 44 15 [no. 10]: rev. 7; SAOC 44 44: tablet rev. 11′, case rev. 12′.
Samsuiluna 17	Witness: SAOC 44 45: tablet rev. 8; SAOC 44 46: tablet rev. 9, case rev. 9.
Samsuiluna 18	Witness: BE 6/2 48 [no. 16]: 43.

Samsuiluna 23	Witness: Cornell 23 [no. 51]: 48 (PfN restored with reasonable certainty); SAOC 44 83: tablet rev. 10.
Samsuiluna 24	Witness: PBS 13 66: rev. 3′.
Samsuiluna 25	Witness: OIMA 1 28: 39.
Samsuiluna 26	Witness: *ARN* 103: vi 26.
Samsuiluna 27	Witness: PBS 8/2 146: 45.
Samsuiluna 28	Witness: PBS 8/1 91: 22; PBS 8/2 138: 22.
Samsuiluna x	Witness: *ARN* 110: rev. 7′; Cornell 6 [no. 26]: iv 12.
Ili-ma-AN 1	Witness: SAOC 44 12: rev. 7.
Ili-ma-AN 2	Witness: BE 6/2 68: 26.
n.d.	Witness: OIMA 1 67: 4′ (partially restored); SAOC 44 87: rev. 10′; SAOC 44 88: rev. 6′; SAOC 44 89: rev. 10.

father of ma-an-nu-um-me-šu-li-ṣur and ^{d}nin-urta-mu-ba-lí-iṭ

Samsuiluna 8	Cornell 18 [no. 28]: 7 (partially restored).
Samsuiluna 10	OECT 8 11 [no. 31]: 2; OECT 8 16 [no. 30]: seal.
Samsuiluna 11	Cornell 8 [no. 35]: 10; OECT 8 6 [no. 34]: 7.
Samsuiluna 12	BE 6/2 38 [no. 40]: 10; Cornell 7 [no. 44]: 10 (partially restored); OECT 8 1: 8; OECT 8 2 [no. 38]: 9; OECT 8 5 [no. 39]: 8; OECT 8 9 [no. 41]: 8; OECT 8 10 [no. 45]: 13; TIM 4 54 [no. 43]: 6.
Samsuiluna 13	OECT 8 7 [no. 50]: 8 (dup.? Cornell 16 [no. 48]: 8); OECT 8 8 [no. 49]: 11.
Samsuiluna 23	Cornell 23: [no. 52]: seal.
Samsuiluna 29	BE 6/2 64 [no. 52]: 5, 7, seal.
n.d.	Cornell 11 [no. 47]: 8.

be-el-šu-nu

father of dingir-ma-an-sum

Samsuiluna x	Cornell 6 [no. 26]: iv 10.

da-mi-iq-ì-lí-šu (also written dam-qí-ì-lí-šu)

son of ^{d}nin-urta-ma-an-sum

Samsuiluna 11	Witness: SAOC 44 77: rev. 4′.
Samsuiluna 13	Witness: Cornell 16 [no. 48]: 22 (dup.? OECT 8 7 omits).

father of ^{d}en-líl-gal-zu

Samsuiluna 11	BE 6/2 30: 8.
Samsuiluna 12	BE 6/2 38 [no. 40]: 3.

^{d}da-mu-a-zu

NI

Ḫammurapi 31	Neighbor (house property) of ^{d}nanna-me-ša$_{4}$: OECT 8 4 [no. 25]: 16.

^{d}da-mu-e-ri-ba-am
gudu$_4$ ^{d}nin-líl-lá

Samsuiluna 11	Witness: Cornell 8 [no. 35]: 18 (partially restored).
Samsuiluna 14	Witness: BE 6/2 44: 21.

^{d}da-mu-i-din-nam (also written ^{d}da-mu-i-din-na-am)
dub-sar

Ḫammurapi 30	Witness: *ARN* 65 [no. 8]: 41.
Ḫammurapi 31	Witness: OECT 8 4 [no. 25]: 36.
Ḫammurapi 33	Witness: BE 6/2 10: 47.
Ḫammurapi 37	Witness: BE 6/2 14: 32.

dingir-ma-an-sum
son of be-el-šu-nu

Samsuiluna x	Witness: Cornell 6 [no. 26]: iv 9.

é-a-i-din-nam
son of ma-ri-er-ṣe-tim

Samsuiluna 12	Seller of temple office to ma-an-nu-um-me-šu-li-ṣur: TIM 4 54 [no. 43]: 3, 4, 11, seal.

father of lugal-ḫé-gál and ^{d}nin-urta-e-mu-qá-a-a

Samsuiluna 12	BE 6/2 38 [no. 40]: 6.
Samsuiluna 24.	PBS 13 66: 5 (collated).

NI; father of the original sellers of a house lot now redeemed by ^{d}nin-urta-ra-ḫi-im-ze-ri-im

Samsuiluna 29	BE 6/2 64 [no. 52]: 4.

el-le-tum
father of li-pí-it-ištar

Samsuiluna 12	TIM 4 54 [no. 43]: 18.

el-me-šum
wife of ì-lí-ip-pa-al-sà-am

Samsuiluna 11	Co-adopter of ^{d}nin-urta-mu-ba-lí-iṭ, with her husband: OECT 8 21 [no. 32]: 2, 10, 13, 20.

é-lú-ti
father of lú-^{d}ba-ú

Lipit-Enlil 5	OECT 8 20 [no. 23]: 4.

agrig, father of lú-^{d}en-líl-lá

Rim-Sin 56	Neighbor (house property) of ilum-iriš (AN.APIN): *ARN* 46: 25.

Rim-Sin IIb	OECT 8 19 [no. 29]: 21.
Samsuiluna 12	OECT 8 1 18.
Samsuiluna 13	BE 6/2 41: 20 (partially restored).
Samsuiluna 29	BE 6/2 64 [no. 52]: 21.

šu-ḫa-a

Sin-iqišam 4	Neighbor (field property) of ^{d}nanna-me-ša$_4$: OECT 8 18 [no. 53]: 11 (dup. OECT 8 17 [no. 24]: 10 omits title).

^{d}en-líl-gal-zu

son of a-gu-ú-a, brother of ^{d}nin-urta-mu-ša-lim

Rim-Sin 48	Witness: *ARN* 36: 23.
Ḫammurapi 31	Witness: OECT 8 4 [no. 25]: 32.

son of da-mi-iq-ì-lí-šu (also written dam-qí-ì-lí-šu)

Samsuiluna 11	Witness: BE 6/2 30: 8.
Samsuiluna 12	Neighbor (house property) of ma-an-nu-um-me-šu-li-ṣur: BE 6/2 38 [no. 40]: 2.

^{d}en-líl-gú-gal

father of nì-gur$_{11}$-^{d}nanna

Sin-iqišam 4	OECT 8 17 [no. 24]: 49 (dup. OECT 8 18 [no. 53]: 47).

^{d}en-líl-ma-an-sum

father of li-pí-it-ištar

Samsuiluna 12	OECT 8 5 [no. 39]: 22.

gudu$_4$

Samsuiluna 12	Witness: OECT 8 10 [no. 45]: 23a (case only).

^{d}en-líl-mu-ba-lí-iṭ

dub-sar

Samsuiluna 12	Witness: OIMA 1 23: rev. 2′; SAOC 44 78: tablet rev. 8′, case 10; SAOC 44 79: tablet rev. 11, case rev. 11′.
Samsuiluna 14	Witness: SAOC 44 81: tablet rev. 10, case rev. 11.
Samsuiluna 23	Witness: BE 6/2 58: 23.
Samsuiluna 24	Witness: PBS 13 66: rev. 3′ (partially restored).
Samsuiluna 25	Witness: OIMA 1 28: 40.
Samsuiluna 26	Witness: PBS 8/2 136: 20 (case rev. 8′).
Samsuiluna 27	Witness: PBS 8/2 127: 3; SAOC 44 14: rev. 3.
Samsuiluna 28	Witness: PBS 13 19: 8.
Samsuiluna 29	Witness: BE 6/2 64 [no. 52]: 25.
Samsuiluna x	Witness: SAOC 44 85: rev. 8′.
n.d.	Witness: SAOC 44 87: rev. 9′ (name and profession partially restored); SAOC 44 88: rev. 7′.

en-na

father of na-bi-^{d}en-líl

Lipit-Enlil 5	OECT 8 20 [no. 23]: 27.

giri$_{3}$-né-ì-sa$_{6}$ (also written giri$_{3}$-né-ì-sà)

father of ma-ri-er-ṣe-tim

Samsuiluna 11	Cornell 20 [no. 37]: 17′; OECT 8 6 [no. 34]: 18.
Samsuiluna 12	OECT 8 1 20; OECT 8 2 [no. 38]: 21.
Samsuiluna 13	OECT 8 7 [no. 50]: 23; OECT 8 8 [no. 49]: 21.
n.d.	PBS 8/1 94: i 15.

ḫI.TAR-^{d}iškur

bur-gul

Ḫammurapi 42	Witness: BE 6/2 11: 27.
Samsuiluna 11	Witness: *ARN* 86: rev. 8′; OECT 8 6 [no. 34]: 20.
Samsuiluna 12	Witness: Cornell 7 [no. 44]: 21; OECT 8 2 [no. 38]: 23; OECT 8 9 [no. 41]: 22; OECT 8 10 [no. 45]: 25 (tablet has dub-sar, case has bur-gul); OIMA 1 23: rev. 3′.
Samsuiluna 13	Witness: OECT 8 7 [no. 50]: 26; PBS 8/2 153 [no. 5]: 24.

ḫu-mu-rum (also written ḫu-um-mu-ru-um)

father of ^{d}adad-ta-a-a-ar

Samsuiluna 11	SAOC 44 73: tablet obv. 10.
Samsuiluna 13	OECT 8 7 [no. 50]: 24.
Samsuiluna 26	PBS 5/1 100: iii 31.

ḫu-pil-[ ]

son of [ ]-na-tum

Samsuiluna 11	Witness: OECT 8 21 [no. 32]: 29.

i-[ ]

father of ib-ni-é-a

Samsuiluna 6	Cornell 4 [no. 27]: rev. 12′.

father of [ ]-e-ri-ba-am

Samsuiluna 11	Cornell 19 [no. 36]: rev. 1′.

i-bi-^{d}en-líl

son of ^{d}sin-i-qí-ša-am, older brother of ^{d}nanna-a-a

Samsuiluna 8	Seller of house property to ma-an-nu-um-me-šu-li-ṣur: Cornell 18 [no. 28]: 3, 5, 12 (restored), seal.
Samsuiluna x	Co-inheritor of temple offices, house, and field property, with his brother, from his father and also(?) from ì-lí-a-wi-li and ^{d}sin-še-mi: Cornell 6 [no. 26]: ii 10, iii 11, seal.

father of arad-^{d}en-líl-lá

Samsuiluna 12	OECT 8 2 [no. 38]: 6, seal.

father of ì-lí-i-din-nam

Samsuiluna 11	SAOC 44 75: tablet obv. 4, 5, 11, seal.
Samsuiluna 12	OECT 8 2 [no. 38]: 22.
n.d.	PBS 8/1 94: i 19.

father of ^{d}nin-urta-mu-uš-ta-al, na-ma-ar-šu-lu-mu-ur, and mu-na-wi-rum

Rim-Sin IIb	Partition of his estate (consisting of temple offices) by his sons: OECT 8 19 [no. 29]: 19, seal (both partially restored).
Samsuiluna 10	Settlement of his debts to ma-an-nu-um-me-šu-li-ṣur by his sons who gave the creditor a temple office: OECT 8 11 [no. 31]: 4, 12, 19, seal.
Samsuiluna 11	Cornell 12 [no. 33]: 10 (partially restored), seal.

simug

Samsuiluna 13	Witness: OECT 8 7 [no. 50]: 25.

i-bi-^{d}nin-šubur

dub-sar

Samsuiluna 12	Witness: Cornell 21 [no. 46]: 22.
Samsuiluna 13	Witness: OECT 8 7 [no. 50]: 27.

ib-ni-é-a

son of i-[ ]

Samsuiluna 6	Witness: Cornell 4 [no. 27]: rev. 12′.

NI

Samsuiluna 12	Witness: BE 6/2 38 [no. 40]: 21.

i-da-tum

son of ^{d}sin-ma-gir

Samsuiluna 11	Witness: Cornell 19 [no. 36]: rev. 3′.

i-din-ištar

son of ma-an-nu-um-me-šu-li-ṣur and na-ru-ub-tum, nephew of ^{d}nin-urta-mu-ba-lí-iṭ

Samsuiluna 29	Co-seller of house property, with his mother and father of brother of, to ^{d}nin-urta-ra-ḫi-im-ze-ri-im who was redeeming it: BE 6/2 64 [no. 64]: 8, 16, seal.

i-din-^{d}sin

NI

Samsuiluna x	His sons were neighbors (field property) of i-bi-^{d}en-líl: Cornell 6 [no. 26]: i 14.

i-di-šum

bur-gul

Samsuiluna 1	Witness: TIM 4 24: 18.
Samsuiluna 3	Witness: SAOC 44 69: tablet rev. 8.
Samsuiluna 6	Witness: PBS 8/2 132: 18.
Samsuiluna 11	Witness: SAOC 44 73: tablet rev. 11, case rev. 2′.
Samsuiluna 12	Witness: BE 6/2 39: 24.
Samsuiluna 13	Witness: OECT 8 8 [no. 49]: 22; PBS 8/2 133: 33.
Samsuiluna 14	Witness: SAOC 44 81: tablet rev. 9, case 10; SAOC 44 82: rev. 7′.
Samsuiluna 26	Witness: BE 6/2 59: 19′; TIM 4 19: 12.
Samsuiluna 29	Witness: BE 6/2 64 [no. 52]: 24.
Ili-ma-AN 2	Witness: PBS 8/1 89: 21.
n.d. (after Samsuiluna 25)	Witness: OIMA 1 29: 26′ (case$^{?}$ *ARN* 114: 5′).*

ì-lí-a-wi-li

brother of ^{d}sin-i-qí-ša-am, father of brother of i-bi-^{d}en-líl and ^{d}nanna-a-a

Samsuiluna x	His inheritance share is divided(?) by his nephews: Cornell 6 [no. 26]: iii 8, 13, 17.

NI

Samsuiluna 6	Witness: Cornell 4 [no. 27]: rev. 11′.

ì-lí-e-ri-ba-am

son of ^{d}sin-ma-gir, brother of lu-mur-ša-^{d}šamaš

Samsuiluna 12	Co-seller of temple offices, with his brother, to ma-an-nu-um-me-šu-li-ṣur: OECT 8 5 [no. 39]: 4, 6, 13, seal.

ì-lí-ḫa-zi-ri (also written ì-lí-ḫa-zí-ri)

son of a-wi-ia-tum

Samsuiluna 12	Witness: OECT 8 5 [no. 39]: 20.
n.d.	Co-seller of temple office, with a-píl-^{d}sin, to ma-an-nu-um-me-šu-li-ṣur: Cornell 11 [no. 47]: 4, 6, 13, seal.
n.d.	List of eren$_{2}$. PBS 8/1 94: i 12.

ì-lí-i-din-nam

son of i-bi-^{d}en-líl

Samsuiluna 11	Seller of temple offices to a-at-ta-a: SAOC 44 75: tablet obv. 4, 5, 11, case 4, 5, 10, seal.

* If *ARN* 111 + *ARN* 114 + *ARN* 115 + N1249 is the case to OIMA 1 29, then the date of this text is Samsuiluna 26.

Samsuiluna 12	Witness: OECT 8 2 [no. 38]: 22.
n.d.	List of $eren_2$: PBS 8/1 94: i 12 (partially restored).

father of ᵈsin-li-di-iš

Samsuiluna 12	OECT 8 9 [no. 41]: 5, 13, seal.

ì-lí-ip-pa-al-sà-am

son of ᵈnin-urta-mu-ša-lim, brother of ᵈnuska-ni-šu

Samsuiluna 11	Witness: OECT 8 21 [no. 32]: 28.
Samsuiluna 12	Witness: OECT 8 9 [no. 41]: 21.
Samsuiluna 13	Witness: BE 6/2 41: 21.

son of ᵈsin-ma-gir, husband of el-me-šum

Samsuiluna 11	Seller of temple office to ma-an-nu-um-me-šu-li-ṣur: OECT 8 6 [no. 34]: 3, 5, 12, seal.
Samsuiluna 11	Co-adopter of ᵈnin-urta-mu-ba-lí-iṭ, with his wife: OECT 8 21 [no. 32]: 1, 9, 12, 19, seal.

ì-lí-iš-na-di

father of [ ]-bi-ᵈen-líl

Samsuiluna 11	Cornell 19 [no. 36]: rev. 2′.

illati (written ILLAT-ti)

father of ip-qú-er-ṣe-tim

Ḫammurapi 31	OECT 8 4 [no. 25]: 7.

im-[ ] (cf. im-gur-ᵈnin-urta)

NI

Samsuiluna 23	Neighbor (house property) of ma-an-nu-um-me-šu-li-ṣur: Cornell 23: [no. 52]: 12.

im-gur-ᵈnin-urta (also written im-gu-ru-um)

father of ma-an-nu-um-ma-ḫir-šu

Ḫammurapi 31	OECT 8 4 [no. 25]: 34.
Ḫammurapi 33	BE 6/2 10: 43.
Samsuiluna 10	OECT 8 16 [no. 30]: 20.

NI

Samsuiluna 23	Neighbor (house property) of ma-an-nu-um-me-šu-li-ṣur: Cornell 23: [no. 52]: 12.

im-gur-ᵈsin

dub-sar

Sin-iqišam 4	Witness: OECT 8 17 [no. 24]: 54 (dup. OECT 8 18 [no. 53]: 52).

Samsuiluna 12 — Witness: Cornell 7 [no. 44]: 22; OECT 8 10 [no. 45]: 26.

Samsuiluna 13 — Witness: OECT 8 8 [no. 49]: 23.

i-na-é-kur-ra-bi

NI

Samsuiluna 6 — With ma-an-nu-um-me-šu-li-ṣur, ^{d}nin-urta-mu-ba-lí-iṭ, and ^{d}sin-ma-gir he is adopted by ^{d}nanna-a-a, to whom support is promised: Cornell 4 [no. 27]: 7, 17, rev. 6′ (restored), seal.

^{d}inanna-ma-an-sum

dub-sar, father of ^{d}en-líl-lú-sa$_6$, ^{d}nanna-a-rá-mu-un-ge-en, ur-du$_6$-kù-ga, and ur-^{d}šul-pa-è-a

Samsuiluna 6 — Partition of his estate by his sons: BE 6/2 26: iv 13, seal.

Samsuiluna 12 — TIM 4 54 [no. 43]: 17.

i-na-ša-me-e-wu-súm

NI

Ḫammurapi 31 — Co-payee of silver as šà-mul to ^{d}nuska-á-maḫ: OECT 8 4 [no. 25]: 8.

in-bi-ì-lí-šu

son of ^{d}nin-urta-mu-uš-ta-al and la-ma-sá-tum

Samsuiluna 11 — Co-seller of temple office, with his mother, to ma-an-nu-um-me-šu-li-ṣur: Cornell 20 [no. 37]: 1′ (partially restored), 3′, 11′, seal.

ip-qá-tum

father of ^{d}nin-urta-iriš(APIN)

Samsuiluna 11 — Cornell 8 [no. 35]: 7, 8, seal; Cornell 19 [no. 36]: rev. 4′.

ip-qú-é-a

father of la-ma-súm

Samsuiluna 6 — Cornell 4 [no. 27]: 1, seal.

ip-qú-er-ṣe-tim

son of illatī

Ḫammurapi 31 — Co-payee of silver as šà-mul to ^{d}nuska-á-maḫ and co-seller of temple office to a-ḫa-mar-ši: OECT 8 4 [no. 25]: 7, 25, 28.

KA-^{d}da-mu

son of da-da-kal-la

Lipit-Enlil 5 — Witness (patronymic poorly written): OECT 8 20 [no. 23]: 25.

Sin-iqišam 4	Witness: OECT 8 17 [no. 24]: 51 (dup. OECT 8 18 [no. 53]: 49).

KA-^{d}en-líl-lá (also written KA-^{d}en-líl)
father of arad-^{d}en-líl-lá

Sin-iqišam 4	OECT 8 17 [no. 24]: 53 (dup. OECT 8 18 [no. 53]: 51).

father of kù-^{d}nanna

Lipit-Enlil 5	OECT 8 20 [no. 23]: 24.

ka-kù-ga
NI

Sin-iqišam 4	Neighbor (house property) of ^{d}nanna-me-ša$_4$: OECT 8 17 [no. 24]: 1 (dup. OECT 8 18 [no. 53]: 1).

kú-^{d}nanna
son of KA-^{d}en-líl-lá

Lipit-Enlil 5	Witness: OECT 8 20 [no. 23]: 24.

kù-^{d}nin-imma$_3$
dub-sar

Samsuiluna 4	Witness: BE 6/2 22: 15.
Samsuiluna 6	Witness: OIMA 1 14: 17.
Samsuiluna 8	Witness: BE 6/2 28 [no. 4]: 34.
Samsuiluna 10	Witness: SAOC 44 32: rev. 5′.
Samsuiluna 11	Witness: BE 6/2 30: 13.
Samsuiluna x	Witness: Cornell 6 [no. 26]: iv 11.

la-a-lum
father of warad-ištar

Samsuiluna 12	Cornell 7 [no. 44]: 7, 14 (partially restored), seal.

la-lu-ú-um
father of ^{d}nin-urta-iriš(APIN), husband of a-lí-a-bu-ša

Samsuiluna 11	Cornell 19 [no. 36]: 10 (largely restored), seal.

la-ma-sà-tum
mother of in-bi-ì-lí-šu, wife of ^{d}nin-urta-mu-uš-ta-al

Samsuiluna 11	Co-seller of temple office, with her son, to ma-an-nu-um-me-šu-li-ṣur: Cornell 20 [no. 37]: 4′, 12′.

la-ma-súm
daughter of ip-qú-é-a

Samsuiluna 6	Marriage to ^{d}nanna-a-a: Cornell 4 [no. 27]: 1, 13, rev. 3′, seal.

li-pí-it-^{d}en-líl

son(?) of ma-ri-er-ṣe-tim and ri-ba-tum, brother(?) of ^{d}utu-^{d}en-líl-lá and ^{d}nin-urta-ni-šu

Samsuiluna 12	Co-seller of his father's temple offices, with his brothers and mother, to ma-an-nu-um-me-šu-li-ṣur: OECT 8 10 [no. 45]: 9, 18, seal.

li-pí-it-ištar

son of el-le-tum

Samsuiluna 12	Witness: TIM 4 54 [no. 43]: 18.

son of ^{d}en-líl-ma-an-sum

Samsuiluna 12	Witness: OECT 8 5 [no. 39]: 22.

son of na-ra-am-^{d}adad

Samsuiluna 12	Witness: Cornell 7 [no. 44]: 20.
Samsuiluna 27	Witness: PBS 8/2 146: 44 (partially restored).

lú-^{d}ba-ú*

son of é-lú-ti

Lipit-Enlil 5	Adopted by ur-^{d}lum-ma: OECT 8 20 [no. 23]: 3, 15.
Sin-iqišam 4	His adoptive brothers, ^{d}nanna-me-$ša_4$ and ad-da-kal-la, inherit from him: OECT 8 17 [no. 24]: seal.

lú-^{d}en-líl-lá

agrig ^{d}en-líl-lá, son of é-lu-ti

Rim-Sin IIb	Witness: OECT 8 19 [no. 29]: 21.
Samsuiluna 10	Witness: OECT 8 11 [no. 31]: 23; OECT 8 16 [no. 30]: 17.
Samsuiluna 11	Witness: Cornell 8 [no. 35]: 19 (partially restored); Cornell 12 [no. 33]: 22; Cornell 20 [no. 37]: 16′; OECT 8 21 [no. 32]: 26.
Samsuiluna 12	Witness: BE 6/2 38 [no. 40]: 20; Cornell 7 [no. 44]: 18; OECT 8 1 [no. 42]: 1: 18; OECT 8 2 [no. 38]: 19; OECT 8 9 [no. 41]: 19; OECT 8 10 [no. 45]: 23.
Samsuiluna 13	Witness: BE 6/2 41: 20; OECT 8 7 [no. 50]: 19 (dup.? Cornell 16 [no. 48]: 19); OECT 8 8 [no. 49]: 19.
Samsuiluna 29	Witness: BE 6/2 64 [no. 52]: 21.
n.d.	Witness: SAOC 44 89: tablet rev. 7.

NI

Samsuiluna 23	Witness: Cornell 23: [no. 52]: 44.

* See note on p. 96.

lugal-a-ma-ru
gudu$_4$ ^{d}nin-líl-lá

Samsuiluna 11 — Witness: Cornell 8 [no. 35]: 20 (partially restored).

Samsuiluna 26 — Witness: BE 6/2 59: 15′; OIMA 1 29: 20′; PBS 8/2 136: tablet 18, case rev. 5′.

NI

Sin-iqišam 4 — Neighbor (field property) of ^{d}nanna-me-ša$_4$: OECT 8 17 [no. 24]: 8 (dup. OECT 8 18 [no. 53]: 8).

lugal-ḫ̮é-gál
son of é-a-i-din-nam, brother of ^{d}nin-urta-e-mu-qá-a-a

Samsuiluna 12 — Co-seller of house property, with his brother, to ma-an-nu-um-me-šu-li-ṣur: BE 6/2 38 [no. 40]: 4, 7, 15 (restored), seal.

lugal-iti-da
father of arad-^{d}nanna

Lipit-Enlil 5 — OECT 8 20 [no. 23]: 28

lú-^{d}inanna
agrig, father of ur-^{d}lum-ma

Lipit-Enlil 5 — OECT 8 20 [no. 23]: 2, seal.

lú-ì-si-in^{ki}-na
son of ^{d}utu-ḫ̮é-gál

Lipit-Enlil 5 — OECT 8 20 [no. 23]: 26.

lu-mur-ša-^{d}šamaš
son of ^{d}sin-ma-gir, brother of ì-lí-e-ri-ba-am

Samsuiluna 12 — Co-seller of temple office, with his brother, to ma-an-nu-um-me-šu-li-ṣur: OECT 8 5 [no. 39]: 3, 6, 12, seal.

lú-^{d}nanna
dub-sar

Rim-Sin IIb — Witness: OECT 8 14: 11.

Samsuiluna 11 — Witness: BE 6/2 29: 14; Cornell 8 [no. 35]: 22 (partially restored); Cornell 20 [no. 37]: 18′.

lú-nibru^{ki}
son of ur-du$_6$-kù-ga, brother of ^{d}sin-še-mi

Samsuiluna 8 — Witness: Cornell 18 [no. 28]: 19.

Samsuiluna 10 — Neighbor (house property) of his brother: OIMA 1 16: 2.

lu-^{d}nin-urta
aga-uš

Rim-Sin IIb	Witness: OECT 8 19 [no. 29]: 24.
Samsuiluna 10	Witness: OECT 8 11 [no. 31]: 25.

lú-si-gar
father of ^{d}sin-li-di-iš

Sin-iqišam 4	OECT 8 18 [no. 53]: 50 (dup. OECT 8 17 [no. 24]: 52 omits dumu).

lú-^{d}sin-na (also written lú-^{d}sin)
NI

Sin-iqišam 4	Neighbor (house property) of ^{d}nanna-me-ša$_{4}$ and ad-da-kal-la: OECT 8 17 [no. 24]: 4, 26 (dup. OECT 8 18 [no. 53]: 4, 24).

ma-an-nu-um-ma-ḫir-šu (also written me-an-nu-(um-)ma-ḫir-šu and ma-nu-um-ma-ḫir-šu)
son of im-gur-^{d}nin-urta (also written im-gu-ru-um)

Ḫammurapi 31	Witness: OECT 8 4 [no. 25]: 34.
Ḫammurapi 33	Witness: BE 6/2 10: 43.
Samsuiluna 10	Witness: OECT 8 16 [no. 30]: 19.

NI

Samsuiluna 23	Witness: Cornell 23: [no. 52]: 46.

ma-an-nu-um-me-šu-li-ṣur (also written ma-an-nu-um-me-e-šu-li-ṣur)
son of a-wi-li-ia, husband of na-ru-ub-tum, father of i-din-ištar, brother of ^{d}nin-urta-mu-ba-lí-iṭ

Samsuiluna 6	Adoption, together with his brother and ^{d}sin-ma-gir and i-na-é-kur-ra-bi, by ^{d}nanna-a-a, to whom support was promised: Cornell 4 [no. 27]: 4, 14, rev. 4′, seal.
Samsuiluna 8	Buyer of property from i-bi-^{d}en-líl: Cornell 18 [no. 28]: 18: 6 (partially restored).
Samsuiluna 10	Recipient of temple offices from mu-na-wi-ru-um in exchange for his (inherited) house property: OECT 8 16 [no. 30]: 3, seal.
Samsuiluna 10	Recipient of temple office from ^{d}nin-urta-mu-uš-ta-al, na-ma-ar-šu-lu-mu-ur, and mu-na-wi-ru-um in settlement of their father's debt to him: OECT 8 11 [no. 31]: 1, 14.
Samsuiluna 11	Buyer of temple offices from ^{d}nin-urta-mu-uš-ta-al: Cornell 12 [no. 33]: 11 (mostly restored, patronymic not given, but attribution probable).
Samsuiluna 11	Buyer of temple office from ì-lí-ip-pa-al-sà-am: OECT 8 6 [no. 34]: 6.

Samsuiluna 11	Buyer of temple offices from ^{d}nin-urta-iriš(APIN): Cornell 8 [no. 35]: 9.
Samsuiluna 12	Buyer of field property from arad-^{d}en-líl-lá: OECT 8 2 [no. 38]: 8.
Samsuiluna 12	Buyer of temple office from lu-mur-ša-^{d}šamaš and ì-lí-e-ri-ba-am: OECT 8 5 [no. 39]: 8.
Samsuiluna 12	Buyer of house property from lugal-ḫé-gál and ^{d}nin-urta-e-mu-qá-a-a: BE 6/2 38 [no. 40]: 9.
Samsuiluna 12	Buyer of temple offices from ^{d}sin-li-di-iš: OECT 8 9 [no. 41]: 7.
Samsuiluna 12	Buyer of house property from ri-im-tum and a lí-a-ḫu-ú-a: OECT 8 1 [no. 42]: 7.
Samsuiluna 12	Buyer of temple office from é-a-i-din-nam: TIM 4 54 [no. 43]: 5.
Samsuiluna 12	Buyer of temple offices from ^{d}utu-^{d}en-líl-lá, li-pí-it-^{d}en-líl, ^{d}nin-urta-ni-šu, and ri-ba-tum: OECT 8 10 [no. 45]: 12.
Samsuiluna 12	Buyer of temple offices from warad-ištar: Cornell 7 [no. 44]: 9 (partially restored).
Samsuiluna 13	Buyer of temple offices from ^{d}nin-urta-ma-an-sum: OECT 8 8 [no. 49]: 10.
Samsuiluna 13	Buyer of temple office from ^{d}nin-urta-ra-ḫi-im-zé-ri: OECT 8 7 [no. 50]: 7 (dup.? Cornell 16 [no. 48]: 7).
Samsuiluna 23	Co-inheritor of house property and temple offices, with mu-na-wi-ru-um, from ^{d}nuska-á-maḫ (partially restored); recipient of the preferential portion: Cornell 23: [no. 52]: 27, seal.
Samsuiluna 29	Previous buyer of house property from sons of é-a-i-din-nam (see BE 6/2 38 [no. 40], dated to Samsuiluna 12); the property now redeemed by ^{d}nin-urta-ra-ḫi-im-ze-ri-im: BE 6/2 64 [no. 52]: 5, 8, seal.
n.d.	Buyer of temple office from ì-lí-ḫa-zi-ri and a-píl-^{d}sin: Cornell 11 [no. 47]: 7′.

ma-ri-er-ṣe-tim (also written DUMU.KI, DUMU-er-ṣe-tim, and ma-a-ri-er-ṣe-tim) son of giri$_3$-né-ì-sa$_6$ (also written giri$_3$-né-ì-sà)

Samsuiluna 11	Witness: Cornell 20 [no. 37]: 17′; OECT 8 6 [no. 34]: 18.
Samsuiluna 12	Witness: OECT 8 1 [no. 42]: 20; OECT 8 2 [no. 38]: 20.
Samsuiluna 13	Witness: OECT 8 7 [no. 50]: 22; OECT 8 8 [no. 49]: 20.
n.d.	List of eren$_2$: PBS 8/1 94: i 14.

son of šeš-du$_{10}$-ga, husband of ri-ba-tum, father of ^{d}utu-^{d}en-líl-lá, li-pí-it-^{d}en-líl, and ^{d}nin-urta-ni-šu

Samsuiluna 12	Sale of his temple offices by his wife and sons to ma-an-nu-um-me-šu-li-ṣur: OECT 8 10 [no. 45]: 6, 10 (so case, partially restored), seal.

son of agrig ^{d}en-líl-lá

Samsuiluna 12	Neighbor (field property) of ma-an-nu-um-me-šu-li-ṣur: OECT 8 2 [no. 38]: 3.

father of é-a-i-din-nam

Samsuiluna 12	TIM 4 54 [no. 43]: seal.

father of ^{d}sin-a-ḫu-um

Samsuiluna 29	BE 6/2 64 [no. 52]: 23.

father of ta-ri-ba-tum

Rim-Sin IIb	OECT 8 19 [no. 29]: 23.

mu-na-wi-rum (also written mu-na-wi-ru-um)

son of i-bi-^{d}en-líl, brother of ^{d}nin-urta-mu-uš-ta-al and na-ma-ar-šu-lu-mu-ur

Rim-Sin IIb	Co-inheritor of temple offices, with his brothers, from his father: OECT 8 19 [no. 29]: 18, seal.
Samsuiluna 10	Party to settlement of his father's debt to ma-an-nu-um-me-šu-li-ṣur by transfer of a temple office: OECT 8 11 [no. 31]: 11, 18, seal.

son of (heir?) ^{d}nuska-á-maḫ

Ḫammurapi 31	Co-seller of temple office to a-ḫa-mar-ši: OECT 8 4 [no. 25]: 13, 26, seal.
Samsuiluna 8	Witness: Cornell 18 [no. 28]: 18.
Samsuiluna 23	Co-inheritor of house property and temple offices, with ma-an-nu-um-me-šu-li-ṣur, from ^{d}nuska-á-maḫ: Cornell 23: [no. 52]: 41, seal.

NI

Samsuiluna 6	Witness: Cornell 4 [no. 27]: rev. 14′.

NI

Samsuiluna 10	Recipient of house property from ma-an-nu-um-me-šu-li-ṣur in exchange for temple offices: OECT 8 16 [no. 30]: 10, seal.

mu-ni-ke-en-gi$_4$-šè (also written mu-ni-ke-en-gi-šè)

NI

Sin-iqišam 4	Neighbor (house property) of ^{d}nanna-me-ša$_4$: OECT 8 17 [no. 24]: 3 (dup. OECT 8 18 [no. 53]: 3).

na-bi-^{d}en-líl

son of en-na

Lipit-Enlil 5	Witness: OECT 8 20 [no. 23]: 27.

son of ì-lí-iš-na-di

Samsuiluna 11	Witness: Cornell 19 [no. 36]: rev. 2′ (partially restored).

father of ^{d}sin-ip-ṭù-ra-am

Ḫammurapi 33	PBS 13 67: 18.
Samsuiluna 13	OECT 8 7 [no. 50]: 21 (dup.? Cornell 16 [no. 48]: 21); PBS 8/2 182: 17.

na-ma-ar-šu-lu-mu-ur

son of i-bi-^{d}en-líl, brother of ^{d}nin-urta-mu-uš-ta-al and mu-na-wi-rum

Rim-Sin IIb	Co-inheritor of temple offices, with his brothers, from his father: OECT 8 19 [no. 29]: 14, seal.
Samsuiluna 10	Party to settlement of his father's debt to ma-an-nu-um-me-šu-li-ṣur by transfer of a temple office: OECT 8 11 [no. 31]: 10, 17, seal.

^{d}nanna-a-a

son of ^{d}sin-i-qí-ša-am, younger brother of i-bi-^{d}en-líl

Samsuiluna 6	Marriage to la-ma-súm and adoption of ma-an-nu-um-me-šu-li-ṣur, ^{d}nin-urta-mu-ba-al-lí-iṭ, ^{d}sin-ma-gir, and i-na-é-kur-ra-bi: Cornell 4 [no. 27]: 2, 13, 18, seal.
Samsuiluna x	Co-inheritor of house and field property and temple offices, with his brother, from his father and(?) ì-lí-a-wi-li, his father's brother, and ^{d}sin-še-mi: Cornell 6 [no. 26]: iii 6, 12, seal.

father of ^{d}nin-urta-ra-ḫi-im-zé-ri

Samsuiluna 12	Cornell 21 [no. 46]: 7.

^{d}nanna-a-rá-mu-un-ge-en (also written ^{d}nanna-a-ra-mu-un-ge-en)

son of ^{d}inanna-ma-an-sum, brother of ^{d}en-líl-lú-sa$_6$, ur-du$_6$-kù-ga, and ur-^{d}šul-pa-è-a

Samsuiluna 6	Co-inheritor, with his brothers, from his father: BE 6/2 26: ii 20′, iii 4, 11, 27, 29 (last two places partially restored), seal.
Samsuiluna 12	Witness: TIM 4 54 [no. 43]: 16.

^{d}nanna-ma-an-sum (cf. ^{d}nin-urta-ma-an-sum)

son of a-wi-il-ili(AN)

Sin-iqišam 4	Witness: OECT 8 17 [no. 24]: 50 (dup. OECT 8 18 [no. 53]: 48).

father of ^{d}nin-urta-ra-ḫi-im-ze-ri

Samsuiluna 11	SAOC 44 73: tablet rev. 7.
Samsuiluna 13	OECT 8 7 [no. 50]: 4, 6 (written ^{d}nanna-MIN), seal (dup.? Cornell 16 [no. 48]: 5, seal).

^{d}nanna-me-ša$_4$*

son of ur-^{d}lum-ma(?), older brother of ad-da-kal-la

Sin-iqišam 4	Division, with his brothers, of lú-^{d}ba-ú's share of ur-^{d}lum-ma's property: OECT 8 17 [no. 24]: 23, 25, 30, 31, 32 (partially restored), seal (dup. OECT 8 18 [no. 53]: 20, 23, 28, 30, 31, 43).

father of ^{d}nuska-á-maḫ and nin-kù-zu

Ḫammurapi 31	Giver of silver for house property to his daughter: OECT 8 4 [no. 25]: 2, 10, 17.

na-ra-am-^{d}adad

father of li-pí-it-ištar

Samsuiluna 12	Cornell 7 [no. 44]: 20.
Samsuiluna 27	PBS 8/2 146: 44.

na-ru-ub-tum

mother of i-din-ištar, wife of ma-an-nu-um-me-šu-li-ṣur

Samsuiluna 29	Co-seller of house property, with her son and husband's brother of ^{d}nin-urta-mu-ba-lí-iṭ, to ^{d}nin-urta-ra-ḫi-im-ze-ri-im who was redeeming it: BE 6/2 64 [no. 52]: 9, 16.

nì-gur$_{11}$-^{d}nanna

gudu$_4$, son of ^{d}en-líl-gú-gal

Sin-iqišam 4	Witness: OECT 8 17 [no. 24]: 49 (dup. OECT 8 18 [no. 53]: 47).

nin-du-ga

NI

Sin-iqišam 4	Neighbor (house property) of ad-da-kal-la: OECT 8 17 [no. 24]: 24 (dup. OECT 8 18 [no. 53]: 22).

nin-kù-zu

daughter of ^{d}nanna-me-ša$_4$, sister of ^{d}nuska-á-maḫ

Ḫammurapi 31	Recipient of gift of house property from her father: OECT 8 4 [no. 25]: 3, 18.

^{d}nin-šubur-ma-an-sum

NI

Samsuiluna 13	Seller, previously, of temple offices to ^{d}nin-urta-ma-an-sum: OECT 8 8 [no. 49]: 8a (case only; partially restored).

* See note on p. 96.

^{d}nin-urta-e-mu-qá-a-a

son of é-a-i-din-nam, brother of lugal-ḫé-gál

Samsuiluna 12	Co-seller of house property, with his brother, to ma-an-nu-um-me-šu-li-ṣur: BE 6/2 38 [no. 40]: 5, 8, 16 (restored), seal.
Samsuiluna 24	Co-seller of temple office, with a-at-ta-a and ^{d}nin-urta-ni-šu: PBS 13 66: 5 (collated).

^{d}nin-urta-ga-mil

dub-sar

Samsuiluna 6	Witness: PBS 8/2 132: 19.
Samsuiluna 11	Witness: OECT 8 6 [no. 34]: 21; PBS 8/2 131: rev. 13 (dup. BE 6/2 37: 21′).
Samsuiluna 12	Witness: OECT 8 5 [no. 39]: 24.
Samsuiluna 28	Witness: OIMA 1 32: 22; PBS 8/2 138: 23.

^{d}nin-urta-īriš(APIN)

son of ip-qá-tum

Samsuiluna 11	Seller of temple offices to ma-an-nu-um-me-šu-li-ṣur: Cornell 8 [no. 35]: 7, 8, 14, seal.
Samsuiluna 11	Witness: Cornell 19 [no. 36]: rev. 4′.

son of la-lu-ú-um and a-lí-a-bu-ša

Samsuiluna 11	Seller of temple offices: Cornell 19 [no. 36]: 9, 10 (partially restored), seal.

^{d}nin-urta-ma-an-sum (cf. ^{d}nanna-ma-an-sum)

son of ta-ri-bu-um

Rim-Sin IIb	Witness: OECT 8 19 [no. 29]: 22.
Samsuiluna 10	Witness: OECT 8 11 [no. 31]: 24.
Samsuiluna 12	Seller of temple office to ^{d}nin-urta-ra-ḫi-im-zé-ri: Cornell 21 [no. 46]: 4 (partially restored), 5, 12 (partially restored), seal.
Samsuiluna 12	Witness: SAOC 44 79: tablet rev. 9, case rev. 9′.
Samsuiluna 13	Seller of temple office to ma-an-nu-um-me-šu-li-ṣur: OECT 8 8 [no. 49]: 7, 8a (case only), 9, 14, seal.

father of da-mi-iq-ì-lí-šu (also written dam-qí-ì-lí-šu)

Samsuiluna 11	SAOC 44 77: 4′ (partially restored).
Samsuiluna 13	Cornell 16 [no. 48]: 23 (dup.? OECT 8 7 omits).

father of ^{d}nin-urta-ra-ḫi-im-ze-ri-im

Samsuiluna 13	BE 6/2 40: 28.
Samsuiluna 29	BE 6/2 64 [no. 52]: 3, 11.

Ili-man-AN 2	BE 6/2 68: 10.
n.d.	OIMA 1 45: obv. 6′.

šagin

Samsuiluna x	Witness: Cornell 6 [no. 26]: iv 7 (partially restored).

ugula-⟨dag⟩ (or, ⟨gá⟩)-gi_4-a

Samsuiluna x	Witness: Cornell 6 [no. 26]: iv 2.

^{d}nin-urta-mu-ba-lí-iṭ (also written ^{d}nin-urta-mu-ba-al-lí-iṭ)

son of a-wi-li-ia, brother of ma-an-nu-um-me-šu-li-ṣur

Samsuiluna 6	Adoption by ^{d}nanna-a-a to whom support was promised: Cornell 4 [no. 27]: 5, 15, rev. 5′, seal.
Samsuiluna 11	Adoption by ì-lí-ip-pa-al-sà-am and el-me-šum to whom silver was given: OECT 8 21 [no. 32]: 3, 6, 8, 18.
Samsuiluna 29	Co-seller of house property, with his brother's son and wife, to ^{d}nin-urta-ra-ḫi-im-ze-ri-im who was redeeming it: BE 6/2 64 [no. 52]: 7, 15, seal.

^{d}nin-urta-mu-ša-lim

son of a-gu-ú-a, brother of ^{d}en-líl-gal-zu

Ḫammurapi 31	Witness: OECT 8 4 [no. 25]: 33.

father of ^{d}nuska-ni-šu and ì-lí-ip-pa-al-sà-am

Samsuiluna 8	Cornell 18 [no. 28]: 17.
Samsuiluna 11	Cornell 12 [no. 33]: 23; OECT 8 21 [no. 32]: 27.
Samsuiluna 12	OECT 8 1 [no. 42]: 19; OECT 8 9 [no. 41]: 20.
Samsuiluna 13	BE 6/2 41: 3, 6, 7, 20 (partially restored), seal.

^{d}nin-urta-mu-uš-ta-al

son of i-bi-^{d}en-líl, brother of na-ma-ar-šu-lu-mu-ur and mu-na-wi-rum

Rim-Sin IIb	Co-inheritor of temple offices, with his brothers, from his father; recipient of preferential portion: OECT 8 19 [no. 29]: 8, seal.
Samsuiluna 10	Party to settlement of his father's debt to ma-an-nu-um-me-šu-li-ṣur by transfer of a temple office: OECT 8 11 [no. 31]: 9, 16, seal.
Samsuiluna 11	Seller of temple offices to ma-an-nu-um-me-šu-li-ṣur (mostly restored): Cornell 12 [no. 33]: 8 (partially restored), 9 (mostly restored), 15, seal.

son of ^{d}sin-ma-gir

Samsuiluna 11	Witness: Cornell 12 [no. 33]: 24.

father of in-bi-ì-lí-šu, husband of la-ma-sà-tum

Samsuiluna 11	Cornell 20 [no. 37]: 2′, seal.

^{d}nin-urta-ni-šu

son of ma-ri-er-ṣe-tim and ri-ba-tum, grandson of šeš-du$_{10}$-ga, brother(?) of ^{d}utu-^{d}en-líl-lá and li-pí-it-^{d}en-líl

Samsuiluna 12	Co-seller of his father's temple offices, with his brothers and mother, to ma-an-nu-um-me-šu-li-ṣur: OECT 8 10 [no. 45]: 10, 19, seal.

dub-sar

Rim-Sin 42	Witness: TIM 4 1: 100.
Samsuiluna 11	Witness: Cornell 12 [no. 33]: 26.
Samsuiluna 12	Witness: OECT 8 1 [no. 42]: 22.

^{d}nin-urta-ra-ḫi-im-ze-ri-im (also written ^{d}nin-urta-ra-ḫi-im-zé-ri-im and ^{d}nin-urta-ra-ḫi-im-zé-ri)

son of ^{d}nanna-a-a

Samsuiluna 12	Buyer of temple offices from ^{d}nin-urta-ma-an-sum: Cornell 21 [no. 46]: 6.

son of ^{d}nanna-ma-an-sum (= ^{d}nin-urta-ma-an-sum?)

Samsuiluna 11	Witness: SAOC 44 73: tablet rev. 6.
Samsuiluna 13	Seller of temple office to ma-an-nu-um-me-šu-li-ṣur: OECT 8 7 [no. 50]: 3, 5, 13, seal (dup.$^{?}$ Cornell 16 [no. 48]: 4, 6, 13, seal).

son of ^{d}nin-urta-ma-an-sum (= ^{d}nanna-ma-an-sum?)

Samsuiluna 13	Witness: BE 6/2 40: 28.
Samsuiluna 20	Witness: BE 6/2 52: 25.
Samsuiluna 29	Buyer of neighboring house lot which he redeemed from the brother, wife, and son of ma-an-nu-um-me-šu-li-ṣur: BE 6/2 64 [no. 52]: 2, 10.
Ili-man-AN 2	Buyer of field property from ^{d}utu-an-dùl and i-da-tum: BE 6/2 68: 9.
n.d.	Buyer of field property from two brothers in exchange for temple offices: OIMA 1 45: 5′.
n.d.	Redeemer of offices from the temple of ^{d}en-ki and ^{d}dam-gal-nun-na which had previously been purchased from ^{d}en-iki-mas-sú: BE 6/2 66: 8.

nu-ra-bi (see next entry)

nu-ra-tum

gudu$_4$ ^{d}nin-líl-lá, son of lú-^{d}nin-urta

Samsuiluna 10	Witness: OECT 8 16 [no. 30]: 18 (read nu-ra-tum$^{!}$ for nu-ra-bi).
Samsuiluna 12	Witness: SAOC 44 78: tablet rev. 4′, case rev. 5; SAOC 44 79: tablet rev. 7, case rev. 7′.

Samsuiluna 13	Witness: BE 6/2 42: 18.
n.d.	Witness: OIMA 1 39: rev. 3; SAOC 44 87: rev. 6′ (DN after PfN lost in both instances).

NI

Samsuiluna 23	Witness: Cornell 23: [no. 52]: 45.

^{d}nuska-á-maḫ

son of ^{d}nanna-me-ša$_4$, brother of nin-kù-zu; a-wi-li-ia and mu-na-wi-ru are his heirs.

Ḫammurapi 31	Recipient of payment from a-ḫa-mar-ši, ip-qú-er-ṣe-tim, i-na-ša-me-e-wu-súm, and ^{d}nuska-á-maḫ: OECT 8 4 [no. 25]: 10, 14, seal.
Samsuiluna 8	Cornell 18 [no. 28]: 18.
Samsuiluna 23	Partition of his estate of house property and temple offices by ma-an-nu-um-me-šu-li-ṣur and mu-na-wi-rum: Cornell 23: [no. 52]: 42, seal (both partially restored).

NI

Ḫammurapi 31	Co-payee of silver as šà-mul to ^{d}nuska-á-maḫ: OECT 8 4 [no. 25]: 9.

^{d}nuska-ni-šu

son of ^{d}nin-urta-mu-ša-lim, brother of ì-lí-ip-pa-al-sà-am, father of a-píl-ì-lí-šu

Samsuiluna 8	Witness: Cornell 18 [no. 28]: 17.
Samsuiluna 11	Witness: Cornell 12 [no. 33]: 23; OECT 8 21 [no. 32]: 27.
Samsuiluna 12	Witness: OECT 8 1 [no. 42]: 19; OECT 8 9 [no. 41]: 20.
Samsuiluna 13	Seller of house property, purchased previously from ḫi-du-tum and mu-tum-ilum, to lú-^{d}nanna: BE 6/2 41: 3, 6, 7, 13, 22, seal.

dub-sar

Samsuiluna 6	Witness: Cornell 4 [no. 27]: rev. 18′.
Rim-Sin IIb	Witness: OECT 8 19 [no. 29]: 26.
Samsuiluna 10	Witness: OECT 8 11 [no. 31]: 27; OECT 8 16 [no. 30]: 22.
Samsuiluna 18	Witness: SAOC 44 47: tablet rev. 8.
Samsuiluna 23	Witness: Cornell 23: [no. 52]: 47 (PfN restored with reasonable certainty.

NI

Samsuiluna 6	Witness: Cornell 4 [no. 27]: rev. 15′.

^{d}pa-bíl-sag-ma-an-sum

dub-sar

Samsuiluna 11	Witness: Cornell 19 [no. 36]: rev. 5′.

ri-ba-tum

wife of ma-ri-er-ṣe-tim, mother of ^{d}nin-urta-ni-šu and(?) ^{d}utu-^{d}en-líl-lá and li-pí-it-^{d}en-líl

Samsuiluna 12	Co-seller of her husband's temple offices, with her sons, to ma-an-nu-um-me-šu-li-ṣur: OECT 8 10 [no. 45]: 11, seal.

ri-im-tum

daughter of a-ḫa-mar-ši and a-lí-a-ḫu-ú-a

Samsuiluna 12	Co-seller of house property, with her mother, to ma-an-nu-um-me-šu-li-ṣur: OECT 8 1 [no. 42]: 4, 6, 13 (restored), seal.

ri-iš-é-a

son of ^{d}sin-na-tum (also written sí-na-tum)

Samsuiluna 11	Witness: Cornell 20 [no. 37]: 19′; OECT 8 6 [no. 34]: 19.
Samsuiluna 12	Neighbor (house property) of ma-an-nu-um-me-šu-li-ṣur: OECT 8 1 [no. 42]: 3.

sí-ia-tum

father of a-ḫa-mar-ši

Ḫammurapi 31	OECT 8 4 [no. 25]: 6

^{d}sin-a-ḫu-um

son of mar-er-ṣe-tim

Samsuiluna 29	Witness: BE 6/2 64 [no. 52]: 23.

^{d}sin-be-lí

dub-sar, father of [ ]-nu

Samsuiluna 11	Cornell 8 [no. 35]: 21.

^{d}sin-e-ri-ba-am

NI

Samsuiluna 12	Witness: Cornell 21 [no. 46]: 19.

^{d}sin-ip-ṭù-ra-am

gudu$_4$, son of na-bi-^{d}en-líl

Ḫammurapi 33	Witness: PBS 13 67: 17.
Samsuiluna 13	Witness: OECT 8 7 [no. 50]: 20 (dup.? Cornell 16 [no. 48]: 20); PBS 8/2 182: 16.

NI

Samsuiluna 12	Witness: Cornell 21 [no. 46]: 20.

^{d}sin-i-qí-ša-am (also written ^{d}sin-i-qí-šam)

father of i-bi-^{d}en-líl and ^{d}nanna-a-a, brother of ì-lí-a-wi-li

Samsuiluna 6	Cornell 4 [no. 27]: 2.
Samsuiluna 8	Cornell 18 [no. 28]: 4, seal.
Samsuiluna x	Partition of his estate by his sons, brother, and ^{d}sin-še-mi: Cornell 6 [no. 26]: iii 7, seal.

father of ^{d}sin-ma-gir

Samsuiluna x	Cornell 6 [no. 26]: iv 5.

^{d}sin-li-di-iš

son of ì-lí-i-din-nam

Samsuiluna 12	Seller of temple office to ma-an-nu-um-me-šu-li-ṣur: OECT 8 9 [no. 41]: 4, 6, 12, seal.

son of lú-si-gar

Sin-iqišam 4	Witness: OECT 8 18 [no. 53]: 50 (dup. OECT 8 17 [no. 24]: 52 omits dumu).

^{d}sin-ma-gir

son of arad-^{d}nanna

Samsuiluna 29	Witness: BE 6/2 64 [no. 52]: 22.

son of ^{d}sin-i-qí-šam

Samsuiluna x	Witness: Cornell 6 [no. 26]: iv 4.

father of i-da-tum

Samsuiluna 11	Cornell 19 [no. 36]: rev. 3′.

father of ì-lí-ip-pa-al-sà-am

Samsuiluna 11	OECT 8 6 [no. 34]: 4, 5, seal; OECT 8 21 [no. 32]: 1, seal.

father of lu-mur-ša-^{d}šamaš and ì-lí-e-ri-ba-am

Samsuiluna 12	OECT 8 5 [no. 39]: 5, 7, 14, seal.

father of ^{d}nin-urta-mu-uš-ta-al

Samsuiluna 11	Cornell 12 [no. 33]: 25.

NI

Samsuiluna 6	Adoption by ^{d}nanna-a-a to whom support was promised: Cornell 4 [no. 27]: 6, 16, rev. 6′, seal.

NI

Samsuiluna 6	Witness: Cornell 4 [no. 27]: rev. 13′.

^{d}sin-na-tum (also written sí-na-tum)

father of ri-iš-é-a

Samsuiluna 11	Cornell 20 [no. 37]: 19′; OECT 8 6 [no. 34]: 19.
Samsuiluna 12	OECT 8 1 [no. 42]: 3.

^{d}sin-še-mi

NI

Samsuiluna 6 — Witness: Cornell 4 [no. 27]: rev. 16′.

NI

Samsuiluna x — His inheritance is divided by i-bi-^{d}en-líl and ^{d}nanna-a-a(?): Cornell 6 [no. 26]: iii 18.

šeš-du$_{10}$-ga

father of ma-ri-er-ṣe-tim, grandfather of ^{d}nin-urta-ni-šu and(?) ^{d}utu-^{d}en-líl-lá and li-pí-it-^{d}en-líl

Samsuiluna 12 — OECT 8 10 [no. 45]: 7.

ta-ri-ba-tum

son of ma-ri-er-ṣe-tim

Rim-Sin IIb — Witness: OECT 8 19 [no. 29]: 23.

son of u-bar-^{d}šamaš

Samsuiluna 12 — Witness: Cornell 7 [no. 44]: 19.

bur-gul

Rim-Sin 45 — Witness: TIM 4 26: 20.

Rim-Sin 48 — Witness: PBS 8/1 44: 24.

Rim-Sin 53 — Witness: *ARN* 41: 27.

Ḫammurapi 30 — Witness: *ARN* 65 [no. 8]: 43.

Ḫammurapi 31 — Witness: OECT 8 4 [no. 25]: 37.

ta-ri-bu-um

father of ^{d}nin-urta-ma-an-sum

Rim-Sin IIb — OECT 8 19 [no. 29]: 22.

Samsuiluna 10 — OECT 8 11 [no. 31]: 24.

Samsuiluna 12 — Cornell 21 [no. 46]: 5 (restored), 13 (partially restored), seal; SAOC 44 79: tablet rev. 9, case rev. 9′.

Samsuiluna 13 — OECT 8 8 [no. 49]: 8, seal.

u-bar-ru-um

gala

Ḫammurapi 31 — Witness: OECT 8 4 [no. 25]: 35.

NI

Samsuiluna 8 — Neighbor (house property) of ma-an-nu-um-me-šu-li-ṣur: Cornell 18 [no. 28]: 2.

NI

Samsuiluna x — His sons were neighbors (house property) of i-bi-^{d}en-líl: Cornell 6 [no. 26]: i 12.

u-bar-^{d}šamaš
father of ta-ri-ba-tum

Samsuiluna 12	Cornell 7 [no. 44]: 19.

ur-du$_6$-kù-ga
father of lú-nibru^{ki}

Samsuiluna 8	Cornell 18 [no. 28]: 19.

ur-^{d}lum-ma*
son of lú-^{d}inanna, father(?) of ^{d}nanna-me-ša$_4$ and ad-da-kal-la

Lipit-Enlil 5	Adopter of lú-^{d}ba-ú: OECT 8 20 [no. 23]: 1, 15, 17, seal.
Sin-iqišam 4	Partition of lú-^{d}ba-ú's share of his estate by ^{d}nanna-me-ša$_4$ and ad-da-kal-la: OECT 8 17 [no. 24]: 19, 41 (dup. OECT 8 18 [no. 53]: 16, 38).

ur-^{d}sa-dàr-nun-na
dub-sar

Lipit-Enlil 5	Witness: OECT 8 20 [no. 23]: 29.

^{d}utu-^{d}en-líl-lá
son(?) of ma-ri-er-ṣe-tim and ri-ba-tum, grandson(?) of šeš-du$_{10}$-ga, brother(?) of li-pí-it-^{d}en-líl and ^{d}nin-urta-ni-šu

Samsuiluna 12	Co-seller of his father's temple offices, with his brothers and mother, to ma-an-nu-um-me-šu-li-ṣur: OECT 8 10 [no. 45]: 8, 17, seal.

^{d}utu-ḫé-gál
father of lú-ì-si-in^{ki}-na

Lipit-Enlil 5	OECT 8 20 [no. 23]: 26.

warad-ištar
son of la-a-lum

Samsuiluna 12	Seller of temple offices to ma-an-nu-um-me-šu-li-ṣur: Cornell 7 [no. 44]: 7, 8, 14 (restored), seal.

wa-ru-ru-tum
NI

Sin-iqišam 4	Owner of orchard: OECT 8 17 [no. 24]: 19, 41 (dup. OECT 8 18 [no. 53]: 16, 38).

* See note on p. 96.

[ ]-e-ri-ba-am
son of i-[ ]
Samsuiluna 11 Witness: Cornell 19 [no. 36]: rev. 1′.

[ ]-na-tum
father of ḫu-pil-[ ]
Samsuiluna 11 OECT 8 21 [no. 32]: 29.

[ ]-nu
son of ^{d}sin-ba-lí dub-sar
Samsuiluna 11 Witness: Cornell 8 [no. 35]: 21.

Copies of Cornell Texts in the Mannum-mešu-liṣṣur Archive

Cornell 4 (no. 27)

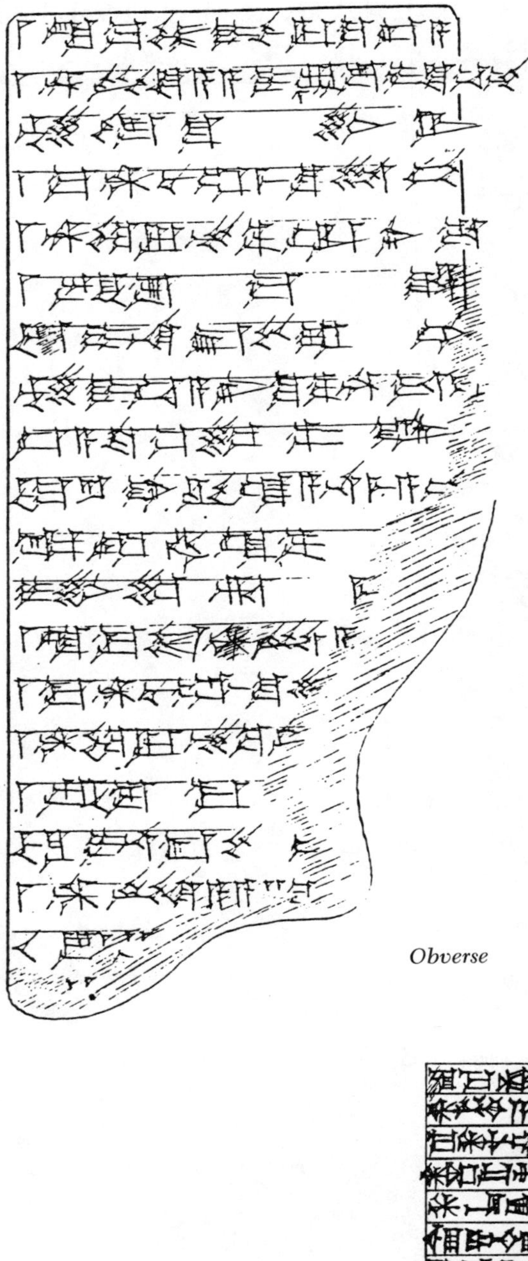

Obverse

SEAL COPY: D. I. OWEN

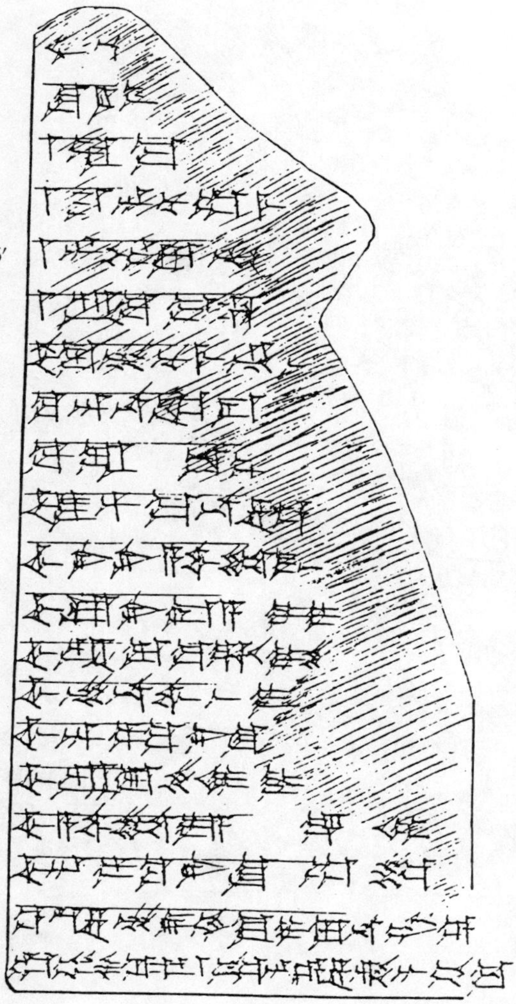

COPY: A. GOETZE

Reverse

Cornell 6 (no. 26)

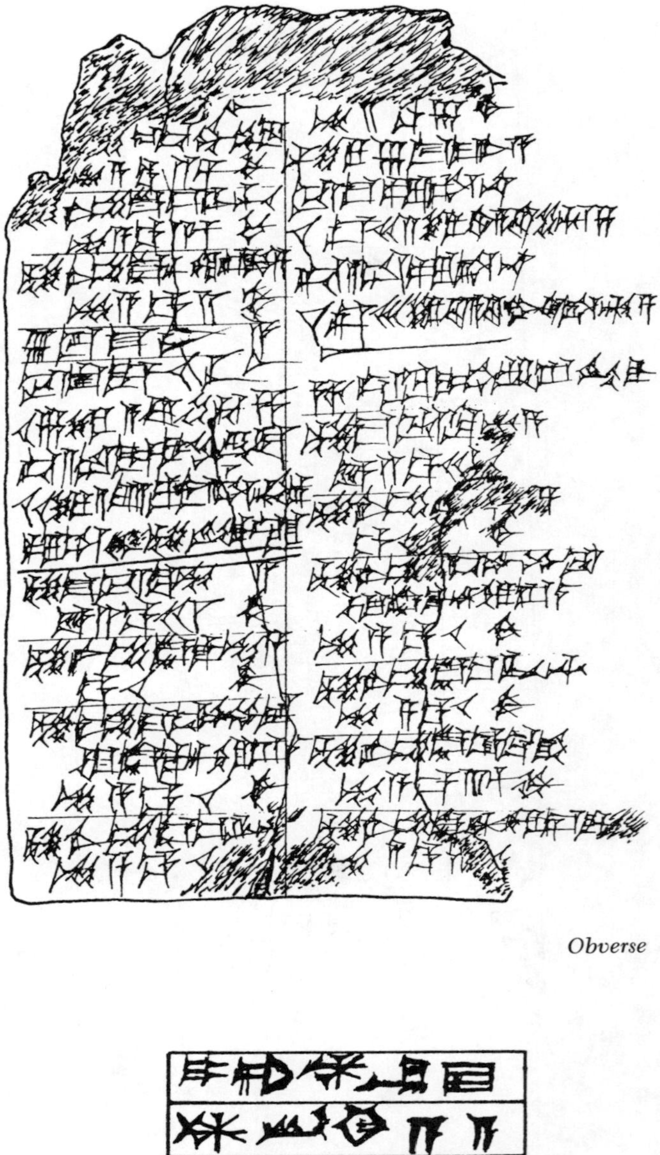

Obverse

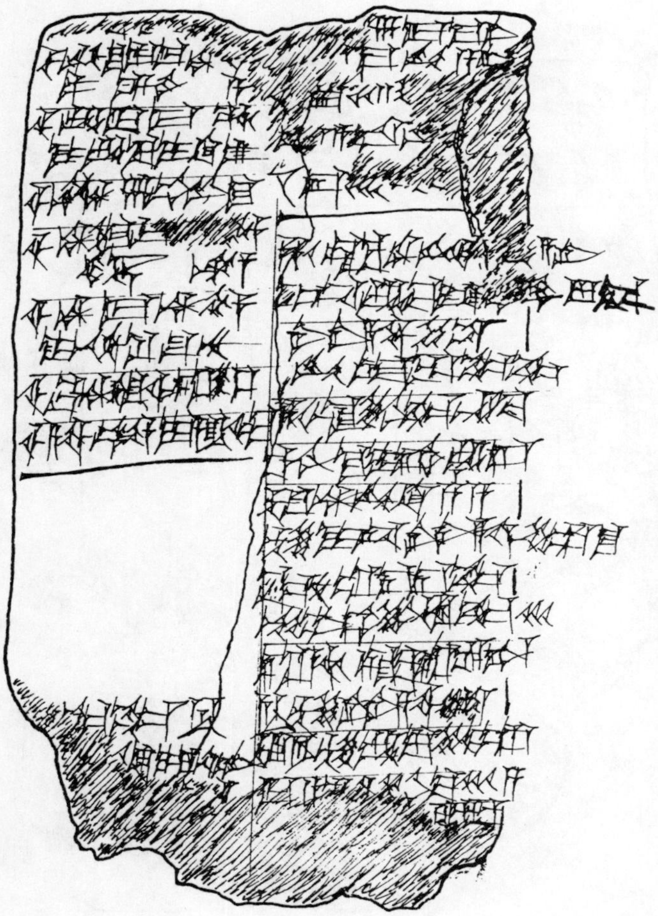

Reverse

Cornell 7 (no. 44)

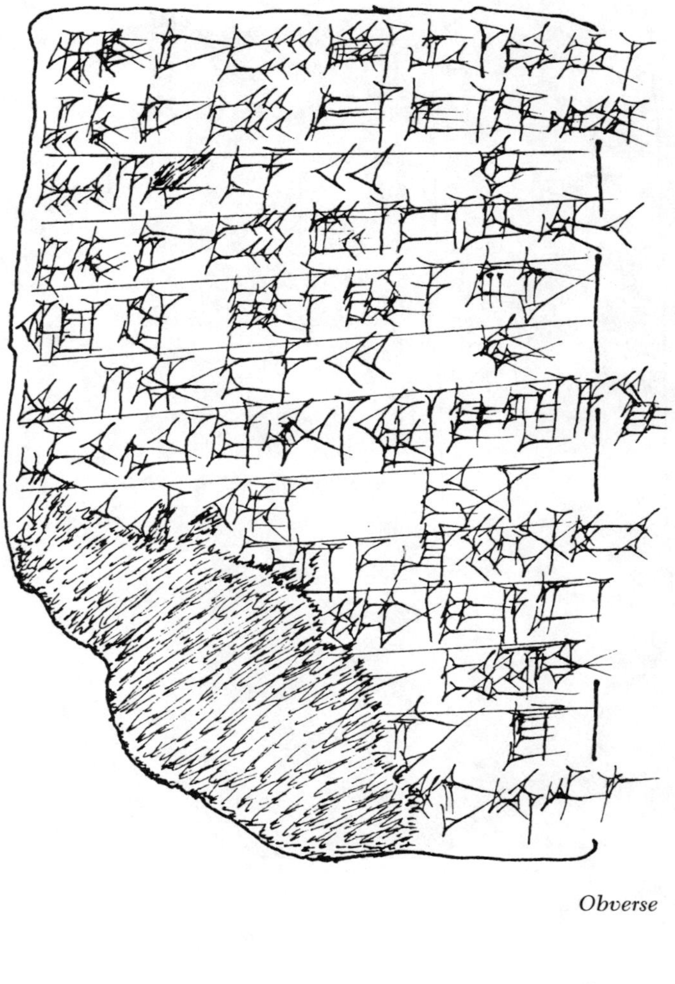

Obverse

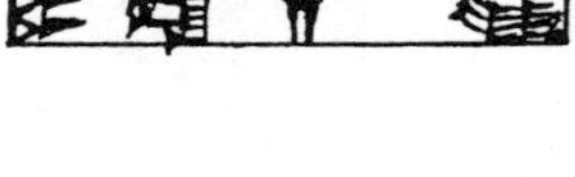

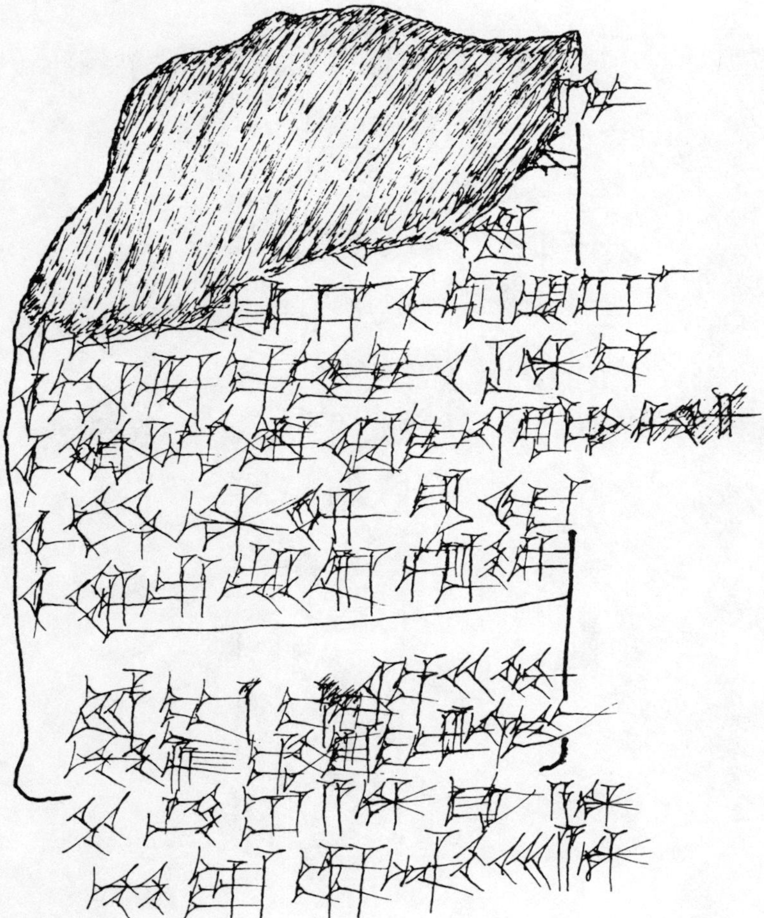

Reverse

Cornell 8 (no. 35)

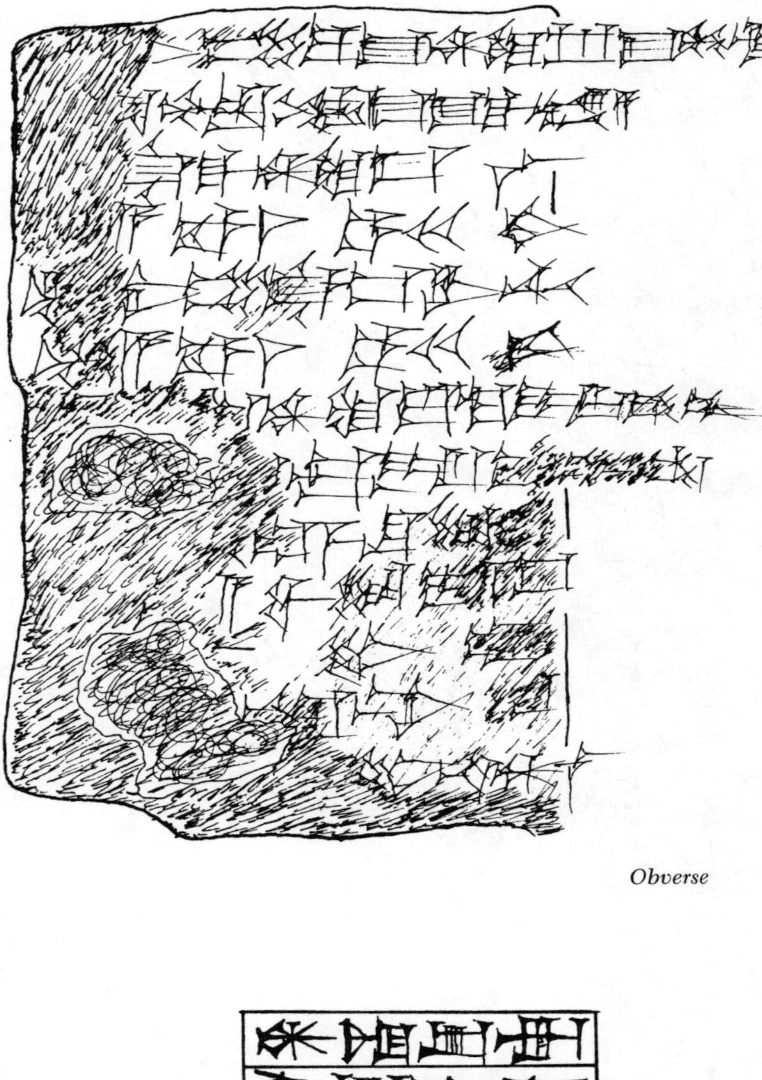

Obverse

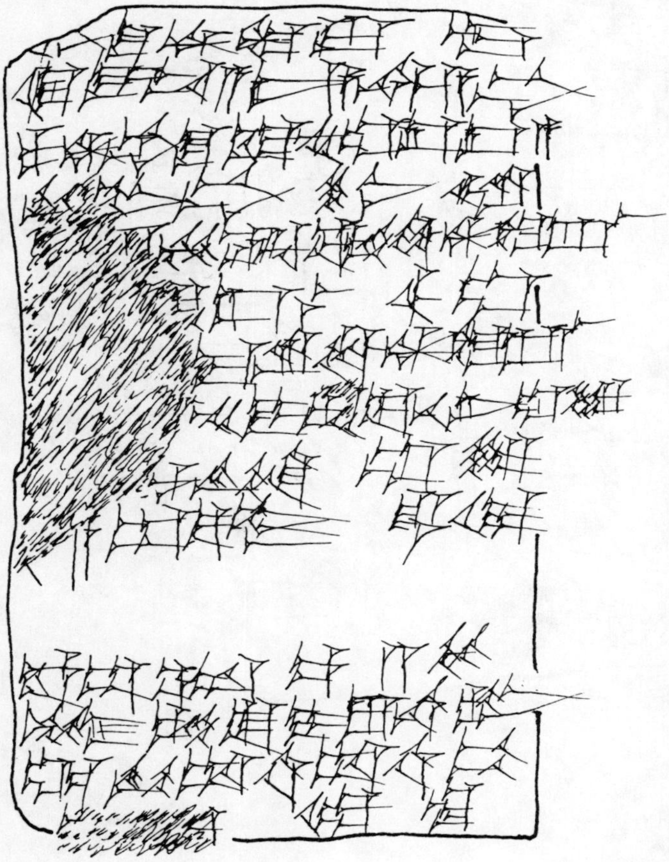

Reverse

Cornell 11 (no. 47)

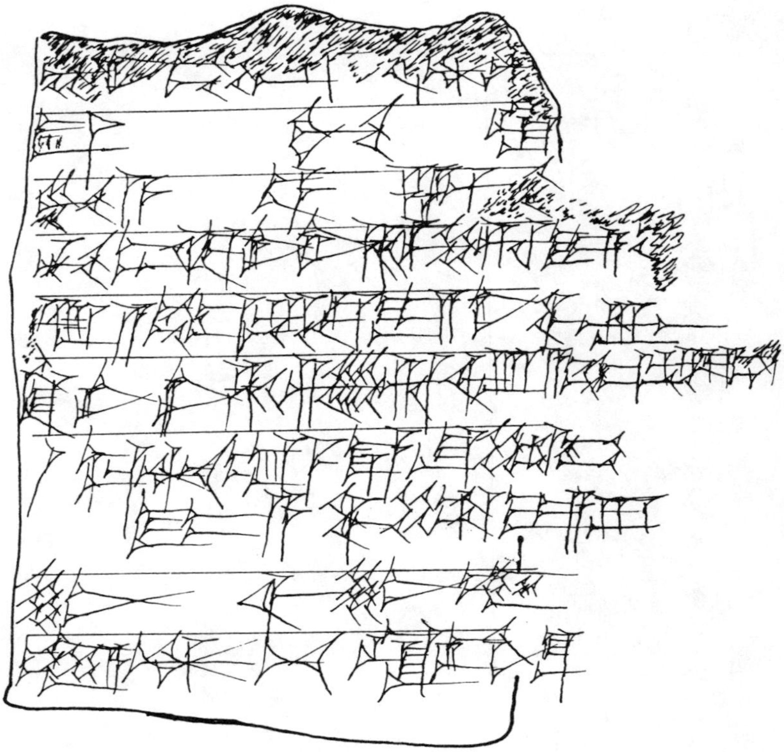

Obverse

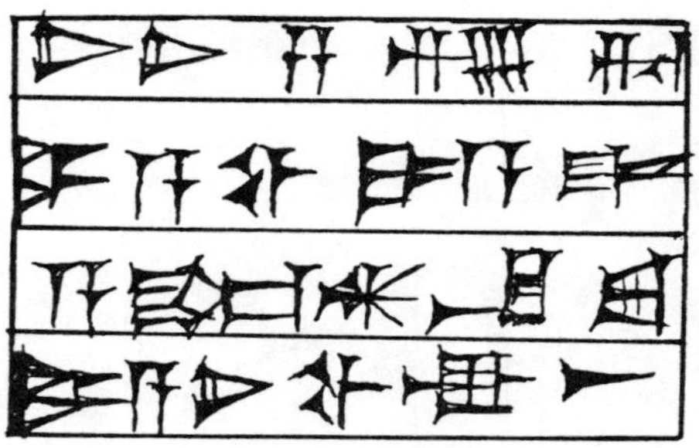

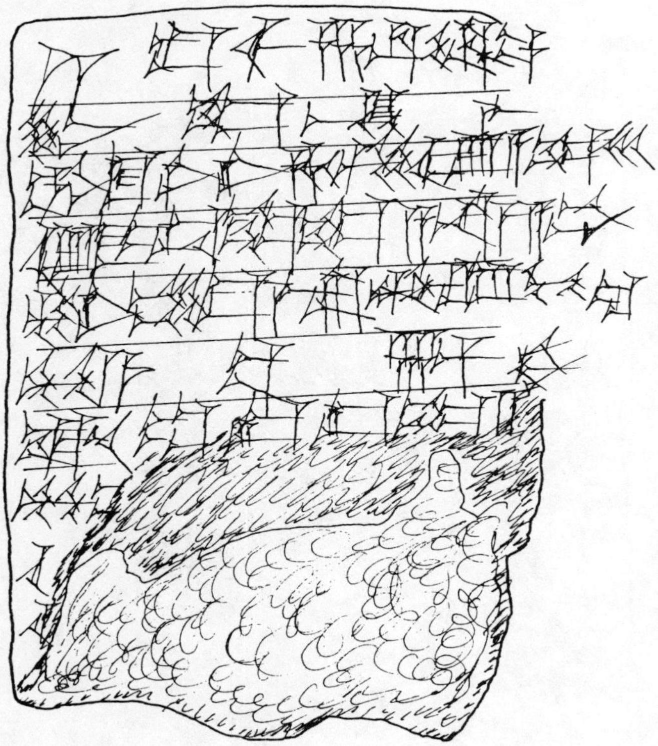

Reverse

Cornell 12 (no. 33)

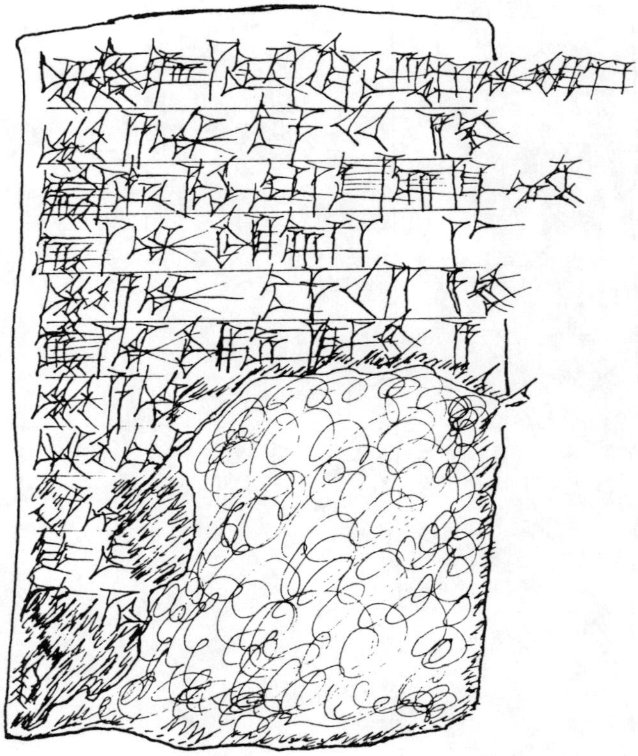

Obverse

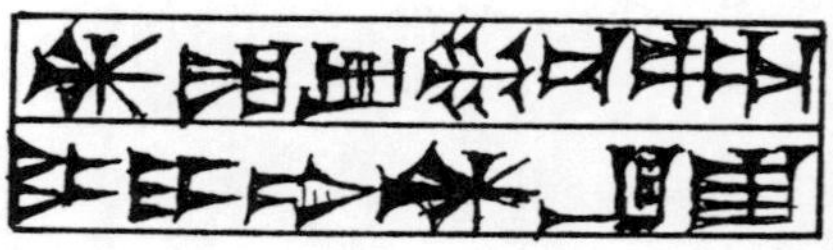

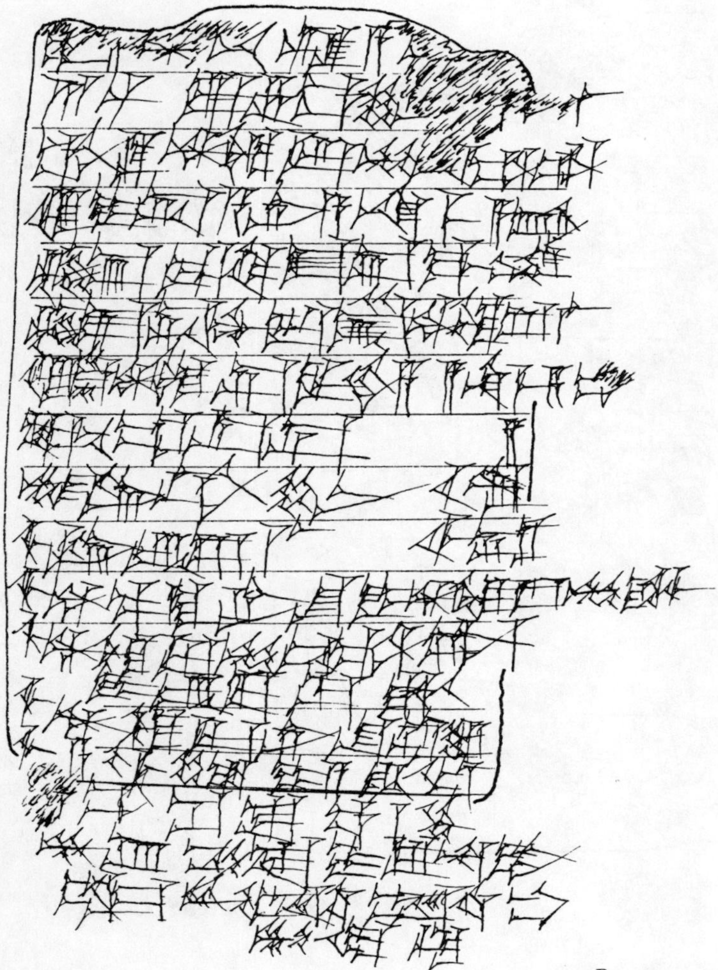

Reverse

Cornell 16 (no. 48)

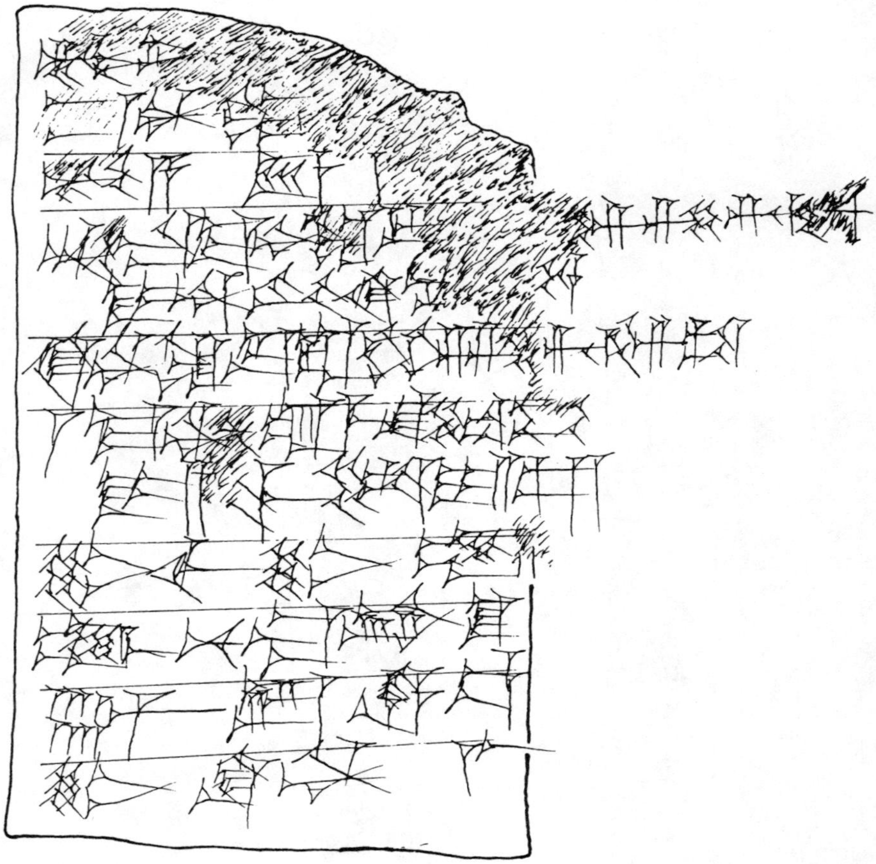

Obverse

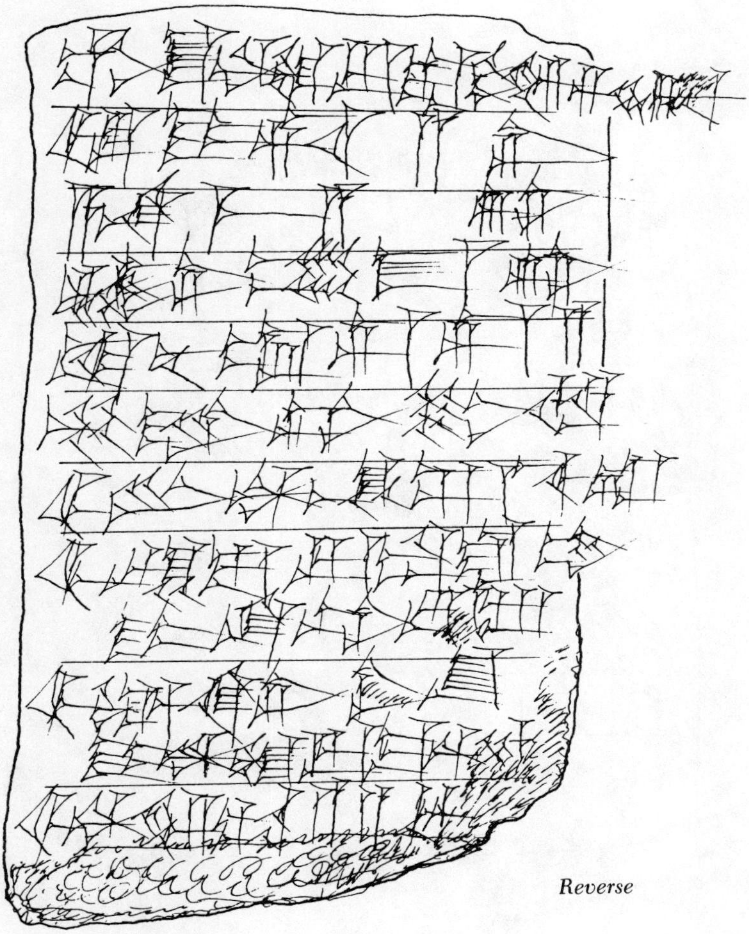

Reverse

Cornell 18 (no. 28)

Obverse

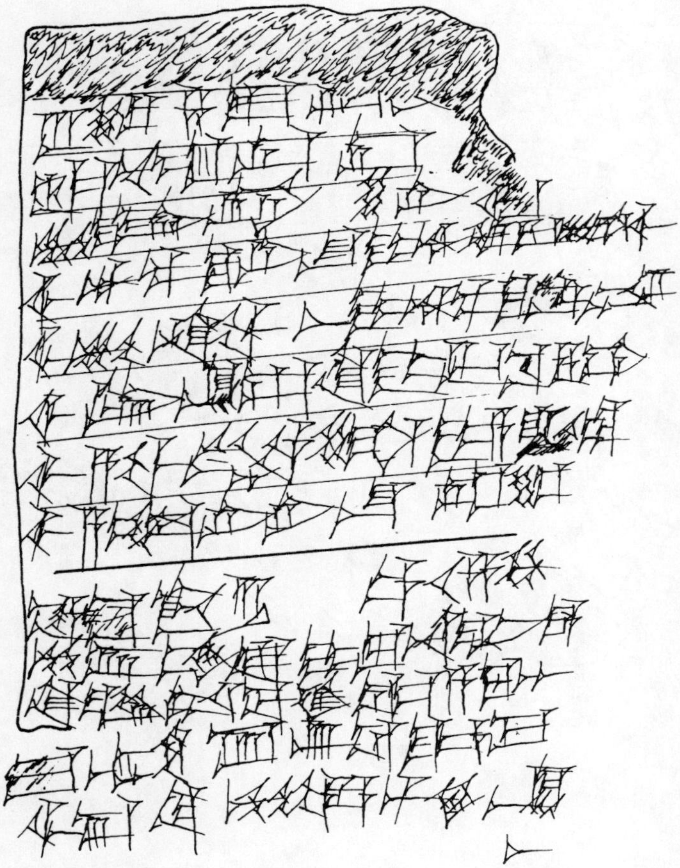

Reverse

Cornell 19 (no. 36)

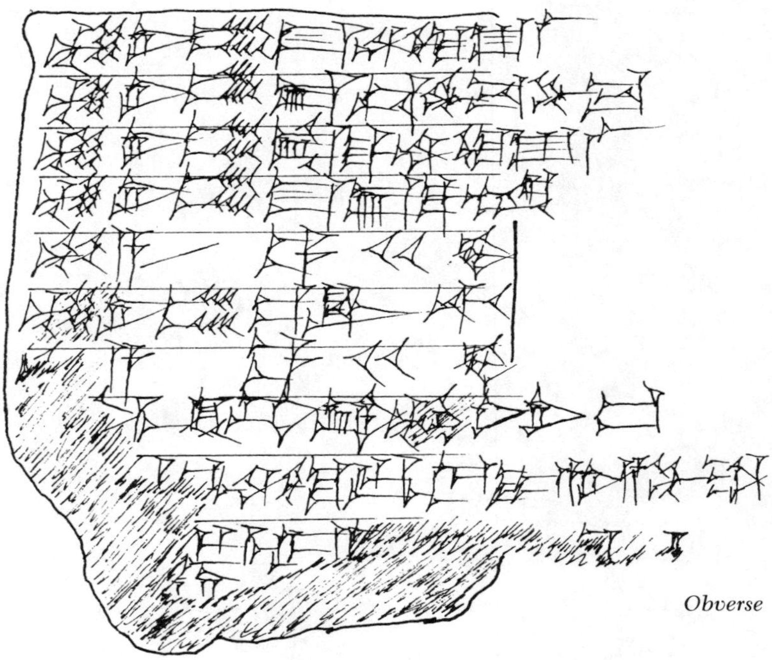

Obverse

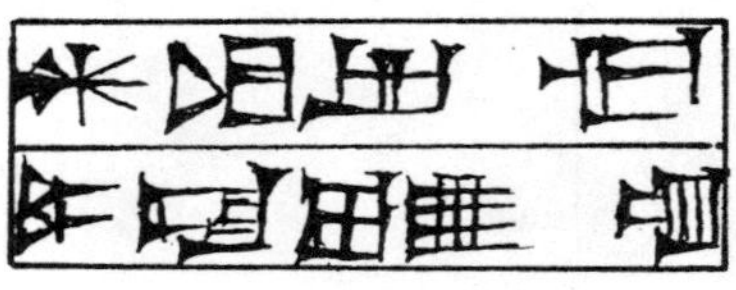

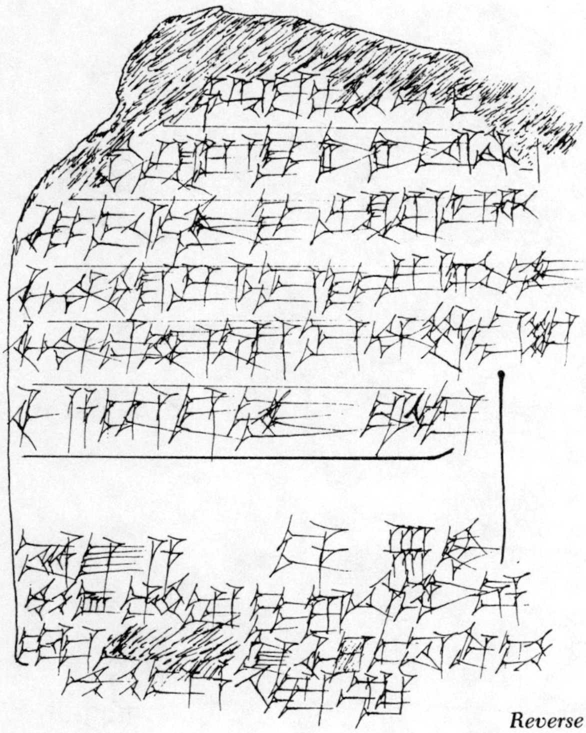

Reverse

Cornell 20 (no. 37)

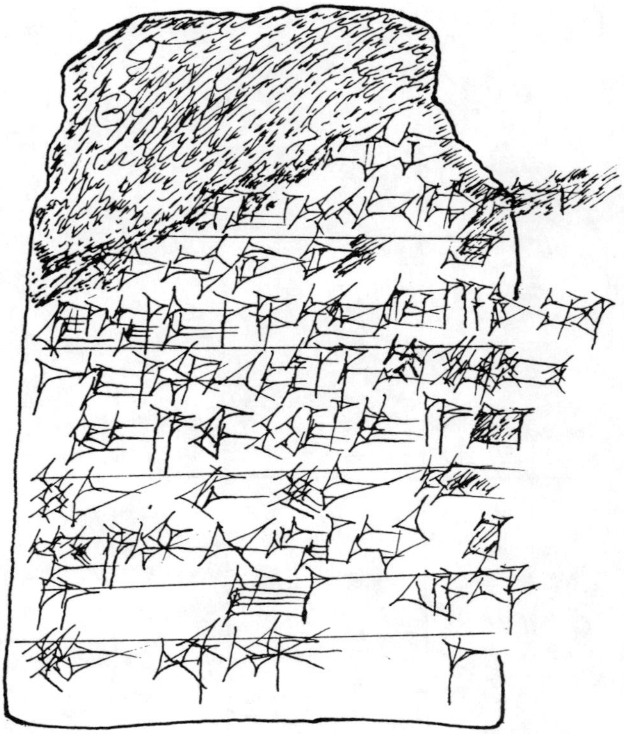

Obverse

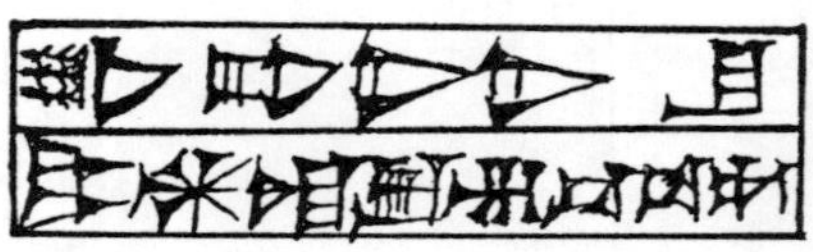

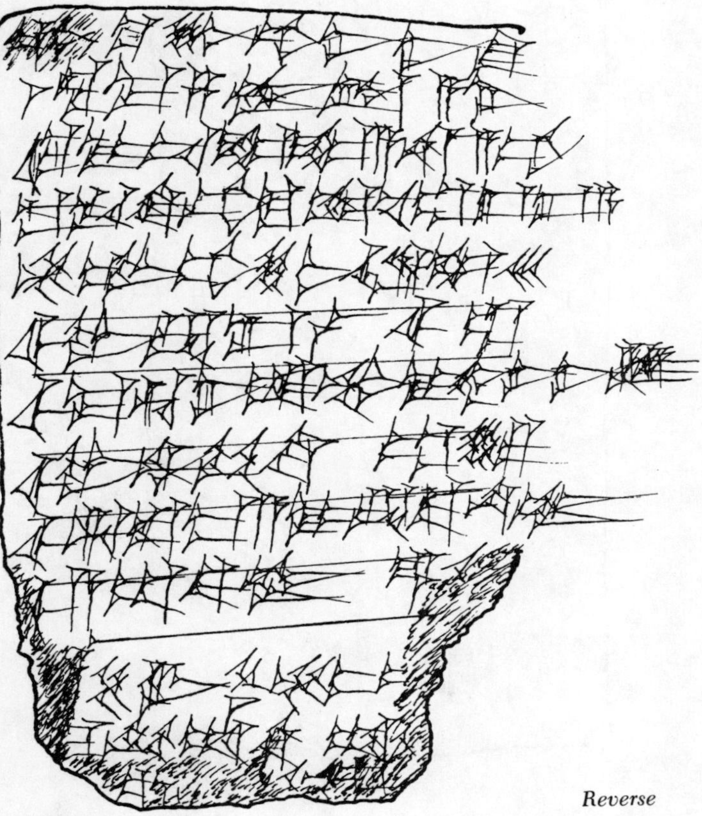

Reverse

Cornell 21 (no. 46)

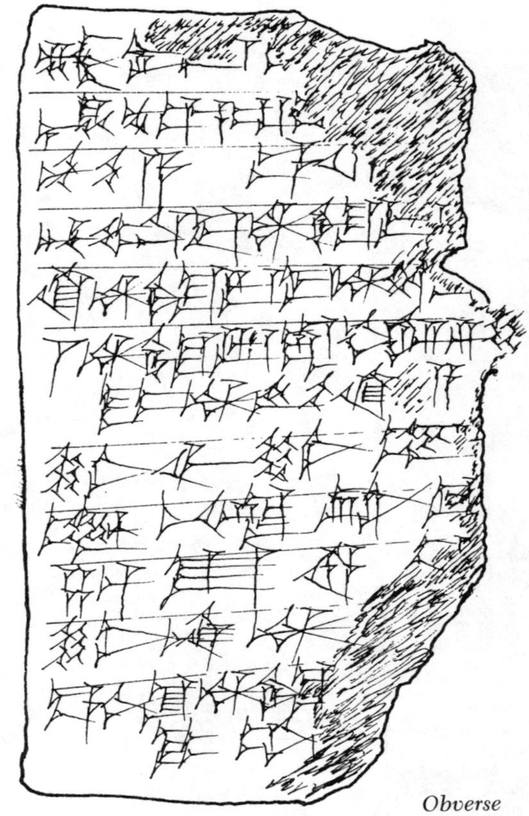

Obverse

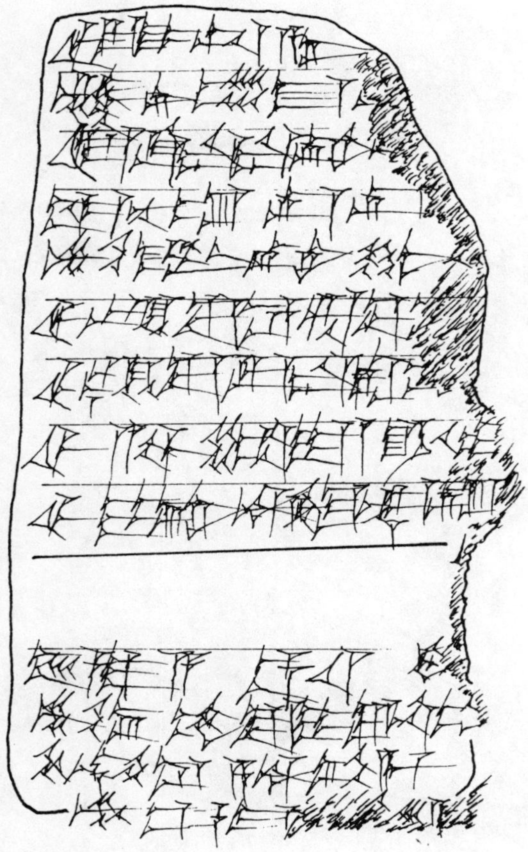

Reverse

Cornell 23 (no. 51)

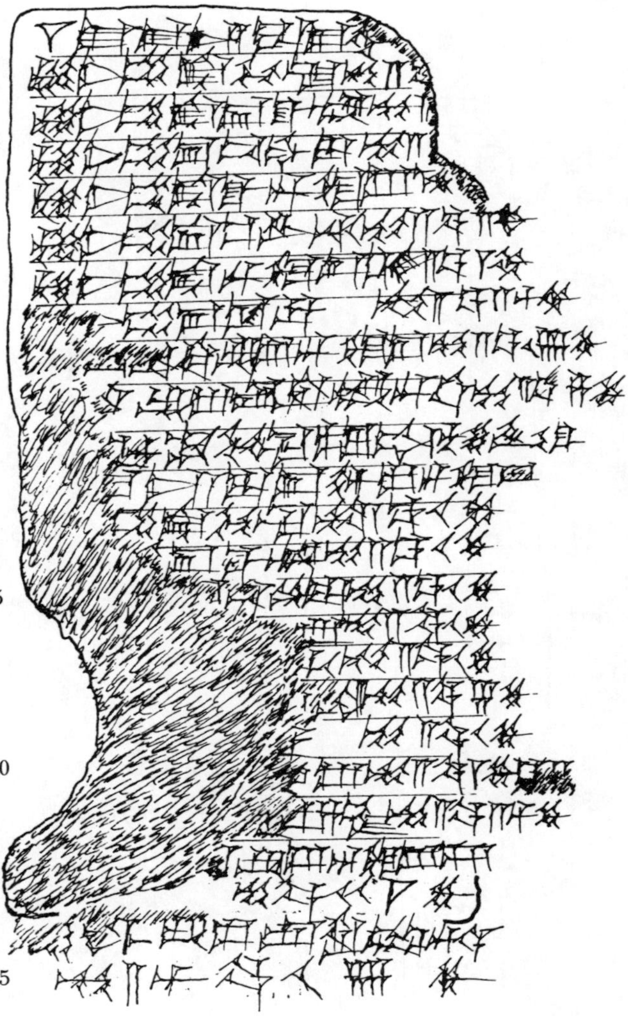

Obverse

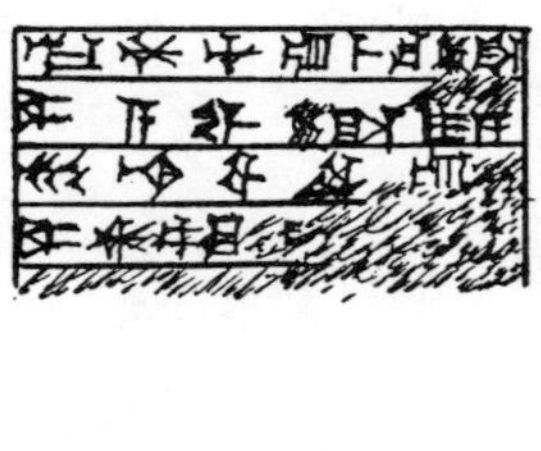

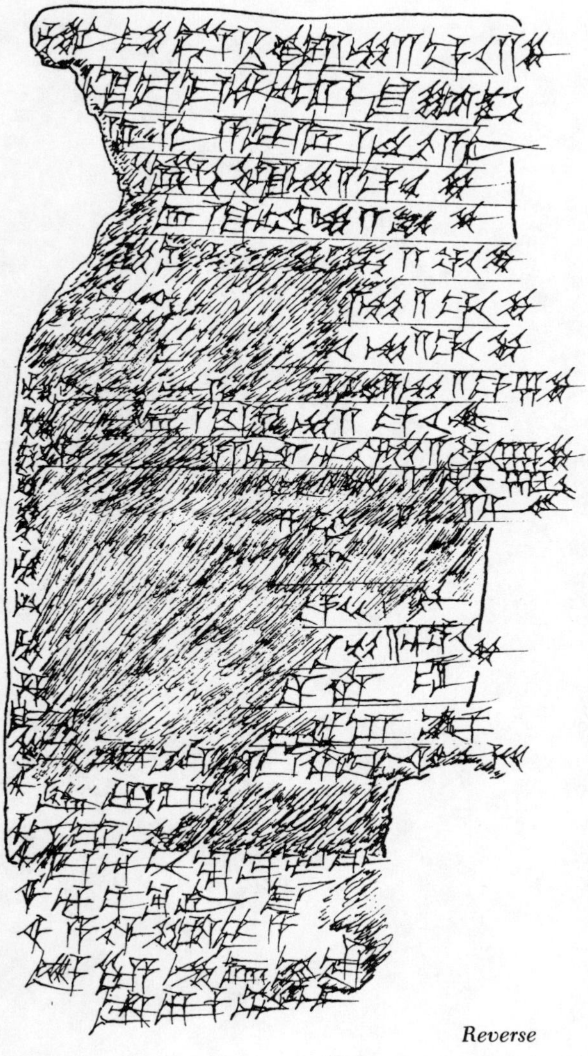

Reverse

Obverse

Right Edge

Upper Edge

Cornell 4 (no. 27)

Left Edge

Reverse

Cornell 4 (no. 27)

Obverse

Right Edge

Cornell 6 (no. 26)

Reverse

Right Edge

Cornell 6 (no. 26)

Left Edge

Lower Edge

Cornell 6 (no. 26)

Obverse

Right Edge

Lower Edge

Cornell 7 (no. 44)

Reverse

Right Edge

Lower Edge

Cornell 7 (no. 44)

Plate 8

Reverse

Right Edge

Cornell 7 (no. 44)

Case/envelope

Obverse

Right Edge

Cornell 8 (no. 35)

Reverse

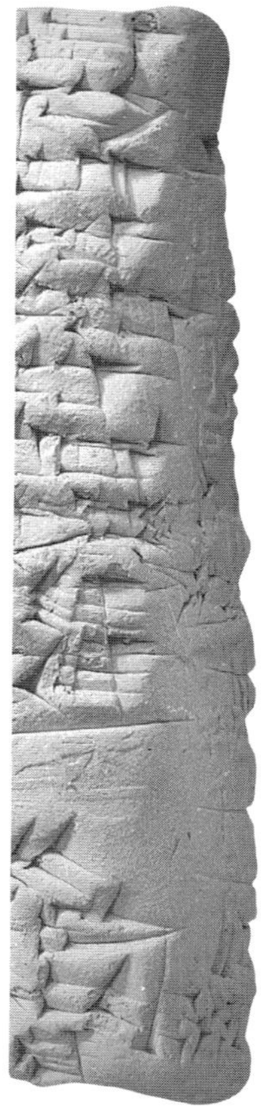

Right Edge

Upper Edge

Cornell 8 (no. 35)

Plate 11

Left Edge

Obverse

Cornell 8 (no. 35)

Case/envelope

Plate 12

Obverse

Right Edge

Lower Edge

Cornell 11 (no. 47)

Reverse

Right Edge

Left Edge

Cornell 11 (no. 47)

Obverse

Right Edge

Left Edge

Cornell 12 (no. 33)

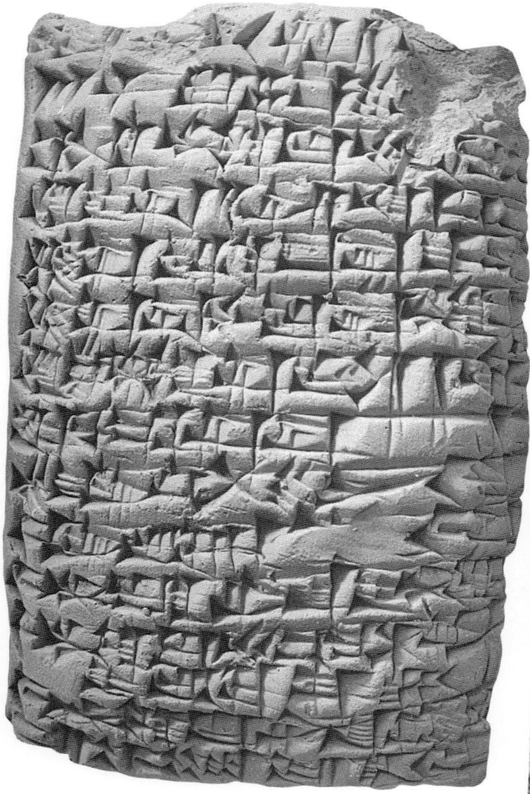

Reverse

Right Edge

Lower Edge

Cornell 12 (no. 33)

Plate 16

Obverse

Right Edge

Cornell 12 (no. 33)

Case/envelope

Reverse

Lower Edge

Cornell 12 (no. 33)

Case/envelope

Right Edge

Obverse

Cornell 16 (no. 48)

Reverse

Right Edge

Left Edge

Cornell 16 (no. 48)

Obverse

Right Edge

Left Edge

Cornell 18 (no. 28)

Reverse

Right Edge

Lower Edge

Cornell 18 (no. 28)

Plate 22

Obverse

Right Edge

Left Edge

Cornell 19 (no. 36)

Right Edge

Reverse

Lower Edge

Cornell 19 (no. 36)

Plate 24

Obverse

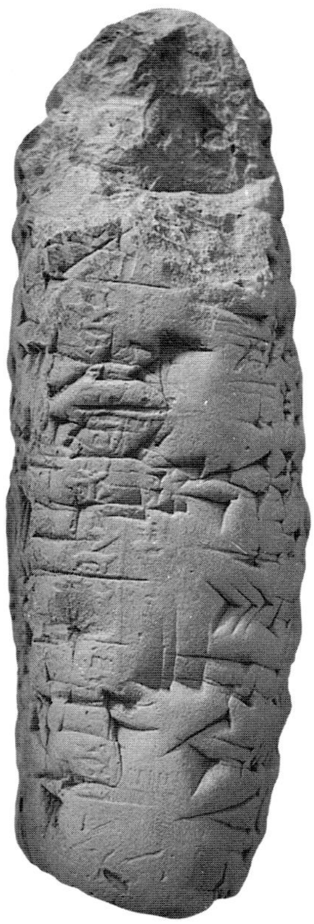

Right Edge

Cornell 20 (no. 37)

Reverse

Right Edge

Lower Edge

Cornell 20 (no. 37)

Obverse

Reverse

Left Edge

Cornell 21 (no. 46)

Obverse *Right Edge*

Lower Edge

Cornell 23 (no. 51)

Reverse

Right Edge

Upper Edge

Cornell 23 (no. 51)

Obverse

Right Edge

Upper Edge

Reverse

Lower Edge

Left Edge

OECT 8 1 (no. 42)

Left Edge

Obverse

Lower Edge

Reverse

Right Edge

Upper Edge

OECT 8 2 (no. 38)

Left Edge

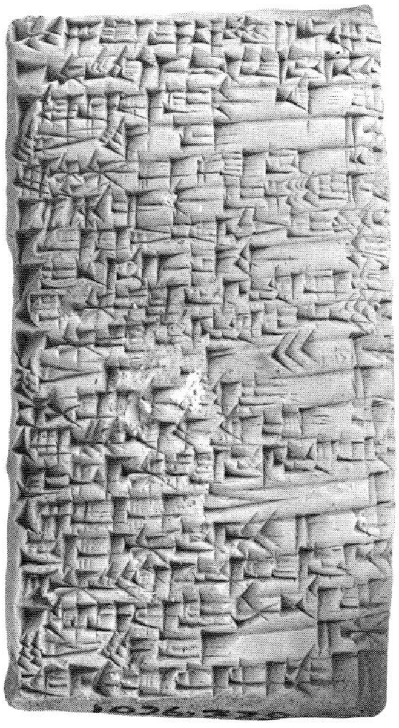

Obverse

Lower Edge

OECT 8 4 (no. 25)

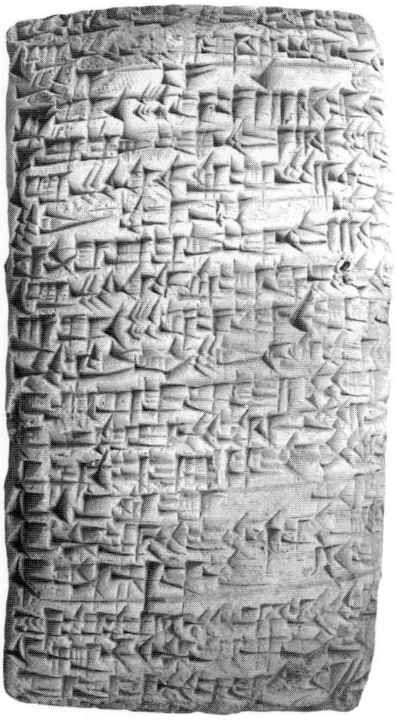

Reverse

Right Edge

Upper Edge

OECT 8 4 (no. 25)

Obverse

Right Edge

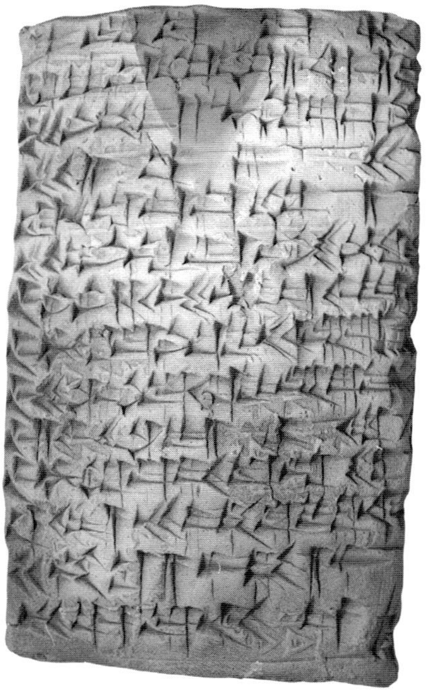

Reverse

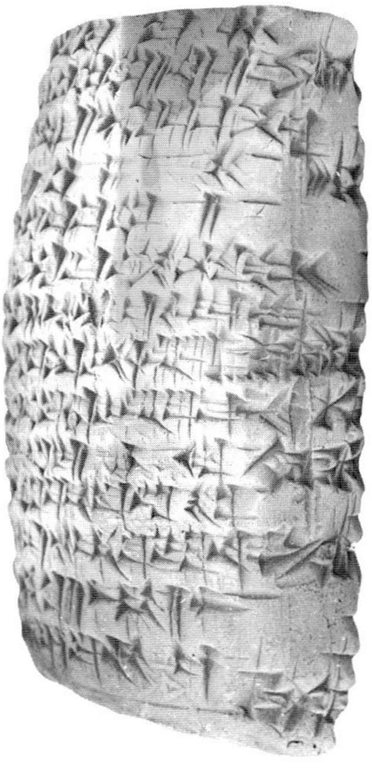

Right Edge

OECT 8 5 (no. 39)

Left Edge

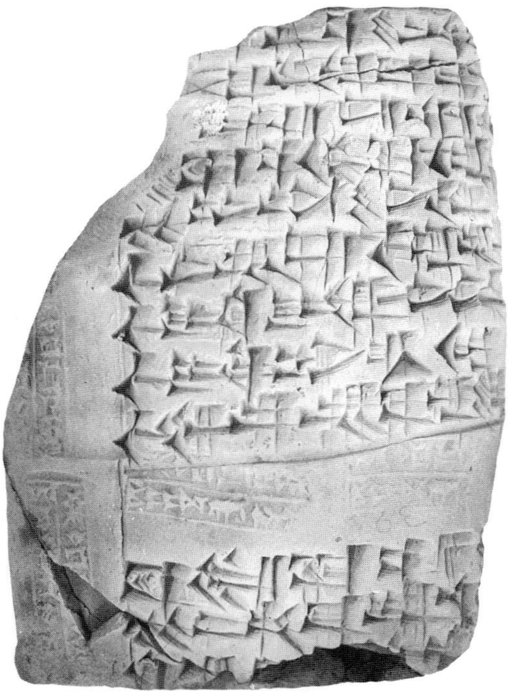

Reverse

Case/envelope

Lower Edge

Left Edge

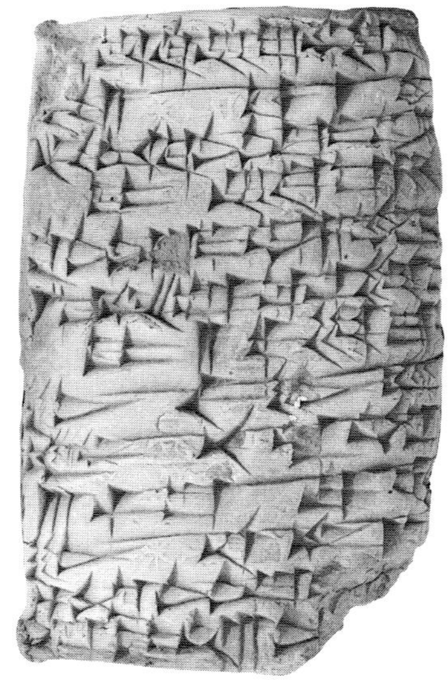

Obverse

Right Edge

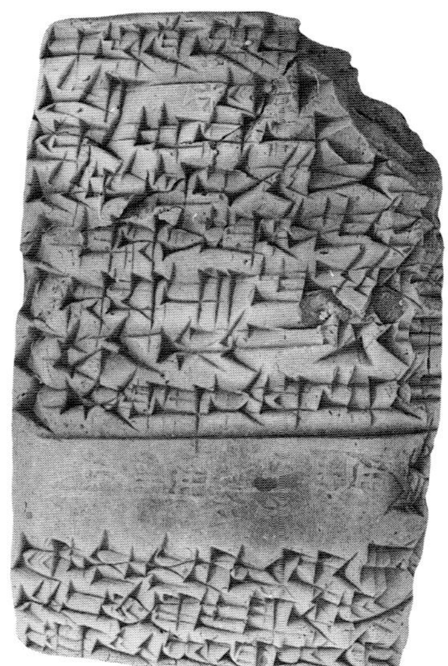

Reverse

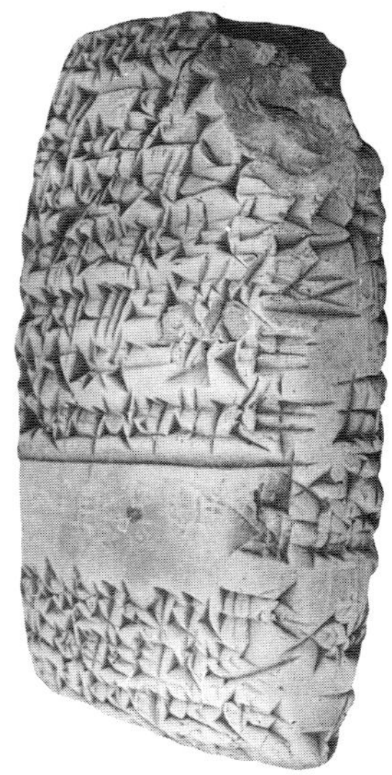

Right Edge

Upper Edge

OECT 8 6 (no. 34)

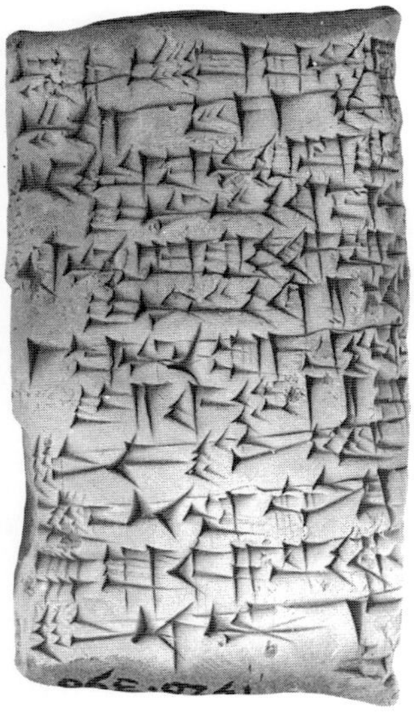

Obverse

Right Edge

Lower Edge

Right Edge

Reverse

Right Edge

Upper Edge

Left Edge

OECT 8 7 (no. 50)

Plate 39

Left Edge

Reverse

Right Edge

Upper Edge

Reverse

Obverse

OECT 8 7 (no. 50)

Case/envelope

Obverse

Right Edge

Lower Edge

Left Edge

OECT 8 8 (no. 49)

Reverse

Right Edge

Upper Edge

Obverse

Right Edge

Left Edge

Lower Edge

OECT 8 8 (no. 49)

Case/envelope

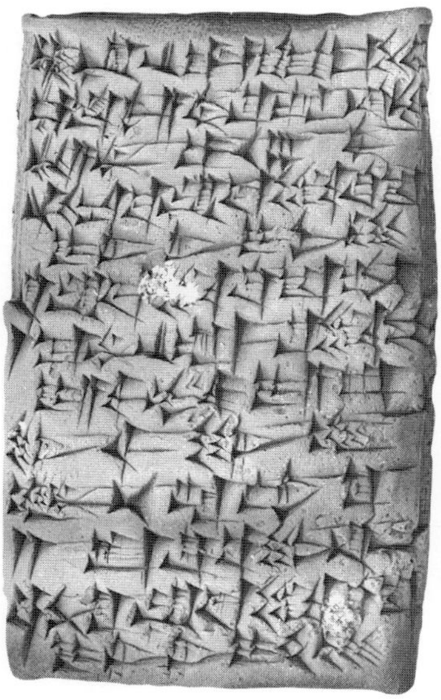

Obverse

Right Edge

Lower Edge

Left Edge

OECT 8 9 (no. 41)

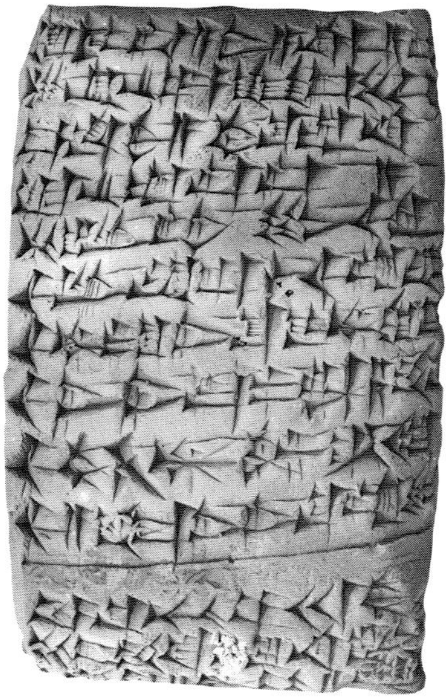

Reverse

Right Edge

Upper Edge

OECT 8 9 (no. 41)

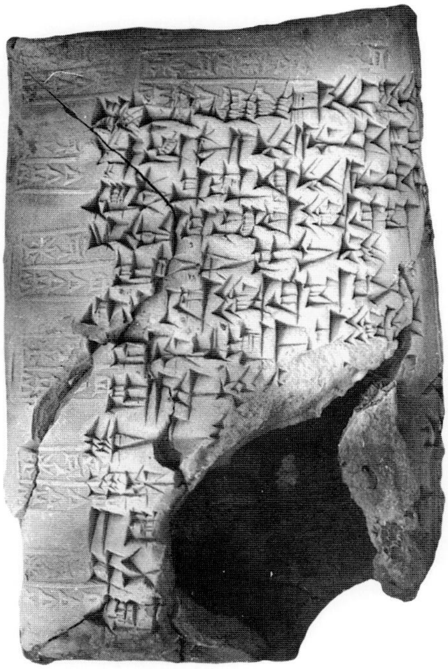

Obverse

Right Edge

Lower Edge

OECT 8 9 (no. 41)

Case/envelope

Plate 46

Reverse

Right Edge

Upper Edge

Left Edge

OECT 8 9 (no. 41)

Case/envelope

Left Edge

Obverse

Right Edge

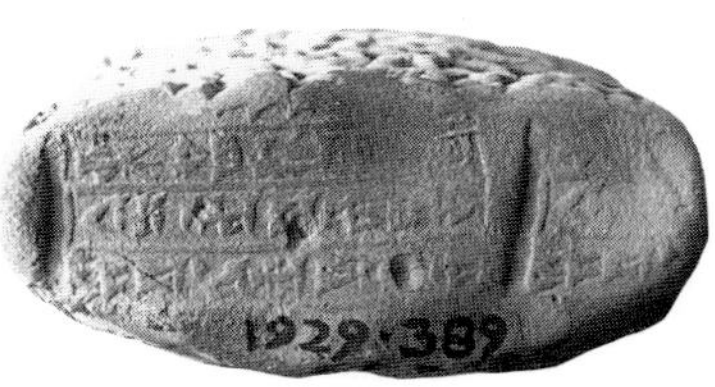

Lower Edge

OECT 8 10 (no. 45)

Reverse

Right Edge

Upper Edge

OECT 8 10 (no. 45)

Obverse

Reverse

Left Edge

Upper Edge

OECT 8 10 (no. 45)

Case/envelope

Left Edge

Obverse

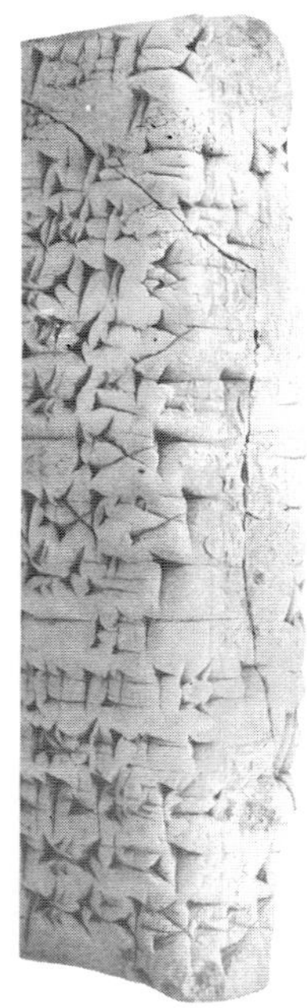

Right Edge

Lower Edge

OECT 8 11 (no. 31)

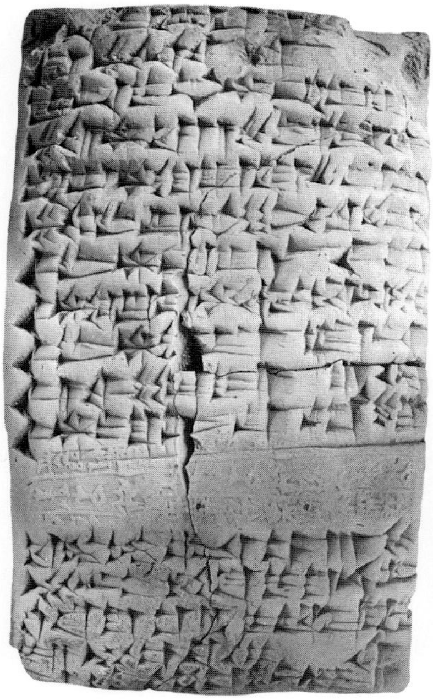

Reverse

Right Edge

Upper Edge

OECT 8 11 (no. 31)

Left Edge

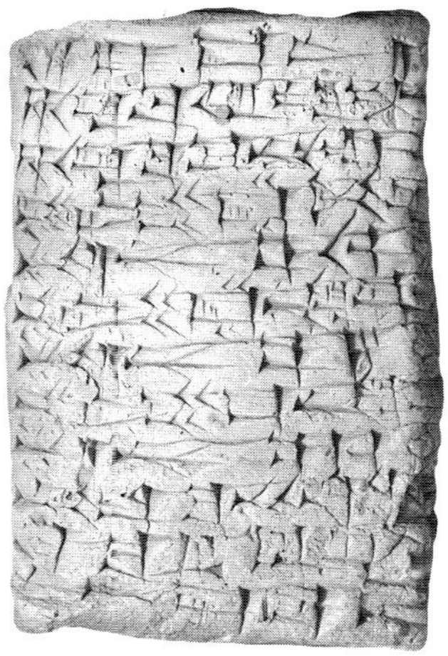

Obverse

Right Edge

Lower Edge

Reverse

Right Edge

Upper Edge

OECT 8 16 (no. 30)

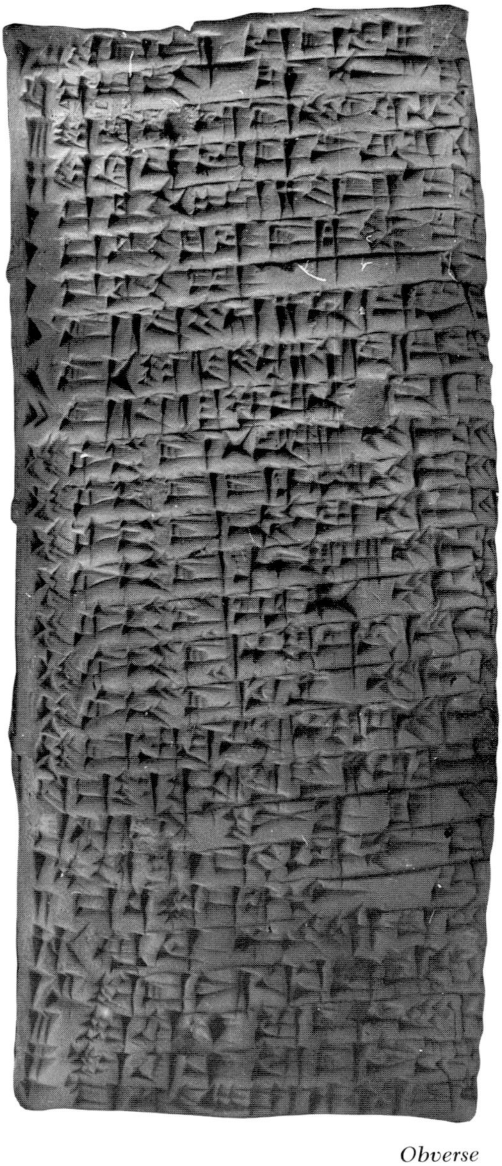

Obverse

Right Edge

OECT 8 17 (no. 24)

Reverse

Right Edge

OECT 8 17 (no. 24)

Left Edge

Upper Edge

Lower Edge

Detail

OECT 8 17 (no. 24)

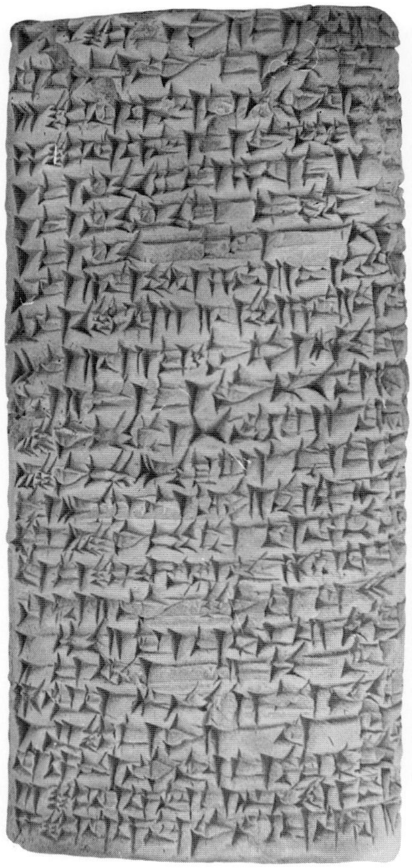

Obverse

Right Edge

Left Edge

OECT 8 18 (no. 53)

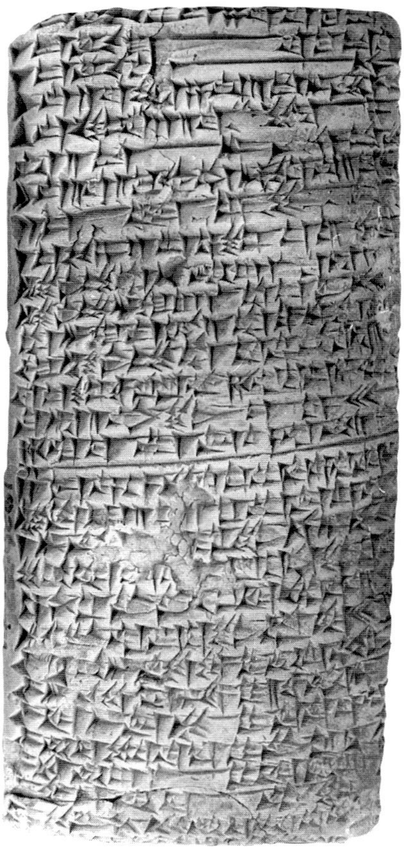

Reverse

Lower Edge

Upper Edge

OECT 8 18 (no. 53)

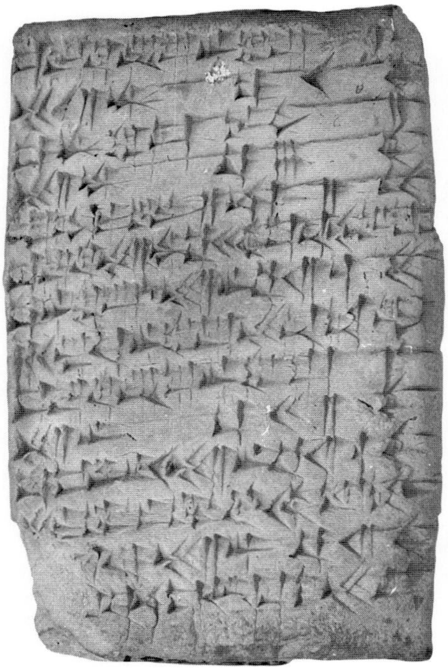
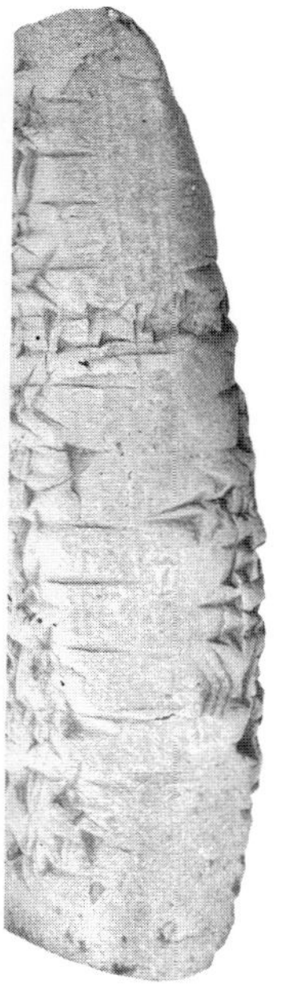

Obverse *Right Edge*

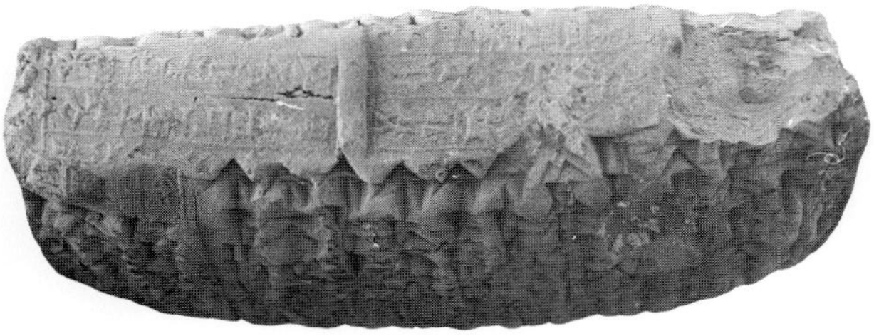

Left Edge

OECT 8 19 (no. 29)

Upper Edge

Reverse *Right Edge*

OECT 8 19 (no. 29)

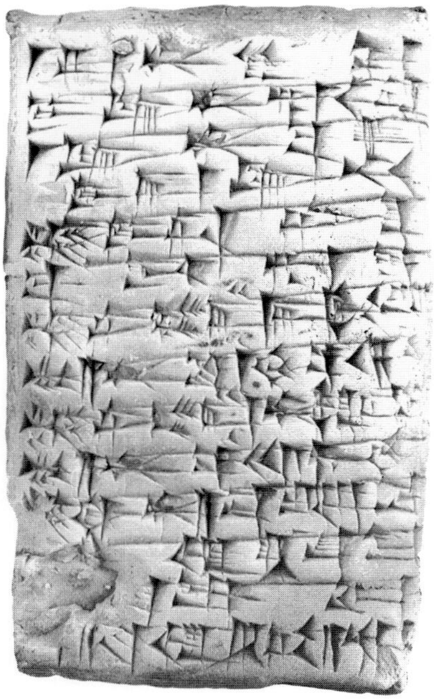

Obverse

Right Edge

Left Edge

OECT 8 20 (no. 23)

Upper Edge

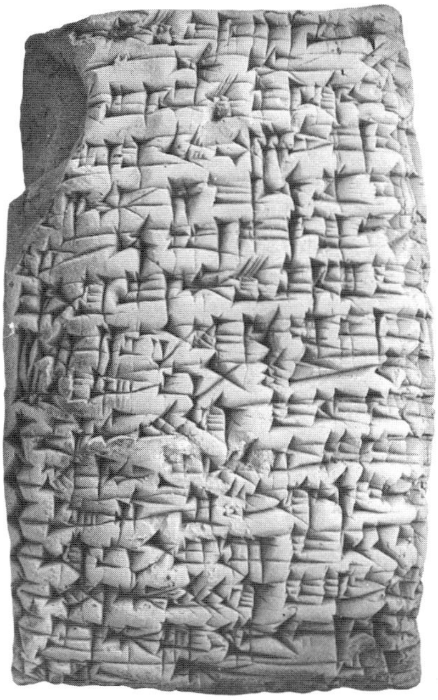

Reverse *Right Edge*

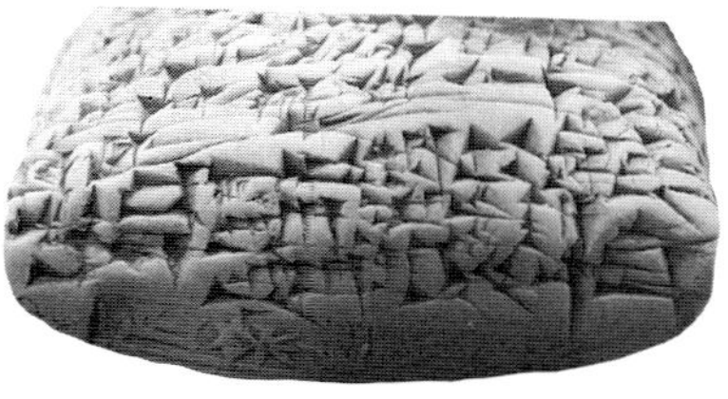

Lower Edge

OECT 8 20 (no. 23)

Left Edge

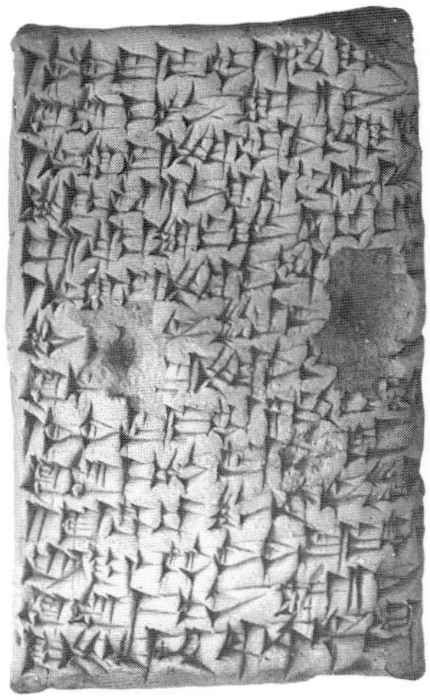

Obverse

Right Edge

Upper Edge

Lower Edge

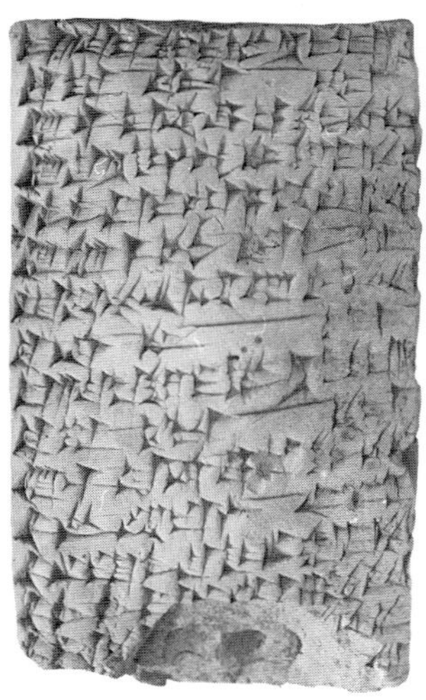

Reverse

Right Edge

OECT 8 21 (no. 32)